Paradox® 3.5

Self-Teaching Guide

Wiley SELF-TEACHING GUIDES (STG's) are designed for first time users of computer applications and programming languages. They feature concept-reinforcing drills, exercises, and illustrations that enable you to measure your progress, and learn at your own pace. Other Wiley Self-Teaching Guides:

MICROSOFT WORD 5.5 FOR THE PC, Ruth Ashley and Judi Fernandez

Q&A, David Angell and Brent Heslop

FOXPRO 2.0, Ellen Sander

ALDUS PERSUASION FOR IBM PC's AND COMPATIBLES, Karen Brown and Diane Stielstra

PERFORM, Peter Stephenson

QUARK XPress, Paul Kaitz and Luther Sperberg

WORDPERFECT 5.0/5.1, Neil Salkind

MICROSOFT WINDOWS 3.0, Keith Weiskamp and Saul Aguiar

TURBO C++, Bryan Flamig

MASTERING MICROSOFT WORKS, David Sachs, Babette Kronstadt, Judith Van Wormer, and Barbara Farrell

PC DOS 4, Ruth Ashley and Judi Fernandez

PC DOS—3rd Edition, Ruth Ashley and Judi Fernandez

QUICKPASCAL, Keith Weiskamp and Saul Aguiar

To order your STG's, you can call Wiley directly at (201) 469–4400, or check your local bookstores.

Mastering computers was never this easy, rewarding, and fun!

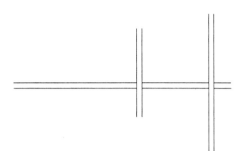

Paradox® 3.5

Self-Teaching Guide

Gloria Wheeler

John Wiley & Sons, Inc.

New York • Chichester • Brisbane • Toronto • Singapore

Publisher: Therese A. Zak
Editor: Katherine Schowalter
Managing Editor: Ruth Greif
Typesetting, Editing, and Production Services: Northeastern Graphic Services, Inc.

PARADOX is a registered trademark of Borland International.

Library of Congress Cataloging-in-Publication Data

Wheeler, Gloria
    Paradox 3.5: self-teaching guide/Gloria Wheeler.
        p. cm.
    Includes index.
    ISBN 0-471-54016-1

Printed in the United States of America

10 9 8 7 6 5 4 3 2 1

To my children, who constantly inspire me
to see things from a new perspective.

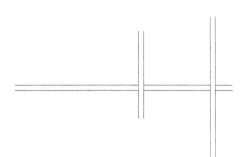

Contents

Chapter 7   *Creating Graphs*   *197*

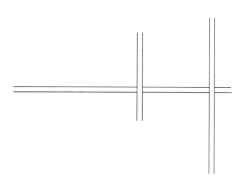

Introduction

This guide contains ten chapters designed to take you step-by-step through the intricacies of Paradox. The sequence of chapters is designed to help you build skills from one chapter to the next so that you can expand your ability to work with Paradox.

While it is best to examine the chapters in order, this book is designed so that you can look up the specific task you need to accomplish. This can be done after you know the basics. The most important basic is learning to create and edit a table, which takes you through Chapter 4.

Some of the tables created in the beginning chapters are used repeatedly; however, enough information is given in subsequent chapters so that you can re-create the tables, without going back to previous chapters. Even better, use your own tables and carry out the steps for certain tasks. The information will mean more to you when you are accomplishing what you need to do.

Chapter Formats

Each chapter begins with an introduction and the main headings found in the chapter. At the end of every chapter, you will find a summary that lists the subjects covered in the chapter in more detail. Following the summary are a series of exercises designed to take you through most of the tasks covered in the chapter. Specific computer response is given for each exercise in order to build confidence in your abilities.

The tasks included in each chapter are listed step-by-step. You will be able to accomplish any one of them. After each set of steps that complete a task, you will find self-checks that encourage review of what you have just learned, as well as hands-on experience with the program. These practice sessions will build your confidence even further as your understanding of Paradox grows.

Who Is This Book For?

The beginning Paradox user will get the most from this book. Details, explanations, and tips abound that enhance your understanding of a database in general and a relational database specifically. The beginning computer user will also find this book a welcome place to start learning about databases.

Because this is an introductory book, you will not learn everything there is to know about Paradox. You will learn important details about creating and editing a database table, doing a query, searching and sorting data, and creating reports and graphs. Once you have gone through this book, you will have a greater understanding of the documentation that comes with Paradox. If you want information about specific commands, refer to the Paradox documents or to Wiley's *Paradox 3.5 Command Reference* by Jonathan Kamin.

System Requirements

This book assumes you have a personal computer that is an IBM or an IBM compatible, with a hard disk drive plus one disk drive for 5.25 or 3.5 disks. You are using DOS 2.0 or higher, with at least 512K of internal memory (RAM). You have a monochrome or color monitor with adapter. In order to see graphics on screen, you need a CGA, EGA, VGA, or Hercules graphics card. Likewise, you need a printer with graphics capabilities if you want to print graphs.

Paradox

Borland continues to produce software programs that combine power with simplicity. Hence the name Paradox. What may seem like a contradiction becomes the fact in Paradox. The consistent and clear menu system allows you to use just what you need to get the job done. But, when you need additional power for complex tasks, Paradox can handle that too. A beginner can be as comfortable with Paradox as an experienced user.

Topics Covered in This Book

Chapter 1 begins with an overview of a database intended to explain the concept to beginners. Many of the terms used in this book in relation to Paradox are defined. Explore the Paradox keyboard to become familiar with the basic methods of communicating with the program.

Using the Paradox menu system becomes a primary focus of Chapter 2. If you can make menu selections, you can use Paradox! You create your first table, get help if you need it, and learn how to handle errors and warnings. After the first table is created, you leave Paradox, using the **Exit** command.

After you have created one simple table, the next step is to learn how to plan all the database tables you will need. In Chapter 3, the task of planning database tables is covered. You create another table in this chapter and then start to use the table in various ways. You begin to understand the advantage of an electronic database through these exercises.

Once you have created a table, how do you change it? How do you correct mistakes? These questions are answered in Chapter 4. The many ways to edit and restructure a table are addressed. Many examples are offered that help you keep your database as accurate and correct as possible.

Now that you have created and corrected database tables, the next task is to get specific information from that table. A database query gets the information you need. In Chapter 5 you learn how to create a query with single and multiple conditions, how to query multiple tables, and how to save queries for later use.

When you are ready to present the data table or the query result to your boss, coworkers, or friends, take advantage of the Paradox report generator. With a single keystroke you can create instant reports. You can also create custom reports that say exactly what you want them to say. In Chapter 6 you will learn the details of creating a report.

To further advance your presentation abilities, learn to use the easy graph functions with Paradox. As with the report generator, Paradox offers an instant graph that is very basic, plus enhanced custom graphs. You use the Paradox menus to create sophisticated graphs for presenting data in Chapter 7.

What are really advanced editing options are the topics of Chapter 8. With Paradox you can find data instantly by using the **Zoom** command. Plus, Paradox lets you look up data in one table from another table. Sorting data by single and multiple fields will be easy, after you complete Chapter 8.

Up to this point, everything in the book has been dealing with the database table. In Chapter 9 you will learn about the Form screen, where you can create invoices and other forms. In this chapter you will also learn about the use of the free form report, which is used to generate mailing labels.

The subject of Chapter 10 is the Paradox script. A script is a series of commands that Paradox performs in an automated fashion. When you need to repeat steps or get somewhere in the menus in a hurry, you can take advantage of instant scripts or named scripts.

Paradox Installation

Beginning with Chapter 1, it is assumed that you have Paradox 3.5 installed and running on your personal computer. If you have not installed Paradox 3.5, turn to Appendix A and follow the directions for installing the program.

New Features Found in Paradox 3.5

Following are some new features found in Paradox 3.5:

VROOMM with turbo drive gives you faster performance with less memory, including manipulating larger tables and more complex procedures.

Paradox is designed to adapt to your hardware, automatically enhancing performance.

Paradox will link to SQL database servers, including translating queries into SQL commands, while you never have to learn SQL.

Improved custom color for all Paradox screen elements.

Paradox more effectively uses greater memory by accessing extended memory in protected mode.

As many as nine tables can be included in a multi-table form.

Variables and PAL functions can be supported in reports and forms.

Acknowledgments

Special thanks to Laura Lewin and Katherine Schowalter at John Wiley; Matt Wagner and Carol Underwood at Waterside Productions; and Nan Borreson at Borland International.

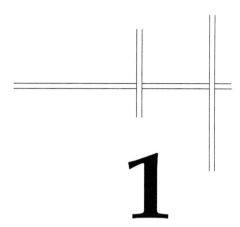

Introducing Paradox

Y̲ou are ready to embark on the process of using your computer to collect and maintain information. But even more important is the process of getting that information out of your computer in some kind of useful format. In this chapter you will learn what a database is and how it works. You will also learn how Paradox works as a database. You will learn about:

- A database
- Paradox terms
- The Paradox keyboard

What Is a Database?

Think of how many databases you use everyday. These databases are *tables* of information. The term table is introduced here because Paradox works with tables of information. Your television listing is a database table. The categories of information in this table are channel, time, name of the program, and duration. Your address book is a table of information, with each entry having the category of name, address, and phone number. So while you may not think of these everyday items as databases, that is what they are.

Figure 1.1 shows how the information from an address book could be arranged in a database table. As you will read later in this chapter, the "Name," "Address," and "Phone" are column labels. Each entry in the address book is in a row.

Paradox moves you to the electronic database table. When you work with Paradox, you work with tables of information. You will view tables, create tables, query (ask questions about) tables, and relate one table to another.

Paradox is built on the *relational model* of a database. This is a collection of data organized into one or more tables, structured in a relational manner. Each table holds information that is very closely related. This information is usually accessed as a group and may be related by sharing common fields. With a relational database, you may link one table to another table.

Here is an example. You have two database tables. One holds the order number, the product ordered, the date shipped, and the name of the customer. Another table holds the names of your customers and their addresses and phone numbers. Link these two tables by asking for a list of the name and address of all customers who ordered product X, shipped during the month of September. Even though one database has the customer name and the product shipped and the other database has the customer name and address, you can pull out the information you need by linking the two database tables.

Tip A relational database works with tables and only tables. A query regarding a table or several tables of information generates an answer table. Your original data remains intact and useful for many years, while specific combinations of information can be requested for your review.

Name	Address	Phone Number
Geoffrey Best	1888 Plantation Way	555–1221
Eleanor Poitier	166887 Anjou Court	555–1056
Carlo Borja	4925 Valencia Lane	555–1500

Figure 1.1. An address database

1. True or False? A Paradox database is a collection of data or information organized into a table.
2. What database model does Paradox use?
3. How does Paradox organize your collection of data?

1. True.

2. A relational database.

3. In tables.

Paradox Terms and Concepts

In order to work with Paradox effectively, review the terms that follow. If you are familiar with other database programs, some of these terms will be similar or only slight variations.

Columns

A table holds a fixed number of columns, each of which holds specific data. The information held in a column is sometimes called a field of data. Each column can hold numbers and letters that represent the information you want to maintain. You can view the information in a column in a list format, where the columns are displayed vertically down the page. Once you define the columns necessary in a table of information, you will rarely add or delete a column. Figure 1.2 shows how the columns appear in a list view of your database.

Rows

A row holds information that is closely related to one person, place, or thing. You can add as many rows of information to your database as you need. One row is sometimes referred to as one record in a database. In an address database, the name, address, and phone number of one person would appear on the same row. Figure 1.3 illustrates a row of data, with each type of data being held in one vertical column.

```
Viewing Custid table: Record 1 of 10                              Main

CUSTID      Cust #          Last Name       First Name          Address
    1        123          Mousse          Mickey          987 Holly Wood
    2        124          Goofie          Glen            876 Peaches Lane
    3        125          Placid          Pluto           765 Bucolic Plac
    4        126          Duck            Daphne          654 Tawny Pond
    5        127          Ferdie          Fred            543 15th Street
    6        128          Mortie          Montey          432 Montivideo A
    7        129          Dilly           Daisy           321 Piccadilly S
    8        130          Menace          Minnie          210 Mystery Crt.
    9        131          Jerry           Tom             109 Egg Nog Cent
   10        132          Doodle          Dipsy           909 Topsy Turvy
```

Figure 1.2. A list view of items in a database

```
Viewing Friends table: Record 3 of 3                             Main

FRIENDS         Name                    Address             Phone Number
    1      Geoffrey Best        1888 Plantation Way         555-1221
    2      Eleanor Poitier      166887 Anjou Court          555-1056
    3      Carlo Borja          4925 Valencia Lane          555-1500
```

Figure 1.3. Three columns with several records, labeled

After a table is created, there are a fixed number of columns, but no rows. You add the rows by adding records of information. If you change the entry in a row, it does not affect the remainder of the database. However, if you add, delete, or change a column, the entire table is affected. For example, if you deleted the column containing phone numbers from your address database, the phone numbers for every record would be deleted. If you deleted one phone number in one row or record in the Paradox database, only that one phone number would be deleted. No other phone numbers would be affected.

1. In a database table, are there a fixed number of columns or rows?
2. What is another term for one row in a database?
3. What is another term for one column in a database?

1. *Columns.*
2. *One record.*
3. *A field of information.*

Field Types

An address book contains several types of information. The name information consists of alphabetic characters. The address information consists of alphabetic and numeric characters. The phone number information is numeric only.

When you design a Paradox database, you designate the type of information that can be entered in each field. You have five choices of field types: Alphanumeric, Number, Currency, Date, and Short Number.

Alphanumeric Fields

An Alphanumeric field can contain letters, numbers, and symbols, such as $, &, %, +, and -. An Alphanumeric field can contain from 1 to 255 characters. An address is an example of something you would put in an Alphanumeric field because very often it is both letters and numbers.

Number Fields

A Number field can hold up to 15 digits, including decimal places. Scientific notation is used to store numbers that are greater than 15 digits. Later you will learn different ways to format the way that numbers are displayed. Decimal places will not be displayed in number format unless necessary. Negative numbers appear with a minus sign (-) in front of them.

Tip

Remember, the way a number is formatted only affects the way it is displayed on screen, not the original number. For example, you have the number 1234.560007. You choose to format all numbers in a column with two decimal places. The number will be stored as 1234.560007, but will be displayed as 1234.56.

Currency Fields

Currency fields are displayed with numbers rounded to two decimal places. In this format, negative numbers appear in parentheses and whole number separators are included. For example, the number 1234.560007 would be displayed as 1,234.56. The number - 1234.560007 would be displayed as (1,234.56). The number 1234 would be displayed 1,234.00.

Date Fields

The Date field type can refer to any date ranging from January 1, 100 to December 31, 9999, based on the Gregorian calendar. You can format dates in the standard format, such as MM/DD/YY. Other options are available, as in dd-Mon-yy, DD.MM.YY, or you can use YYY or YYYY as dates beyond the twentieth century. Paradox will not let you enter invalid dates like 3/35/95. Paradox allows you to sort and do arithmetic with the dates you enter in fields.

Short Number Fields

The Short Number fields were designed for use by advanced Paradox users. Short Number fields contain only whole numbers and have a limited range.

They are used in very large tables because they take less disk space than other numeric field types.

1. What field type would you use if you wanted to display a number like this: 1,234.00?
2. The Alphanumeric field type contains:
   a. Letters and numbers
   b. Letters, numbers, and symbols
   c. Letters, numbers, and arrows
3. Which field type is for the advanced Paradox user?

1. *Use the Currency field type.*
2. *b.*
3. *Short Number fields.*

Paradox Terminology

Paradox has its own set of terms to describe the different components of the program. When you perform an action and then get a result, you will need a name for that result.

Objects

Each table created with Paradox has other associated objects that go along with it. One object is a *form*. One way to describe a form is to say that it is a map that shows how one record is to be displayed on the screen. An example of a Paradox form is shown in Figure 1.4.

A *report* is another object that you can design to represent one of your tables. *Graphs* are similar, in that they are the result of the custom graph you design to display the contents of a table. Figures 1.5a, 1.5b, and 1.6 show examples of a report and a graph.

These objects are stored as DOS files. Think of file folders when you

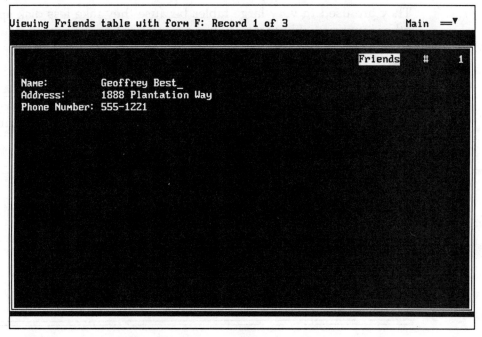

Figure 1.4. A Paradox form

think of DOS files. Each object you create is stored in an electronic file folder called a DOS file.

If you have one table with an associated form, report, and graph, you have a family of files. Paradox will remember which DOS files belong to which family. This family of DOS files is stored in the same "file folder." Very rarely will you have to worry about the DOS files and their names.

Name	Address	Phone Number
Geoffrey Best	1888 Plantation Way	555–1221
Eleanor Poitier	166887 Anjou Court	555–1056
Carlo Borja	4925 Valencia Lane	555–1500

Figure 1.5a. Example of a report (printed)

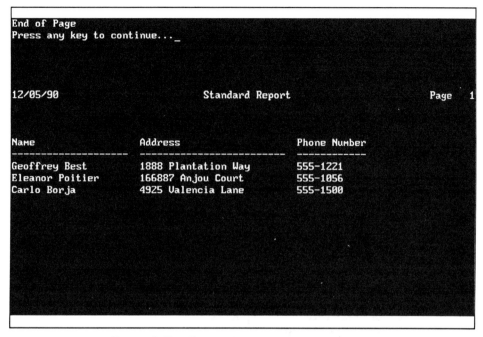

Figure 1.5b. Example of a report (on screen)

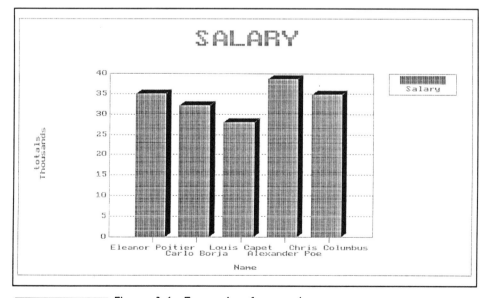

Figure 1.6. Example of a graph

Images

An image is what you see on the computer screen. If a table is too large to fit on the screen, you can move the image so that more of it is visible to you. For example, with a database of ten columns, only five may be visible on the screen at any one time. Use the right arrow key to view columns 6, 7, 8, 9, and 10. If your database is very large with 50 columns and 150 rows, you will see only a small portion of the image at any one time.

You can create, enlarge, shrink, clear, and move images on the screen. When you clear an image on the screen, the data still exists in its original state. (The data is saved in the DOS file.) Your window to view the image is merely closed.

Workspace

Think of an enormous table where you can display all of your data tables. This is the Paradox workspace. Only Paradox holds it all electronically and allows you to see only confined amounts of the table at one time. The screen is a window to this enormous workspace. Different tables can be brought into the workspace and moved around. When you are designing a new report, the workspace will occupy the entire screen. When you are working with other Paradox objects, a set of menu options are displayed across the top of the screen.

1. What are the three Paradox objects?
   a. Form, report, and graph
   b. Query, image, and workspace
   c. Image, form, and graph
2. Together, the three objects found in the answer above are called a
   _____.
3. In what way should you think of the computer screen when working with Paradox?

1. *a.*
2. *Family of files.*
3. *As a window on the workspace.*

A Tour of the Keyboard

The computer keyboard consists of three main work areas. The alphanumeric area is in the center, where you will do most of your typing. This includes the Shift, Ctrl, Alt, and Enter keys.

A group of function keys will appear either at the left of the alphanumeric area or across the top of the keyboard. The function keys, as their name implies, allow you to perform various functions in Paradox. A function key can be used by itself or in combination with the Shift, Ctrl, or Alt keys.

You will find that two function keys are most often used. One is F2, the DO-IT key. Press F2 and you tell Paradox to finalize an action and save the resulting object to disk. When adding new records, or rows, to a table, Paradox does not actually add them to the disk until you press F2. The F2 DO-IT key acts like the Save key that you might find in other software programs.

The F10 key is frequently used to call up the menu. The menu that appears will vary depending on what activity you are working on. Most often, the main menu will appear, allowing you to make a selection for your next action.

To the right of the alphanumeric area, either alone or with a numeric keyboard, are the arrow keys. These, along with the Enter key and the Backspace key, will be the most frequently used keys when using Paradox.

The Tab key is used to move you between rows and columns while working in a Paradox table. The Enter key is used to select a menu option, end a task, move to another field, and insert extra lines in a report or script function.

While in the edit mode, delete data from fields using the Backspace key. Hit the Backspace key and the character to the left of the cursor is deleted. Hold down the Ctrl key and the Backspace key together and you can delete data in the field.

Table 1.1 lists the function keys in Paradox.

Figure 1.7. Areas of the keyboard delineated

Table 1.1 Function Keys and Their Functions

Function Key	Function	Alt	Ctrl
F1	Help		
F2	Execute		
F3	Up Image	Record Script	
F4	Down Image	Play Script	
F5	Example	Field View	
F6	Check	Check Plus	Check Desc
F7	Form Toggle	Instant Report	Instant Graph
F8	Clear Image	Clear All Images from screen	
F9	Edit	Coedit	
F10	Menu	PAL Menu	

1. Which function keys are the most frequently used with Paradox?
2. Which keys on the alphanumeric keyboard will you use most often?
3. What happens if you press the **Ctrl** and the **Backspace** key at the same time?
4. What are the three components to the keyboard?

1. *F2 or DO-IT and* **F10,** *to call up the menus.*
2. *The* **Tab** *key, arrow keys,* **Backspace** *key, and* **Enter** *key.*
3. *You delete a field of information.*
4. *The alphanumeric, function keys, and arrow keys.*

Summary

You have reviewed the basic terminology used with Paradox. While many of the terms are new at this point, they will become second nature as your experience with Paradox grows. The important concept of Paradox tables is the key to your understanding of how Paradox will make your data more useful and revealing. Important concepts covered in this chapter are:

- A database
  - Columns
  - Rows
  - Field types
- Paradox terms
  - Objects
  - Images
  - Workspace
- The Paradox keyboard
  - Function keys

In the next chapter you will create your first Paradox table.

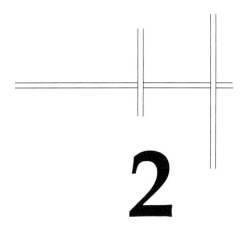

2

Getting Started with Paradox

In Chapter 2, you will learn to create a database table and add records, to get your feet wet with Paradox. You will be able to:

- Select menu items
- Create a table
- Get help from Paradox
- Learn how to handle errors
- Leave Paradox

Starting Paradox

At this point, Paradox should be installed on your computer. (Directions on how to install Paradox can be found in Appendix A.) Once installed, start Paradox by turning on your computer. You will have to log into the Paradox directory through DOS commands. At the "C>" prompt:

Type: CD\PDOX35
Press: **Enter**
Then
Type: PDOX35
Press: **Enter**

 Tip

Your "C>" prompt may be as simple as that, or it may display the name of the directory. Whether you see "C:\" or "C:\PARADOX3" after the **CD** (change directory) command, Paradox will start after you enter the **PARA-DOX3** command.

You will see the opening Paradox screen that you see in Figure 2.1.

1. Turn your computer on. It displays "C\WORKS." Type CD\PDOX35 to get to the Paradox directory. What do you see?
2. What does "C:.>" mean?

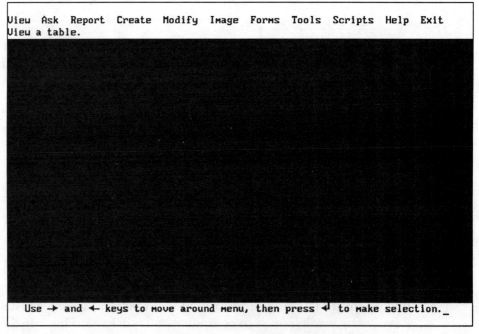

Figure 2.1. Paradox opening screen

1. *C:\PDOX35>.*
2. *You are using the C drive.*

Working with the Menu System

Paradox is a menu-driven database program. In the past you had to program a database to carry out your commands. With Paradox you use a convenient menu system. The menu system makes life simpler for the beginner,
allowing you to select options instead of design them from scratch.

The Main Menu

The Main menu consists of 11 menu items that appear across the top of the
screen. The **View** menu is highlighted. This indicates which menu option
will be selected when you press Enter.

Moving to Menu Items

The opening Paradox screen provides access to nearly all of the functions
available. The reverse-video block at the top of your screen indicates the
current menu selection. Use the right or left arrow keys to move to the de-
sired menu item.

With the **View** option highlighted, press the right arrow key five times.
Notice how the line directly below the Main menu changes with each menu
selection. The **Image** option is now highlighted. The line directly under the
Main menu reads: Resize or reformat images; go to records or values; pick
forms; specify graphs. You've discovered how easy it is to move in the
menus. Now select a menu!

Selecting a Menu Item

There are two ways to select menu items. The first way is to highlight the
item and press Enter; the second way is to press the first letter of the menu
item. Practice menu selection, using both methods.

When the item is highlighted, select that item by pressing the Enter key.

STEP:

With the **Image** option highlighted, press Enter.

Another menu appears. This is the **Image** submenu shown in Figure 2.2. Select an item here just as you would from the Main menu.

To get out of the **Image** submenu, press the Esc key. A little later you will read more about how the Esc key can get you out of certain menu functions. Right now, just press it once and you return to the Main menu with **Image** still highlighted.

As with most tasks in Paradox, there is an easier way to select menu items. Type the first letter in the word that represents a menu item. The menu item **Image** is still highlighted on the screen.

STEP:

Press: R

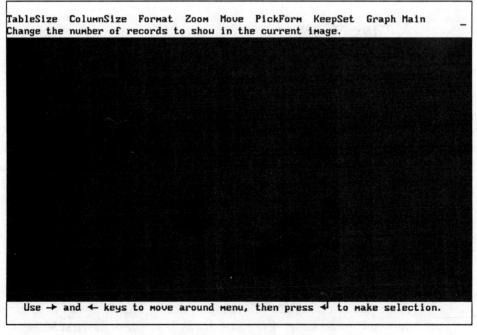

```
TableSize  ColumnSize  Format  Zoom  Move  PickForm  KeepSet  Graph Main        _
Change the number of records to show in the current image.
```



```
Use → and ← keys to move around menu, then press ↵ to make selection.
```

Figure 2.2. The **Image** submenu

The **Report** submenu is now on screen. The items on the **Report** submenu are: **Output, Design, Change, RangeOutput,** and **SetPrinter.**

The word Main appears in the upper right corner of the screen. It indicates that the Main menu is the previous menu. Press the **F10** key. You jump back to the Main menu with the **View** item highlighted.

Try it again! Press **S.** Now the **Script** submenu appears across the top of the screen with the highlighting on **Play.** Press **F10** and you go right back to where you were. You can be confident moving around in the menus.

Tip | As you progress through this book, you will be asked to "Select" menu items. When you are asked to select a menu item, use either of the methods described above. Either move the highlighting to the option and press **Enter,** or press the first letter of the option. You will have "selected" the menu.

With **View** highlighted, press the right arrow key. The line below the menu describes briefly what you will be able to do by choosing that menu option. Eleven menu options are displayed. Table 2.1 lists the menu options and their brief description.

Table 2.1 The Main Menu and a Brief Description of Actions

Option	Result
VIEW	View a table.
ASK	Get a query form to ask questions about a table.
REPORT	Output, design, or change a report specification.
CREATE	Create a new table structure.
MODIFY	Sort or edit a table, enter new records, or restructure a table.
IMAGE	Resize or reformat images, go to records or values, pick forms, or specify graphs.
FORMS	Design or change a form.
TOOLS	Rename, speed up queries, convert data, copy, delete, info, net, and more.
SCRIPTS	Play or record a script.
HELP	Help with using Paradox.
EXIT	Leave Paradox (all changes have been saved for you).

Submenus

After you have selected a menu option, you may get a screen prompt or a submenu. A screen prompt asks you to give Paradox some information, such as the name of a table. A submenu lists the next phase of action you can take. For example, choose **Modify** from the Main menu and the **Modify** submenu appears. This menu consists of the **Sort, Edit, CoEdit, DataEntry, MultiEntry,** and **Restructure** options, as seen in Figure 2.3.

The list of menu choices appears across the top of the screen. The highlighting indicates the current menu selection. Paradox does not always show a menu across the screen. Instead, you may see a prompt or description of activity. In the upper right corner of the screen is an indicator of the menu you can view should you need to see one. Figure 2.4 shows the menu indicator in the upper right corner of the screen.

To see the menu indicated, press F10. There are special menus for editing, creating, and other topics that are called submenus. When Edit is highlighted in the upper right of the screen, press F10 and the **Edit** submenu appears across the top of the screen.

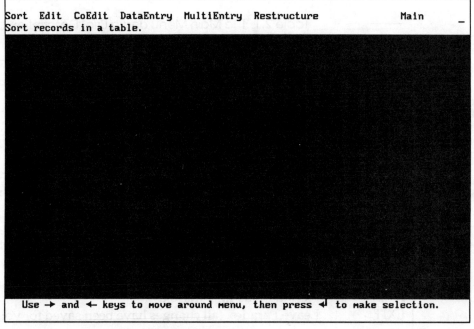

```
Sort  Edit  CoEdit  DataEntry  MultiEntry  Restructure          Main       _
Sort records in a table.
```

```
   Use → and ← keys to move around menu, then press ↵ to make selection.
```

Figure 2.3. The **Modify** submenu

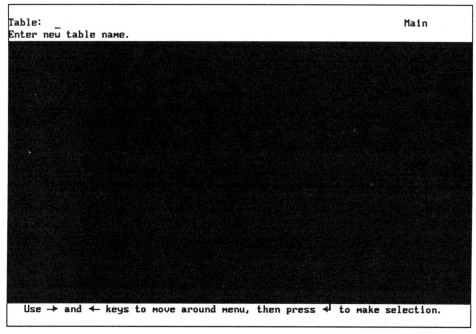

```
Table:  _                                                    Main
Enter new table name.




















     Use → and ← keys to move around menu, then press ◁ to make selection.
```

Figure 2.4. Menu indicator

Some menu strings may be three deep. For example, the menu string **Modify/Edit/ValCheck** indicates the **ValCheck** option of the **Edit** submenu, found on the **Modify** submenu.

If you make mistakes while searching for a menu option you want, press **Esc** to back out of the incorrect menu. You will be taken one step back to the previous menu or submenu.

Using the Escape Key

At the far right, the word Main is visible. This indicator tells you that, if you decide not to create a new table, you can press the **Esc** key and return to the Main menu. Or, press the **F10** Menu key to see the Main menu. Before naming the new table, press the **Esc** key, labeled **Esc** on your keyboard. The screen reverts back to the Main menu and leaves **Create** highlighted. Press **F10** and the screen reverts back to the Main menu, but leaves **View** highlighted.

Tip

Use the **Esc** key to get you out of almost any situation. If you select the wrong menu item, or enter an incorrect field, press **Esc** and you will go back to the previous step. Continue pressing **Esc** and you will go back to the Main menu.

1. Press **F10** and what appears on the screen?
2. What menu item would you choose if you wanted to design a Paradox form?
3. Move the cursor, using the arrow keys, to the **Help** menu item. What appears on the line directly below the menu?
4. Select create from the Main menu. What happens?

1. *A menu appears.*
2. *The **Forms** menu item.*
3. *Help with using Paradox*
4. *A STRUCT table appears, ready for you to create a Paradox table.*

You spent a lot of time practicing using Paradox menus. The effort is worth it! Master Paradox menus and you can master Paradox!

Creating a Paradox Table

You want to create a *Paradox* table. You just answered the question above that tells you the menu item to select in order to create a table. The steps involved in creating a table are:

1. Select **Create** from the Main menu.
2. Name the table.
3. Design the table.

STEP 1:

Using the left and right arrow keys, move the cursor to **Create** and press **Enter.**

Paradox Prompts

You see that your screen changes slightly. The Main menu is replaced with the word "Table:," where below you find the prompt. In this case, the prompt says "Enter new table name." The Paradox program is telling you what you have to do next; in other words, it prompts you for the next piece of information it needs. Every table must have a unique name in Paradox. Expect to see prompts that guide your activity while using Paradox.

The first table we create will be of the names and addresses from Chapter 1. Consider this a list of your personal friends, so we will call the table *Friends*.

STEP 2:

Type: Friends

The screen appears as in Figure 2.5. You have followed the directions given by the prompt by typing the name for the table.

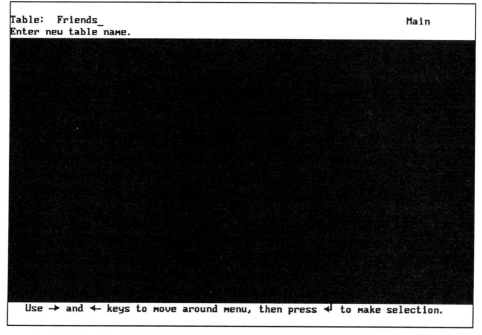

Figure 2.5. Prompt with table name filled in

STEP 3:

Press: **Enter**

Again your screen changes, moving you to the next step in creating a Paradox table. Across the top you can read "Creating new Friends table," so you know exactly what you are doing. At the top right, the word "Create" is highlighted. This tells you that you are in the process of creating a new table. Also, if you hit the **F10** key, the **Create** menu will appear.

Try pressing **F10** right now! "Create" is still highlighted, telling you that you are in the process of creating a table. However, on the left side of the screen, the **Create** submenu has appeared. The options are "Borrow, Help, DO-IT!, and Cancel." As with the Main menu, each menu item has a short description, and the menu item you want to select is highlighted on screen.

We will not be using the **Create** menu right now, so press the **Esc** key. The **Create** menu disappears, and you are right back where you were before you pressed **F10**. See how easily **Esc** helps you back out of a wrong decision or procedure?

Across the top left side of the screen you see the word "STRUCT," followed by "Field Name," and "Field Type." Paradox is ready for your commands for creating the structure of the new table. Under the word "STRUCT" is the number "1," and to the right of that is your blinking cursor. Characters you enter will appear to the left of the blinking cursor.

Defining the Table Structure

Before you actually add data to your Paradox table, you will tell Paradox what the data is going to look like. The first step is to create a Table Definition, where you define the columns (or fields of information).

The two steps to creating a table definition are:

1. Name the field column.
2. Determine what type of data will be entered into that column.

The type of data refers to the field types introduced in Chapter 1. You do not need to look them up, however, since they are very conveniently described on the right side of the screen in which you are now working.

The new table you are creating has three fields or columns of information. As you see above, they are Name, Address, and Phone Number. For this example, we will define each field as holding alphanumeric data.

With the blinking cursor under the heading "Field Name," you know where the information you type will be entered. The arrow head at the right side of the same column helps you keep track of the field you are in. The first field you want to enter is Name.

STEP 1:

> Type: Name
> Press: Enter

The cursor and arrowhead move to the space under "Field Type."

STEP 2:

> Type: A25
> Press: Enter

You have just defined the type of data that can be entered in the first field as alphanumeric. The number "25" represents the number of spaces you are allowing in this field. A name in this field, then, can be up to 25 characters long.

Tip

Before you decide how many characters a field should hold, find out the maximum number of spaces necessary. If all of your data is 10 characters and only one is 25, you might want to shorten the one record and make the field smaller. The reason you want the field as small as possible is so that you don't store a lot of blank spaces on disk. As soon as you define a field size, Paradox stores all the characters and the blank spaces on disk. For the most efficient use of disk space, keep blank spaces to a minimum.

Paradox moves the cursor down to the second field in this database. Define this field by following these steps:

STEP 3:

> Type: Address
> Press: Enter
> Type: A25
> Press: Enter
> Type: Phone
> Press: Enter

Type: A15
Press: **Enter**

Your screen should match the one you see in Figure 2.6, with three fields
defined.

1. Create a table definition. What is the first step?
2. What are the four field types described on your screen?
3. Under the heading Field Type, create an Alphanumeric field that is 25
   spaces long. What do you enter in this space?

1. *Name the column.*
2. *A, N, $, D.*
3. *A25.*

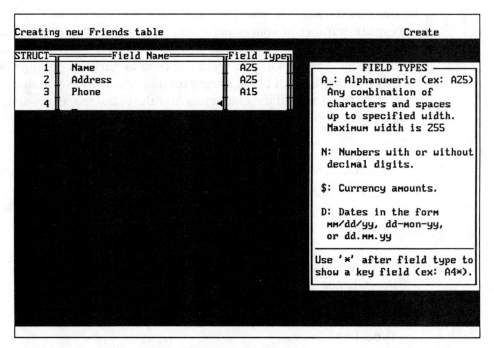

Figure 2.6. Three fields defined

Checking for Errors

Read through the information that appears on your screen and check for errors. If you find an error, use the arrow key to get to the field that holds the error. Press the **Backspace** key to remove incorrect letters to the left of the cursor. Retype the correct information.

Using DO-IT

When the table on your screen looks like the one in the figure above, tell Paradox to create the table.

Press: **F2** DO-IT

By pressing **F2**, you are telling Paradox that you are finished with the table definition and that you want to DO-IT! You have built the structure for your first Paradox table and saved it. But wait! There is no evidence of this table on the screen. It appears to have disappeared.

1. Press the **DO-IT** key. What happens?
2. Press the **Backspace** key while you are in a field. What happens?

1. *Paradox defines the table structure and then saves the table to disk.*
2. *The character to the left of the cursor disappears.*

Retrieving the Friends Table

The table you have built is not lost forever. Through menu selections you can see the table. Start by selecting the **Modify** menu option.

STEP 1:

Press: right arrow key, four times or until **Modify** is highlighted, *or* press **M** for Modify.
Press: **Enter**

A submenu appears from which you choose the **Edit** option.

STEP 2:

Press: the right arrow key one time
Press: **Enter**

Paradox prompts you for information. After the word "Table:," type the name of the table you want to edit.

STEP 3:

Type: Friends
Press: **Enter**

The image of the *Friends* table will appear on the screen, as you see in Figure 2.7. The message that appears on the screen tells you exactly what you are doing, "Editing Friends table." In the upper right-hand corner, you also see the highlighted word "Edit." If you press **F10** at this point, the **Edit** menu will appear at the top of the screen.

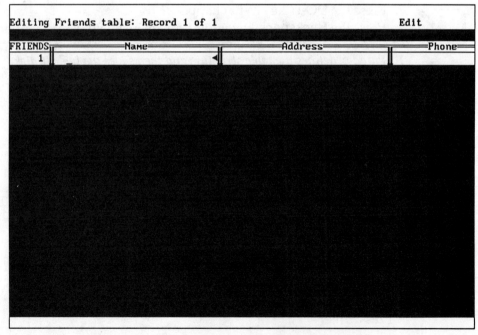

Figure 2.7. The image of the *Friends* table

This screen looks familiar! The format is similar to the screen used to design the table. Notice that the fields you created are now shown across the top of the screen in the order of Name, Address, and Phone.

Tip

Suppose you have forgotten the name of the table you want to retrieve. At the "Table:" prompt, press **Enter** and Paradox will list all the tables you have created so far. Move the highlighting to the table you want and press **Enter**. That table is selected.

1. To edit a table, what do you do?
2. How many rows or records of information appear in the table image?

1. *Select **Modify** and **Edit** and then type the name of the table.*
2. *None.*

Entering Data into a Table

Whenever you add, remove, or change records in a Paradox table, you are editing the table. This is in contrast to editing the table structure, which you had to do to create the table. The screen shows the blinking cursor in the Name field. Add the names and addresses listed earlier by taking these steps:

STEP 1:

Type: `Geoffrey Best`
Press: **Enter**
Type: `1888 Plantation Way`
Press: **Enter**
Type: `555-1221`
Press **Enter**

Each time you press **Enter** in the Phone field, the cursor automatically opens a row for a new record. New records can be added by pressing the **Ins** (Insert) key, as well.

The first record is filled in across the row.

STEP 2:

Add the following two names to the table in row 2 and 3.

Name	Address	Phone
Eleanor Poitier	166887 Anjou Court	555-1056
Carlo Borja	4925 Valencia Lane	555-1500

Figure 2.8 shows how your screen looks at this point.
You have finished entering records.

STEP 3:

Press: F2

Paradox puts the finishing touches on your table by eliminating extra
rows. This time when you press F2, Paradox leaves the table on the screen.
Paradox has put you in the **View** mode, so look over the table to make sure

```
Editing Friends table: Record 3 of 3                        Edit
======Name======    ======Address======    ======Phone======
  Geoffrey Best       1888 Plantation Way      555-1221
  Eleanor Poitier     166887 Anjou Court       555-1056
  Carlo Borja         4925 Valencia Lane       555-1500
```

Figure 2.8. Table with three names entered

it is designed the way you want. While in the **View** mode, you cannot change or edit data. Use **View** when you just want to look at the data.

1. After you type the name, press **Enter**. What happens to the cursor?
2. What does Paradox do when you press **F2**?
3. What mode are you in after pressing **F2**?

1. *The cursor moves to the next column on the right.*
2. *Paradox finishes and then saves the table.*
3. *The **View** mode.*

Checking and Editing Errors

Use the keys listed below to edit any errors you may find in the table. Remember, to get to the editing function, select **Modify** from the Main menu and **Edit** from the **Modify** submenu. Type in the name of the table you want to edit—in this case, *Friends.*

Right Arrow or Tab	Moves you to the next field. When you are in the last field of a record, press this key to move to the next blank record.
Left Arrow or Shift-Tab	Moves you to the previous field. When you are in the first field, press this key to move to the last field of the previous record.
Up Arrow	Move to the same field in the previous record.
Down Arrow	Move to the same field in the next record.
Ins **Key**	Look for Ins or Insert on your keyboard to create a new blank record "inserted" just before the one you are in.
Del **Key**	Look for Del or Delete on your keyboard to delete an entire record. Use the Backspace key key to delete a single character in a field. If you press Del accidentally, press Ctrl-U to recover

the record. You hold the **Ctrl** key down and press **U** to make the command work.

Backspace Key   Look for the left-facing arrow in the upper right-hand corner of the alphanumeric area of the keyboard. This key deletes single characters to the left of the blinking cursor.

1. Go to the next field. What key did you press to do so?
2. What happens to the cursor when you press the down arrow key?

1. *The **Tab** key or the right arrow key.*
2. *The cursor moves down one record but stays in the same field.*

The Drives and Directories Where Paradox Saves Tables

When you press **F2** DO-IT to create a table in Paradox, it is saved on the disk. Paradox creates a DOS file for the new table. You need not know the DOS file name, but you need to know that a file is created. The DOS file name becomes necessary if you cannot remember the name of the table for which you are looking. Also, Paradox knows if a file is a table, report, or graph.

The data you enter into tables is organized into files by the computer. Every file has a two-part name: a name and an extension. The name can hold up to eight alphanumeric characters.

The file extension is three characters long and is separated from the file name by a period. The extension is optional, but is often used to distinguish a type of file. For example:

File Name and Extension	Description
DOUGLAS.TXT	The person who saved this file gave it his own name. The TXT extension is a file that contains printable letters and numbers. Very often, you will find a README.TXT file in a software program that updates you on the most recent changes in the product.
PARADOX3.EXE	This is a DOS file, with the EXE extension,

meaning it is an executable file. This file
can be loaded into RAM and executed.

X   This is a valid DOS file, with a single
                           character for the name and no extension.
                           Remember, the extension is optional.

Tip │ A file extension can be especially helpful if you want to find all the files that
    │ relate to a specific group. A user with the initials AWW might put the exten-
    │ sion. AWW on all the files they create. Later, when they ask for a list of their
    │ files, they can ask to see any files with the.AWW extension.

DOS organizes the files you create into "directories." A directory groups related disk files together. Your hard drive has a "root" directory from which all the other directories branch out.

When you start Paradox, you type the command CD. This stands for "Change Directory." When you type CD\PDOX35, you are making PDOX35 your working directory. Make sure you are in the PDOX35 directory while using Paradox so that all of your Paradox files are stored in the Paradox directory.

Getting Help

The Paradox Help function is only one key away. Press F1 and a Help screen is displayed, as shown in Figure 2.9.

The Help screen displays information about how to get around the Help facility when you press F1 while in the Main menu. If you are editing a table and press F1, the Help information will be about editing. You can still move to other areas of the Help facility, but your current activity determines the first screen that appears.

Help menus are set off from the screen workspace by a double line border. Press F1 from the Main menu and you will see these help menu options:

Basics   As the name implies, with this option you get
                           basic information about Paradox. It describes
                           items you see on your screen.

```
Basics  GettingAround  Keys  MenuChoices  Index  Scripts/PAL  Paradox
Basic Paradox terms and concepts._
========================= About the Paradox Help System =========================

   ◆  The double-line border tells you that you're in the Help System.
      Note that the Paradox menu has been replaced by the Help System menu.

   ◆  Press [F1] at any time during a Paradox session.  The Help System
      gives you information about what you were doing when you pressed [F1].

   ◆  Browse the Help System by making Help menu selections.

   ◆  Once you are in the Help System, press [F1] again to get the index.
      (Choose Index, above, for more about how to use the index.)

   ◆  While you're in the Help System, pressing [Esc] takes you to the
      previous help screen or back to Paradox.

   ◆  Choosing Paradox or Back from the Help System menu always returns you
      to Paradox.


   ┌─────────────────────────────────────────────────────────────────────┐
   │ Choose a help menu item.   [F1] for help index.   Paradox to resume. │
   └─────────────────────────────────────────────────────────────────────┘
```

Figure 2.9. The Help screen

GettingAround	This option gives descriptions of efficient ways to move around tables, menus, and the Help facility.
Keys	The use of special keys is covered with this Help topic, that is, the use of the **Shift**, **Ctrl**, and **Alt** keys along with alphabetic and function keys.
Menuchoices	Lists of the menu selections and their action can be seen with this option.
Index	The Help index is like having a manual on the screen. You can look up any activity and find the steps for doing it.
Scripts/PAL	This option, for the more advanced Paradox user, introduces the scripts and PAL features of Paradox.
Paradox	Select this option to exit out of Help into Paradox.

While in any Help screen, press **F1** and the Help index appears on the screen. You will find a summary of all the topics found in Help screens.

1. You want to move around the Help facility effectively. Which Help menu option would you use?
2. What happens when you press **F1**?
3. What screen or image do you have to view before you can access the Help facility?

1. *GettingAround.*
2. *A Help screen appears, with information related to the activity you are doing at the time.*
3. *You can access the Help facility from almost any screen or image.*

Moving in the Help Screen

Moving in the Help screen makes use of familiar keys and their actions. The actions are logical, and most do what you would expect them to do, without looking it up.

Up Arrow	Move highlighting to the previous Help topic.
Down Arrow	Move highlighting to the next Help topic.
Page Down	Move to the next page of the Help facility.
Page Up	Move to the previous page of the Help facility.
Enter	Display Help information you have selected by highlighting a Help topic.
Ctrl-Z	Searches the Help index for the subject you specify.
Alt-Z	Continues the search started with **Ctrl-Z**.

Leaving Help

When you have gotten all the help you need, press the **Esc** key, and keep pressing it until you return to your original activity or to the Main menu.

The other option is to select Paradox from the **Help** submenu to return to the previous screen.

1. While in the Help index, press **Ctrl-Z**. What happens?
2. Name the value for which you want to search. Press **Enter**. What happens?
3. Press the up arrow key while in the Help index. What happens?
4. The highlighting is on the subject you want to explore. Press **Enter**. What happens?

1. *Paradox prompts you to name the subject for which you want to search through the Help index.*
2. *Paradox takes you to that subject in the index.*
3. *The highlighting moves to the previous Help topic.*
4. *The Help screen for that subject appears on screen.*

Errors

Paradox has three types of errors for which you may see a red message appear on the screen and/or hear a beep.

Syntax Errors

Enter instructions that are misspelled, have missing letters or symbols, or are not typed in the correct order, and Paradox will display an error message.

Run Errors

You may spell the command correctly, or select the right command from the menus, but if Paradox cannot carry out your command, you will get a "Run Error" message. One example is trying to print when your printer is not turned on. Another example is trying to view a table that you have not yet created. An example of an error message on screen is seen in Figure 2.10.

When you see an error message, don't panic. Instead, press **Esc** and correct the problem, or retry your procedures.

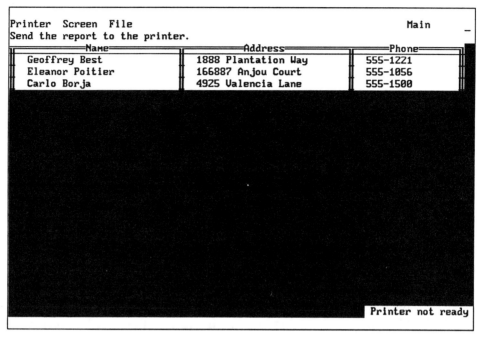

Figure 2.10. Error message on screen

Logic Errors

Your syntax is correct, but the sequence of commands is incorrect. This error will be seen when working with PAL. As your skills advance with Paradox, you will learn about Logic errors.

Tip | If you make an error, Paradox displays an error message, usually in red (if you have a color monitor). Paradox may include a beep to signal you of the error explained in the message.

Leaving Paradox

Your first short table exists in Paradox. Unlike many other software programs, there is no save command in Paradox. The Do-It command finishes the activity and saves the result on disk.

With this built-in safeguard, you never lose files by forgetting to save them before you exit Paradox. The Do-It command also creates the DOS files found in the Paradox directory.

Begin the process of leaving Paradox by:

STEP 1:

Press: the **Esc** key and/or the **F10** key to move to the Main menu.

STEP 2:

Move: the cursor to the **Exit** option
Press: **Enter**
Answer the "Exit" prompt with a yes or no.

STEP 3:

Select: Yes

You are presented with a DOS prompt as you exit Paradox.

Tip | If you are in the **Edit** command, you cannot simply press **Esc** to get to the Main menu. You must first finish and save the table by pressing Do-It. From there, you can back out to the Main menu.

1. Select the **Exit** option from the Main menu. What happens?
2. What command finishes your table and saves it to disk?
3. With Main highlighted in the upper right corner, press **F10**. What happens next?

1. *Paradox prompts you to make sure you want to leave Paradox.*
2. *F2 DO-IT.*
3. *The Paradox Main menu appears across the top of the screen.*

Summary

Congratulations on creating your first simple Paradox table, Doing It, and exiting Paradox. You have started Paradox, explored menu options, learned how to select menu items, and created a table. The value of the **Esc** key, the F2 Do-It key, and the F10 Menu key have been demonstrated. The difference between creating a table structure and editing a table is now clear in your mind. Drives and directories have been introduced. You are familiar with the many Help options available while you are working in Paradox. An example error message is shown so that you are acquainted with this instance, should it ever happen to you. You are ready to move on to more sophisticated use of the Paradox database program.

The main topics covered in this chapter are:

- Selecting menu items
- Creating a table
  - Paradox prompts
  - Defining a table structure
  - Entering data into a table
- Getting help from Paradox
- Learning how to handle errors
- Leaving Paradox

Exercises

With your computer still on and the DOS prompt appearing, follow the steps below as a review of this chapter. You will practice booting Paradox, creating a table, editing a table, asking for help, and then leaving Paradox.

What You Should Do	**How the Computer Responds**
1. At the "C>" prompt, type: CD\PDOX35 Press: **Enter** Type: PDOX35 Press: **Enter** If your screen is already in the Paradox directory, indicated by "C:\PDOX35," simply: Type: PDOX35 Press: **Enter**	1. For an instant, the Paradox title screen appears. Paradox is booted with the Main menu available.
2. Press the right arrow key three times to move to the **Create** option. Press Enter.	2. The "Table:" prompt appears with the word "Main" highlighted in the upper right-hand corner.

3. Type in the name of the table you are going to create. An example for this exercise is "Salary." Press **Enter**.

3. The structure definition appears on the screen with your blinking cursor in the Field Name column. The word "Create" appears in the upper right-hand corner. Down the right side of the screen are the **Field Type** options.

4. Type: `Name`
   Press: **Enter**
   Type: `A25`
   Press: **Enter**

4. "Name" appears in the Field Name column. "A25" appears in the Field Type column, and the blinking cursor moves to the second field to be defined in the table structure.

5. Type: `Salary`
   Press: **Enter**
   Type: `$`
   Press: **Enter**

5. The word "Salary" is entered in the Field Name column, the $ appears in the Field Type column, and the cursor is next to number 3 in the Field Name column.

6. Press the right arrow key four times until **Modify** is highlighted and then press **Enter**. Move the highlighting to **Edit** and press **Enter** again.

6. After you select **Modify**, the **Modify** submenu is displayed. From this menu, you select **Edit** and the "Table:" prompt appears.

7. Type: `Salary`
   Press: **Enter**

7. The *Salary* table appears on the screen ready for your data input. Your blinking cursor is under the Name column.

8. Type: `Eleanor Poitier`
   Press: **Enter**
   Type: `35000`
   Press: **Enter**
   Type: `Carlo Borja`
   Press: **Enter**
   Type: `32000`
   Press: **Enter**

8. The two names are entered in their field columns, with the respective salaries in the *Salary* field. You have entered two records in the table.

9. Press: **F1**

9. The "Editing a Table" Help screen appears with the first item being listed: "To change a record."

10. Move the menu highlighting to "Paradox."
    Press: **Enter**

10. You are instantly returned to the table you are editing.

11. Press: **F2**

11. *Salary* table is saved to disk. Line 3, which was blank on the table, is removed as the table is finished off. You

are now in the **View** mode with the word "Main" in the upper right-hand corner.

12. Press: **F10**

Press: the left arrow key one time

Press: **Enter**

Type: Y for Yes you want to leave Paradox

12. The Paradox screen is removed from the screen as you exit Paradox. The DOS prompt remains on the screen, showing that you are still in the PARADOX directory.

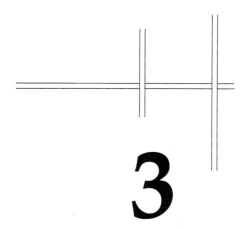

3

Working with Paradox Tables

As you explore more and more of the options in Paradox, you will find that its power and simplicity becomes apparent. In this chapter you will learn to take further advantage of that power by building database tables. You will:

- Plan a database table
- Create a table
- Use tables in a variety of ways

Planning a Table

Power. Paradox has a lot of power. A well-designed table takes full advantage of that power. The best way to harness the power is to plan your tables before you create them. Up to now, the tables you have created are quite simple. As you introduce more data, keep simplicity in mind.

You do not want to create one huge database that will hold all the information you will ever need about a database item in one record. Remember, Paradox is based on a relational model and can handle multiple tables.

Start by deciding what information you need to have in your database. If you have a business, some of the information you might need is customer information, invoices, order information, sales records, and inventory data. Some of these are listed here:

*Customer Info   *Invoice Info   *Sales Records

Think of everything that you need in each of these three categories. List them on a piece of paper so that you can organize your database. Here are some examples:

Customer Info	Invoice Info	Sales Records
First Name	Invoice Number	Sales Person
Last Name	Sale Date	Available Customers
Address	Product Number	Number of Customers
City	Quantity	Monthly Sales
State	Customer Number	Products Sold
Phone Number	Tax	Total Sales
Customer Number	Shipping	Commissions Earned
	Total Sale	

Tip

Predict what information you think you will need in future reports. If you are designing a database for a business, ask the sales manager, the vice president of product development, and the financial manager what information they need. What do they get now? How do they use it? How could it be more useful? If they could design the report, what would they want to know? If this database is for yourself, ask similar questions.

The foregoing lists are not meant to be a complete list of what you might need in each of these three categories, but you can see how useful the process of writing everything down first is. As stated earlier, you might be tempted to put all the information in the lists above into one table. With Paradox, you can create three separate tables according to the columns above and still use any related information.

Take another look at the list of items under the heading Invoice Info. The customer name and address is not necessary here. If you put the customer name and address in this database, the customer who places ten orders in a month will have their name in this database ten times. Repetitive information should be in a separate table.

Using a customer number instead of a name means that you can simply add the number to the database and save the expense of having redundant data in your database. The customer number on the invoice would be the same as that in the customer database. Using the Paradox relational database, you can match those without entering the data two, three, or more times.

Guidelines for Designing a Table

From those with more experience, take these suggestions seriously. You will save yourself a lot of work down the road if you plan your database following these guidelines.

Keep Your Database Simple
Include as few fields in a table as you can, while keeping all the information you need. Too many fields make a table hard to manage. It is better to link many small tables when you are ready to create reports with your data.

Keep Redundancy to a Minimum
After you make lists of the main categories of data and the information that goes into each category, check to make sure the same information is not found in each database. It is one thing if something like a customer number is found in each database. But if name, address, phone number, and zip code are found over and over, you create unnecessary work.

Imagine having customer names and addresses in four separate tables. Then imagine that a customer changes her address. You have to edit four tables, entering the new address in each one. This is redundancy. If, instead, you have one table with the customer name, address, and customer number, and three other tables with customer number alone, how many times do you have to change the address? *Right!* Only one time.

You change the address field one time, and any reference to that data, from any other table, is automatically changed.

Designing Tables to Meet Your Individual Needs

If you have a pile of paperwork on your desk that you want to incorporate into an electronic database, make the electronic database as similar to your pile of paperwork as you can. All the products you sell have an inventory number. Use that same number on your Paradox invoice. For example, if you keep a list on your desk of the patients you've seen and why, make a table called Patients Seen.

Tip ‖ Tie any reference to a patient name to that patient's number. Use the patients number to eliminate redundant information.

Use Descriptive Field Names

This guideline is most important when people other than yourself will be using the database you design. If you put "XYZ" as the field name and that means "Total Monthly Income," other people entering data are going to have a tough time knowing what you mean. Paradox provides space to name fields in a more descriptive way. Using "Total Monthly Income" may make the field too wide, but better too wide than forgotten or misinterpreted.

1. In how many tables would it be best to have the names and addresses of all your customers?
2. What would be a good field name for the field that holds the total sales for a salesperson?
3. Name a field that will hold gross sales.

1. *One.*
2. *Total Sales.*
3. *Gross Sales, Monthly Gross Sales, or Annual Gross Sales.*

Types of Table Relationships

As you write down all the information you need to keep in a database, you will find that there are relationships between tables. A customer number or patient number may appear on three separate tables. A product number may appear on an *Invoice* table, an *Inventory* table, and a *Sales* table.

One example of how tables can be related is a *lookup* table. This is commonly used and very powerful. If you have an inventory of five products with lengthy descriptions, your table might look like this:

Name	Product Description	Quantity	Price
Harvey Gough	Political Map of Medieval Europe	5	$34.95
Ole Olson	Contour Map of Scandinavia	1	24.95
Jake Van Late	Physical Map of the Early Dutch Empire	50	13.99

If you are the data entry person, you do not want to type these long product descriptions every time you get an order. Because you are working with Paradox and the tables are relational, pull the product description out and put a product number in.

Keep the product number and product description on its own database table. You only need to access this table when you add more products or change the products you have now. Here is how the *Product Description* table would look.

Product Number	Product Description
POM1	Political Map of Medieval Europe
POM2	Political Map of Modern Europe (1990)
COM1	Contour Map of Scandinavia
COM2	Contour Map of the Grand Canyon
PHM1	Physical Map of the Early Dutch Empire (1556–1663)

The result is the following table with less typing, less time taken to enter the data, and less chance for error. This method also assures that product descriptions remain consistent with different data entry personnel.

For a company with only five products, this may not seem worthwhile, but if a company has many products, the concept is a lifesaver. Paradox can look up information related to the product number in any table you develop, quickly and accurately.

Name	Product Number	Quantity	Price
Harvey Gough	POM1	5	$34.95
Ole Olson	COM1	1	24.95
Jake Van Late	PHM1	50	13.99

Flexibility is enhanced because any database table can be changed, altered, and redefined. As a business grows and database needs change, Paradox can adapt to these new needs.

Other types of relationships exist between tables. Paradox is most useful because it allows the splitting of data out of a table that can be brought together at a later date. The result is tables that are smaller, simpler, and easier to understand and navigate.

Table Keys

Table keys indicate special fields in a large table used to find records. In a database of 10,000 names, you are searching for someone with the last name of Wicker. One by one, Paradox searches through 10,000 last name fields until it finds Wicker. Not only could this take a very long time, but if no Wicker were in the file, you would have to wait for the search and then get a dismal result.

Paradox creates a special file with key fields. Paradox can look up information much more quickly by using its key field files, which act like an index of your data. Like many of the files Paradox creates, you will not directly access that file. Instead, you deal with the tables, reports, and forms created in Paradox.

Characteristics of Table Keys

You can set up each table with a unique key that helps prevent you from entering redundant information into a table. Keys help you get more accurate data. Some table links may require a key field. A key field helps keep data in order. If you enter data out of order in **Edit** mode, Paradox will put it back in order, by key field, when you press **F2** DO-IT.

Processing speed is enhanced by using key fields. Compare two methods of trying to find the subject of Making Database Graphs, while looking in this book. Without key fields, you would start at the beginning and, page-by-page, look through the book until you found a section on graphs. With key fields (the index), you turn to the back of the book, look up the subject of graphs and turn to page 197.

The Primary Key Field

The main type of key field is the *Primary Key* field. The Primary Key field should be the field you use to find records in the database. This is the field used most often to look up individual records. Examples are last name, customer number, or social security number.

In the table you saw previously that included different kinds of maps, the product number is the field you would want to designate the Primary Key field. That is the main lookup field, plus it is the field that will be present in all tables. Right now we will be concerned only with Primary Key fields.

Primary Key Rules
The following are rules for using primary keys:

1. Put primary keys in the first few fields of a table, with no skipping of fields. The first field should be the primary key in most situations. The second field cannot be the primary key by itself because that would mean you skipped the first field. The second field can be a primary key if the first field is also a primary key field, because you have not skipped a field.
2. All primary keys indicate unique fields in a table. If you select the social security number to be your primary key, then no two records in the table can have the same social security number. If a second record is entered with the same number, Paradox informs you of the repeating data with a special table displaying duplicates. When using the **CoEdit** mode, Paradox allows you to choose between the new or original data noted with a primary key. This helps eliminate errors and keeps you informed of offending records.

Indicating a Primary Key
You make a primary key by adding an asterisk after the description given for the field type, while creating a Paradox table. If the field type was numeric, you would type N*; if alphanumeric, you would type A25*.

If you do not follow these rules when creating a primary key, Paradox will display a warning message when you press **F2** DO-IT.

When to Use Primary Keys

In every table you create, it is recommended that you create a primary key. Keep this in mind when creating tables so that the Primary Key field is the first field. This way you comply with the primary key rules. Without the Primary Key field, you will have to look for your own duplicate records manually. Paradox will let you change your mind if you assign a field as a primary key and decide that a different field should be the primary key.

1. Name the customer number as the primary key. What are the benefits?
2. Which of the following would make the best primary keys?
   a. Social security number
   b. Salary
   c. Customer number
   d. Phone number

1. *That number will be used most often to look up records. Paradox will find and display duplicate customer numbers if any exist.*
2. *a and c.*

Creating a Table

Use the **Create** option on the Main menu to create a table in Paradox. If you are just loading Paradox, follow these steps at the "C>" prompt:

STEP 1:

Type: `CD\PDOX35`
Press: **Enter**

STEP 2:

Type: `PDOX35`
Press: **Enter**

Checking the Directory

If you have been working in Paradox for awhile, do a quick check to make sure you are in the PDOX35 directory. Any tables you create will be stored in the directory in which you are now working. The steps below will show you how to check your working directory while still in Paradox.

STEP 1:

With the main menu on the screen, press **F10**, the Menu key
Select: **Tools**
Select: **More**
Select: **Directory**

The screen will show the "Directory:" prompt, as in Figure 3.1. At the "Directory:" prompt, check the name of the directory. If you are in c:\PDOX35\, leave the directory as is.

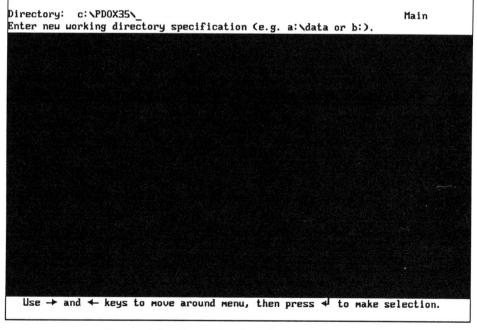

```
Directory:  c:\PDOX35\_                                         Main
Enter new working directory specification (e.g. a:\data or b:).
```

```
   Use → and ← keys to move around menu, then press ↵ to make selection.
```

Figure 3.1. The "Directory:" prompt

STEP 2A:

> Press: **Enter**
> Select: OK

If the "Directory:" prompt shows that you are in another directory:

STEP 2B:

> Type: `C:\PDOX35`
> Press: **Enter**
> Select: OK

On the lower right of the screen, a red (if you have a color monitor) warning line appears, announcing your present working directory. When you start to work, the red line will disappear.

Clearing Table Images

If you were already working in Paradox, clear any table images that appear on the screen so that you can prepare to create a new table.

STEP:

> Press: **Alt-F8 Clear All**

Planning the Table

The table created in the following exercises is for a high school teacher, teaching advanced chemistry. The table will list the students in the class by student number. Their final grade, expressed as a percentage, is included. The student number will be the primary key. The fields are:

Student Number   Last Name   First Name   Grade-%

The student number is designated as the Primary Key field and is the same student number used in all the databases in the school. That way, this table can be linked to any other data information table regarding any student. The student number has two parts, the first being the grade the student is in, followed by their alphabetical rank in the class. A student with the number 12-018 would be a senior, with a last name probably starting with A.

With the highlighting on **View** in the Main menu, start creating the table.

STEP 1:

Select: **Create**

The screen appears, as in Figure 3.2. You are prompted to name the table you want to create.

Naming the Table

The prompt appears to name the table. The name you give the table eventually becomes a DOS file, making the following guidelines necessary when you are naming a table.

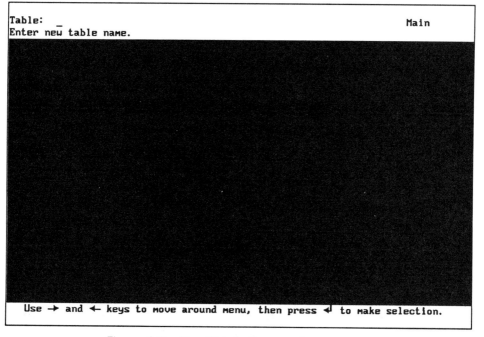

Figure 3.2. The "Table:" prompt

- A table name must be eight or fewer characters in length.
- Only letters, numbers, and the characters $ and _ are allowed.
- No blank spaces are allowed in the table name.
- Table names must be unique. No other table name can be identical to a new table name.

Tip Choose a table name that reflects the subject of the data found in the table. For example, the table created here has a list of advanced chemistry students and their grades. Here are some possible names:

ADVCHEM
AC_GRADE
ACHEMGRD

While any of these may mean something to the teacher who designs them, the first one might be the best to use if others are going to have access to this table. Again, the guideline is to keep it simple.

STEP 2:

Type: ADVCHEM
Press: Enter

1. You have created and saved a table, which is now on screen. Press Alt-F8. What happens?
2. You are ready to create another table. With the images cleared and the Main menu on screen, press **C**. What happens?

1. *All images are cleared from the screen.*
2. *Paradox prompts you to name the table you want to create.*

Deciding Field Names, Types, and Keys

The screen appears with the structure table. At the right are the field types from which you must select. The two sections of the structure definition screen are the Field Name section and the Field Type section.

Field Name Area

The blinking cursor and the arrow indicator are in the column called "Field Name." The name of the field will go in this space. As with the table name, there are some guidelines for naming a field.

- Field names can be no longer than 26 characters.
- Spaces can be used, but the field name cannot start with a blank space. This allows you to use more than one word as a field name.
- The following symbols are not allowed in a field name: double quotes ("), square brackets ([]), braces ({}), left or right parentheses (()), the number sign (#), or the dash-right arrow combination (->).
- A field name can be used only once in a table.

Tip

A field name can be used only once in any one table, as was stated. However, the same field name can be used in two different tables. Recall the example given earlier in this chapter. A product number was created to indicate a specific type of map. One table holds the product number and the description of that product. Another table holds the name of the person who ordered the product, the product number, the quantity ordered, and the price. Later, these two fields can be linked, using the product number field.

Field Type Area

In this area, you describe how the data will be defined in the table. Paradox checks the data entered into each field, making sure it is the right type. If not, a warning is sounded. The field types are described below in more detail than you see on your screen.

Alphanumeric

A
Choose alphanumeric, and any data can be entered using the typing area of the keyboard. Letters, numbers, and some special characters are allowed, such as #, or %. Numbers entered in this field type are usually those found in an address. Numbers entered in an Alphanumeric field cannot be used for mathematical functions.

Define an Alphanumeric field by pressing A first and then the maximum number of spaces allowed in the field. Paradox allows up to 255 spaces in an

Alphanumeric field. If you make the space too small, some of your data will not appear on screen. If you make the space larger than you need, a lot of disk space will be used storing blank spaces.

Number

N

Up to 15 significant digits can be stored in a Number field. The range of numbers that can be used is from 10^{-307} to 10^{+307}. Numbers with this field type can be used for mathematical functions.

Currency

$

Similar to the Number field, numbers in this field can be used for mathematical functions. You will see two decimal places displayed, however. You will also see commas separating large dollar values, with negative numbers enclosed in parentheses.

Date

D

The range of dates you can include in this field are from January 1, 100 to December 31, 9999. The default date format determines how dates are displayed on the screen. The **Image/Format** menu option allows you to change the date format.

Tip

Numbers placed in an Alphanumeric field cannot be used in mathematical functions. Use the Number and Currency fields when you want to add, subtract, multiply, or divide numbers.

The Primary Key

Specify the primary key for the table by typing an asterisk (*) after the field type definition. More than one key can be defined, but remember that they must be in the first columns of the table, with no skipping of columns.

1. You decide that the first Alphanumeric field with 18 spaces should be the primary field. What do you type in the field type category?
2. You decide that a Numeric field that will hold ten numbers will be the primary field. What do you type in the field type category?

1. *A18*.*
2. *N*. (In a number field, you do not enter the number of spaces.)*

Entering the Field Names and Types

The field names have already been listed. With careful planning, the Advanced Chemistry teacher knows the data wanted in this table, which is the primary key, as well as which field types to use.

STEP 3:

> Type: `Student Number`
> Press: **Enter**
> Type: `A6*`
> Press: **Enter**

The first field is defined. Six spaces were used in the field because no student number exceeds six spaces. There is no need to store blank spaces on disk. The asterisk denotes this field as the Primary Key field.

STEP 4:

> Type: `No.`
> Press: **Enter**
> Type: `N`
> Press: **Enter**

This field numbers the entries you make in this table. You can call this field record number, or in another situation it might be an invoice number. The reason you number your entries is as follows. Say you enter 100 names in a specific order, without numbering the records. Later you sort the records so that they appear in a completely different order. How do you get the records back to the order in which you entered them?

You may not need to answer this question with every table you create. Yet, you can save yourself time and frustration by numbering each record before the table becomes unwieldy.

Tip | Decide to number records when you anticipate that the number of entries in any one table will become too large for you to want to type them in again.

STEP 5:

> Type: Last Name
> Press: **Enter**
> Type: A15
> Press: **Enter**

The second field is defined. The third and fourth are defined as follows:

STEP 6:

> Type: First Name
> Press: **Enter**
> Type: A15
> Press: **Enter**
> Type: Grade-%
> Press: **Enter**
> Type: N
> Press: **Enter**

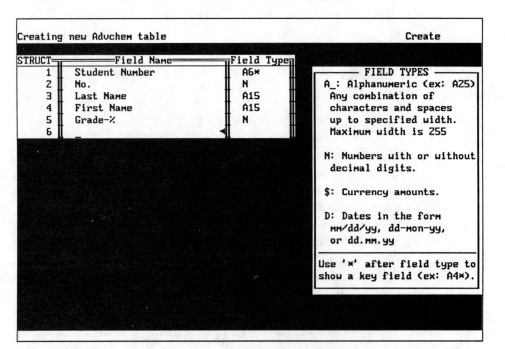

Figure 3.3. The *ADVCHEM* table defined

This completes the table definition. Your screen should look like the one in Figure 3.3.

Tell Paradox to create the *ADVCHEM* table by pressing the F2 DO-IT key.

STEP 7:

Press: **F2 DO-IT**

Paradox returns you to the Main menu.

1. Type an asterisk (*) following the table definition in the Field Type category. What have you done?
2. Press the **F2 DO-IT** key. What happens?

1. *You have defined the primary key.*
2. *Paradox defines the table and saves the structure to disk.*

Using the Table

The structure of the table is created. Now you can start to use it! Start by viewing the table.

Viewing the Table

You might wonder why you want to view the table, when what you really want to do is add records to the table. You are going to go through this short side track to learn about function keys. When you want to edit a table or add records, you select **Modify/Edit**, type the name of the table you want to edit, press **Enter**, and the fields appear across the screen.

Instead, view the table first. After viewing, go directly to **Edit** by using the function key.

STEP 1:

Select: **View**
Type: ADVCHEM
Press: **Enter**

You are viewing the *ADVCHEM* table, with no records in it. You are ready to add records to the table, which is called editing the table.

STEP 2:

Press: **F9** Edit

By pressing the **F9** key, you have moved directly into the **Edit** mode without having to travel through the menus. The cursor is placed in the first field of the table just as if you had backed out of the **View** menu and selected the **Modify** and **Edit** menus, as you see in Figure 3.4.

Editing the Table

There are 15 students in the advanced chemistry class, but start by entering only five names. This gives you a good indication of the quickest ways you can take advantage of a Paradox table. Start adding records to the *ADVCHEM* table:

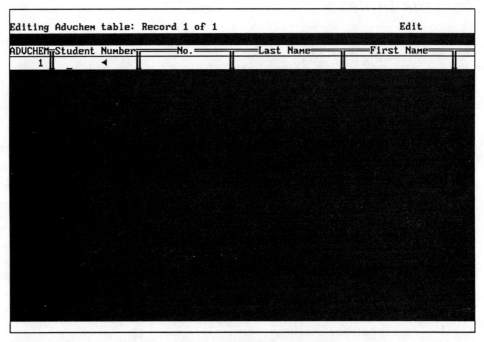

Figure 3.4. Screen ready for editing

STEP 1:

Type: 11-013
Press: **Enter**
Type: 1
Press: **Enter**
Type: Astro
Press: **Enter**
Type: Billy
Press: **Enter**
Type: 88.85
Press: **Enter**

This is the first record entered into the *ADVCHEM* database table. Now, enter the remaining four students.

STEP 2:

Student Number	No.	Last Name	First Name	Grade-%
12-288	2	Galaxy	Andrea	94.88
12-316	3	Moon	Monica	72.34
11-384	4	Pluto	Pete	90.09
12-122	5	Comet	Alvin	98.92

That's it for the *ADVCHEM* table. Finish the table and save it to disk.

STEP 3:

Press: **F2** DO-IT
The table appears on the screen, as in Figure 3.5.

Tip

Notice the asterisk that appears in the far right column. This indicates to you, the user, that there is more data in a column that you cannot see on screen. When you move the blinking cursor to that column, the asterisk disappears and only the data in the column is visible.

```
Viewing Advchem table: Record 1 of 5                              Main

ADVCHEM┬Student Number┬        ═No.═         ┬       ═Last Name═     ┬═First Name═┬
    1 ║  11-013_      ║         1            ║        Astro          ║  Billy    ║  ×
    2 ║  11-384       ║         4            ║        Pluto          ║  Pete     ║  ×
    3 ║  12-122       ║         5            ║        Comet          ║  Alvin    ║  ×
    4 ║  12-288       ║         2            ║        Galaxy         ║  Andrea   ║  ×
    5 ║  12-316       ║         3            ║        Moon           ║  Monica   ║  ×
```

Figure 3.5. The *ADVCHEM* table on screen

1. While in the **View** mode, press **F9** Edit key. What happens?
2. What is the name given to the **F9** key?
3. Press **Enter** after typing in the data for the Grade-% field. What happens?

1. *Paradox puts you in the **Edit** mode. Changes and additions can be made in the table.*
2. *A function key.*
3. *Paradox opens the next row to enter data for the next record.*

Using Function Keys

In the section above, you used the **F9** Edit and the **F2** DO-IT keys. Most of the time, a function key is set up to do in one keystroke what might take several keystrokes. For example, while viewing a table, pressing **F9** puts Paradox in **Edit** mode. The alternative is to select **Modify** from the menu, select **Edit** from the submenu, and then type the name of the table you want to edit at the prompt.

The Paradox function keys are listed here with a brief description of what function they control.

Tip

In most books written about computers and in the documentation that comes with software programs, there is a convention for describing how keys are pressed. In the list below, you will see Alt-F5 as a function key. This convention means that you press the Alt key, hold it down while pressing the F5 key. Additional examples are: Ctrl-F3 or Shift-F6. The hyphen between keys means hold the first down and then press the second.

F1 HELP	Press F1 and you open the door to the extensive Paradox Help facility. Press this key when you first start Paradox and you get a Help opening screen. Press it anytime while working in Paradox and you get information on your present task.
F2 DO-IT!	Press F2 and Paradox finishes an action and saves the table or table structure to disk.
F3 UP IMAGE	Open two or more tables and they appear simultaneously on the screen. Press F3 and you move up one table image. The image in which you are working is the one that appears highlighted on the screen.
F4 DOWN IMAGE	With the highlighting on one table image, press F4 and you move down one table image on the screen.
F5 EXAMPLE	Use F5 with the **Ask** option from the Main menu. It is used to generate a query. Learn more about this function key as you continue reading this book.
F6 CHECK	Use F6 with the **Ask** option from the Main menu. With this function, you can check the columns you want to see in an answer query.
F7 FORM TOGGLE	Press F7 and you switch (toggle) from the list view of a table and the form view. The list view displays several records in rows and columns on the screen. The form view displays one record in a specified format.

F8 CLEAR IMAGE	Open two or more tables and you may have too much clutter on your screen. Highlight an unwanted table by pressing **F3** or **F4** and then press **F8** to remove that image from the screen. You do not lose the data; it is simply cleared from the screen.
F9 EDIT	While viewing a table, press **F9** to go into the **Edit** function in Paradox.
F10 MENU	Press **F10** and a menu is displayed as indicated by the highlighted menu indicator in the upper right-hand corner of the screen. If Main is highlighted and you press **F10**, the Main menu appears on screen.
Alt-F3 INSTANT SCRIPT RECORD	Use the **Alt-F3** combination to record keystrokes for a script. Scripts are used to automate tasks with Paradox. Learn more about scripts in Chapter 10.
Alt-F4 INSTANT SCRIPT PLAY	Record the script with **Alt-F3** and then play the script back, using **Alt-F4**.
Alt-F5 FIELD VIEW	Press **Alt-F5** to see the entire contents of a field while in the **View** or **Edit** mode.
Alt-F6 CHECK PLUS	Use **Alt-F6** while filling in a query form. Learn more about queries in Chapter 5.
Alt-F7 INSTANT REPORT	Highlight the active table in the workspace and then press **Alt-F7** to create and print an instant report.
Alt-F8 CLEAR ALL	Press **F8** and you clear one highlighted image. Press **Alt-F8** and every image on the screen is cleared.
Alt-F9 COEDIT	Often used to start an edit in the network version of Paradox. Other Paradox users can access tables while you edit them. **CoEdit** holds characteristics that are useful in a single-user environment, as well.
Alt-F10 PAL MENU	Displays the **Paradox Application Language** menu (PAL). Using PAL is discussed under the topic of "The Advanced Paradox User."

1. Press Alt-F7. What happens?
2. With several images on screen, press F4. What happens?

1. *Paradox prints an Instant Report.*
2. *The cursor moves down one image on the screen.*

Printing a Quick Report

The table is created, and you have learned about function keys. Combine your knowledge of function keys with your table to create a report of the data entered into the *ADVCHEM* table. While in the **View** mode:

STEP:

Press: **Alt-F7** Instant Report

Paradox will send the table on screen to the printer, creating a neat report of the data you have entered. This report is seen in Figure 3.6a and b.

This is the simplest, most basic method of getting a report with Paradox. As you progress through this book, you will learn more sophisticated methods. Right now, give yourself a pat on the back for creating your first Paradox report!

Creating a Quick Graph

The blinking cursor is in the *ADVCHEM* table. Move the cursor to the field "Grade-%" to create a graph of the student's grades.

Press: **Ctrl-F7** Graph

A graph appears instantly on screen, showing the student's scores by their student number. The graph on your screen should match the one in Figure 3.7.

```
End of Page
Press any key to continue..._




12/05/90                    Standard Report                        Page   1



Student Number  No.      Last Name         First Name       Grade-%
--------------  ------   ----------------  ----------------  -------
11-013               1   Astro             Billy                 89
11-384               4   Pluto             Pete                  90
12-122               5   Comet             Alvin                 99
12-288               2   Galaxy            Andrea                95
12-316               3   Moon              Monica                72
```

Figure 3.6a. The instant report

Removing the Graph from the Screen

Admire the graph you have created. You have created an instant picture of
the data on the table, but now it is time to go back to the table.

STEP:

Press: Any key

Student Number	No.	Last Name	First Name	Grade-%
11–013	1	Astro	Billy	89
11–384	4	Pluto	Pete	90
12–122	5	Comet	Alvin	99
12–288	2	Galaxy	Andrea	95
12–316	3	Moon	Monica	72

Figure 3.6b. The instant report (printed)

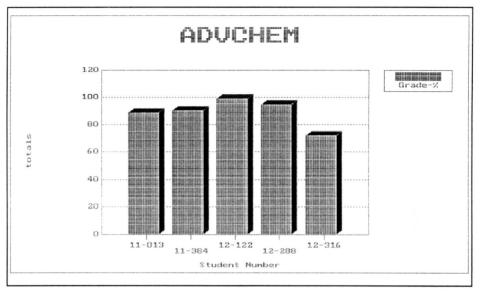

Figure 3.7. The instant graph

Follow this step and Paradox removes the graph from the screen and puts you back in the **View** mode, with the *ADVCHEM* table on screen. The cursor is where you left it before you created the graph.

Removing the Table Image from the Screen

Once again, practice using a function key. You have finished working in AD-VCHEM for now. Clear the image of *ADVCHEM* from the screen by pressing one key.

STEP:

Press: **F8** Clear Image

Paradox immediately puts you in the Main menu, where you can select the next task. The workspace is blank so that you can prepare to create another table or attack another task in Paradox.

1. Press **Ctrl-F7**. What happens?
2. Press **F8**. What happens?

1. *You have created a graph on screen.*
2. *The table image that the cursor is in is cleared from the screen.*

Summary

Review what you want to get out of a database and how that database will be used. Talk to others who will be using the database. Keep the database as simple as possible. These are the guidelines for planning a database table, given in this chapter. In addition, you want to keep redundancy to a minimum, write descriptive table and field names, and design the database for your individual needs. If it makes sense to you and the way you work and it keeps your work simple, then do it that way.

You have learned how to define a primary key in a database table in order to increase the speed for finding records. A primary key also helps you match, list, and sort records. Add an asterisk after the field type to mark a primary key.

In this chapter you created a more sophisticated table than you have previously. You planned it, named it, determined the structure, including defining a primary key, and edited it.

With this table in Paradox, you used it in a variety of ways. You practiced viewing it, editing it, printing the table, graphing the table, and removing the image from the screen. In addition, you learned how the many Paradox function keys can save keystrokes. All of this was covered in this chapter under the three main headings below:

- Plan a database table
- Create a table
- Use tables in a variety of ways

Exercises

What You Should Do	How the Computer Responds
1. Remove any images from the screen. Press **F8**.	1. Main menu appears with workspace clear.
2. Retrieve *ADVCHEM* table by selecting **Modify** and then **Edit**. Type ADVCHEM and press **Enter**.	2. The list view of the *ADVCHEM* table appears on screen, with the blinking cursor in the last field. You are ready to edit *ADVCHEM*.
3. Press the arrow keys to move the cursor to the name "Andrea."	3. The blinking cursor moves to the field column.
4. Go to the end of the word "Andrea" and press the **Backspace** key one time.	4. The letter "a" is erased. Leaving "Andre" instead of "Andrea."
5. Press: **Alt-F7**	5. Paradox sends the table to the printer, where you get a neat printed copy of your table.
6. Move the blinking cursor in the table to the "Grade-%" column. Press **Ctrl-F7**.	6. Paradox graphs the numerical data in the "Grade-%" column on screen.
7. Press: any key.	7. Paradox clears the graph image from the screen, returning you to the table screen.
8. Press: **F2**	8. Paradox saves the *ADVCHEM* table to disk with the one change you have made. The table is finished, and you are in the **View** mode.
9. Press: **F8**	9. The *ADVCHEM* table image is cleared from the screen, leaving the workspace clear. The Main menu appears and you are ready to perform another task.
10. Press: the left arrow key one time Press: **Enter**	10. Exit is selected from the Main menu.
11. Select **Y** if you are ready to leave Paradox. Select **N** to return to the Main menu.	11. Select **Y** and Paradox displays the DOS prompt. Select **N** and you return to the Paradox Main menu.

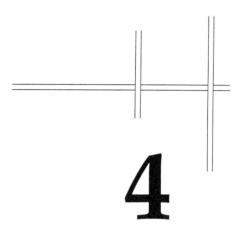

4

Entering Information

In Chapter 4 you will find ways to add, delete, and change the information entered into a table. Adding and changing information is called *editing*. You can edit Paradox records in the table view or the form view. This chapter will focus on the table view. Beyond editing, you will learn to restructure and redefine a table. Information is included on how redefining or restructuring affects the table and its relationships to other tables. The main topics you will find in this chapter are:

- Editing table records
- Restructuring a table

Editing Table Records

As you prepare to add, delete, or change records in a Paradox table, take a look at some of the editing terminology used in Paradox.

Editing Terms

Edit Session

Press the **F9** Edit key and you begin the edit session. You must complete an edit before you can continue with other Paradox functions. The edit session has a definite beginning and end. If mistakes are made during an edit session, they can be corrected before the session ends.

Undo

If you make an edit and then decide you want the original information, using the **Undo** function cancels the edit.

Tabular Edit

A tabular edit is one done in the Table view, as opposed to the Form view. In a tabular edit, you can change the data as it appears in the Table view.

Form Edit

While in Form view, an edit is called a *form edit*. You can edit the data in a form, but you can also edit the design, structure, and contents of a form. It is important to distinguish between these two.

Field View

Use the field view to update a field's data by replacing or inserting new information. You must tell Paradox that you intend to use field view for editing purposes.

Basic Edit View

This mode of updating fields is used most often. This mode allows you to delete old data and insert new data or add new records to the end of a table. You cannot use this mode to add data to the middle of a field.

Validity Checks

Paradox checks the data you enter into a field. If you try to enter letters in a number field type, Paradox will inform you that this is not allowed. Paradox may also check the range of information you have entered. A validity check also helps you with a lookup.

Lookup

Paradox checks to make sure that what you enter in a field in one table matches an entry in another table. The table you are trying to match is called the lookup table.

Multiple Record Entry   You can choose to create and add records as a group. This gives you a concise view of the records you intend to add.

1. Select the **Undo** option from the **Edit** menu. What happens?
2. While in the **View** mode, press The **F9** key. What happens?

1. *An edit you just made is returned to its original status.*
2. *You are put in the **Edit** mode.*

Editing a Table

Editing a table, as opposed to editing a form, is most useful if the table has few fields and records. Few fields means few enough to view on no more than two horizontal screens. That is, if three columns are visible on one screen, press the right arrow key and three more fields are visible. This is the maximum amount of jumping around you will want to have to do to edit in the tabular format.

Few records would mean no more than two vertical screens of records. With more fields or records in a table, go to Chapter 9 for information on editing in a form.

Tip ‖ If you find you are having to jump around a great deal while editing in **List** view, switch to **Form** view for easier editing.

Before you can edit, you have to have Paradox on the screen. If you have not already done so, start Paradox.

Starting Paradox

Follow these steps at the "C>" prompt:

STEP 1:

Type: `CD\PDOX35`
Press: **Enter**

STEP 2:

> Type: PDOX35
> Press: **Enter**

Now that you are in Paradox, start the edit.

Starting a Tabular Edit Using Paradox Menus

One way to get into the **Edit** mode with Paradox is to use the menu system.

STEP 1:

> From the Main menu, press the right arrow key four times, highlighting **Modify**.
> Press: **Enter** or **M**

STEP 2:

From the **Modify** submenu, press the right arrow key one time, until **Edit** is highlighted and press **Enter** or **E**.

The quickest way to get to the **Edit** mode using the menus is to:

STEP:

> Press: **M** and then **E**
> At the "Table:" prompt, type the name of the table you wish to edit.

Starting a Tabular Edit Using the Function Key

You already know that using the **F9** Edit key puts you in the **Edit** mode quickly, but try pressing **F9** now. Paradox beeps you and nothing happens.

The reason nothing happens is that in order to use the **F9** Edit key, you must first be viewing a table. To use the function key for editing, you must follow these steps:

STEP:

> Select: **View**
> Type: ADVCHEM

Press: **Enter**
Press: **F9**

You are now in the **Edit** mode. During the course of this chapter, the F9 key will be used to access the **Edit** mode.

1. Select **View**, type ADVCHEM, press **Enter**, press **F9**. What have you started?
2. Press **M** and then **E**, type ADVCHEM, press **Enter**. What have you started?

1. *A tabular edit.*
2. *A tabular edit. There are two ways to start a tabular edit.*

Creating the ADVCHEM Table

If you created *ADVCHEM* in the last chapter, you can skip this section. If you want to follow along in this chapter, create *ADVCHEM* by following the steps below. For more details in how to create *ADVCHEM* or defining and creating any table, read Chapter 3.

From the Main menu:

STEP 1:

Select: **Create**
Type: ADVCHEM
Press: **Enter**

The table definition screen appears. Define the table:

STEP 2:

Type: Student Number
Press: **Enter**
Type: A6*
Press: **Enter**

The first field is defined.

STEP 3:

> Type: No.
> Press: **Enter**
> Type: N
> Press: **Enter**

STEP 4:

> Type: Last Name
> Press: **Enter**
> Type: A15
> Press: **Enter**

STEP 5:

> Type: First Name
> Press: **Enter**
> Type: A15
> Press: **Enter**
> Type: Grade-%
> Press: **Enter**
> Type: N
> Press: **Enter**

STEP 6:

> Press: **F2 DO-IT**

With the table defined, add the records that should have previously been entered and then continue to edit, first by viewing and then by going to the **Edit** mode.

STEP 7:

> Select: **View**
> Type: ADVCHEM
> Press: **Enter**

STEP 8:

> Press: **F9 Edit**

STEP 9:

Type: 11-013
Press: **Enter**
Type: 1
Press: **Enter**
Type: Astro
Press: **Enter**
Type: Billy
Press: **Enter**
Type: 88.85
Press: **Enter**

The first record is entered in *ADVCHEM*.

STEP 10:

Add the remaining records listed here:

Student Number	No.	Last Name	First Name	Grade-%
12-288	2	Galaxy	Andrea	94.88
12-316	3	Moon	Monica	72.34
11-384	4	Pluto	Pete	90.09
12-122	5	Comet	Alvin	98.92

STEP 11:

Press: **F2 DO-IT**

The *ADVCHEM* table is now available for the further edit practice found in this chapter.

Viewing a Table

In order to edit *ADVCHEM*, you need to be in the **View** mode. After selecting **View**, type in the name of the table you want to edit, or:

STEP 1:

Select: **View**

Paradox prompts you to name the table you want to view.

STEP 2:

Type: ADVCHEM
Press: **Enter**

ADVCHEM appears on the screen, as seen in Figure 4.1.

Distinguishing the Edit Screen

Look at Figure 4.1. On the message line at the top of the screen is the message: "Viewing Advchem table: Record 1 of 5." At the far right of the screen, the word "Main" is highlighted. To start editing, press **F9** and the screen changes slightly.

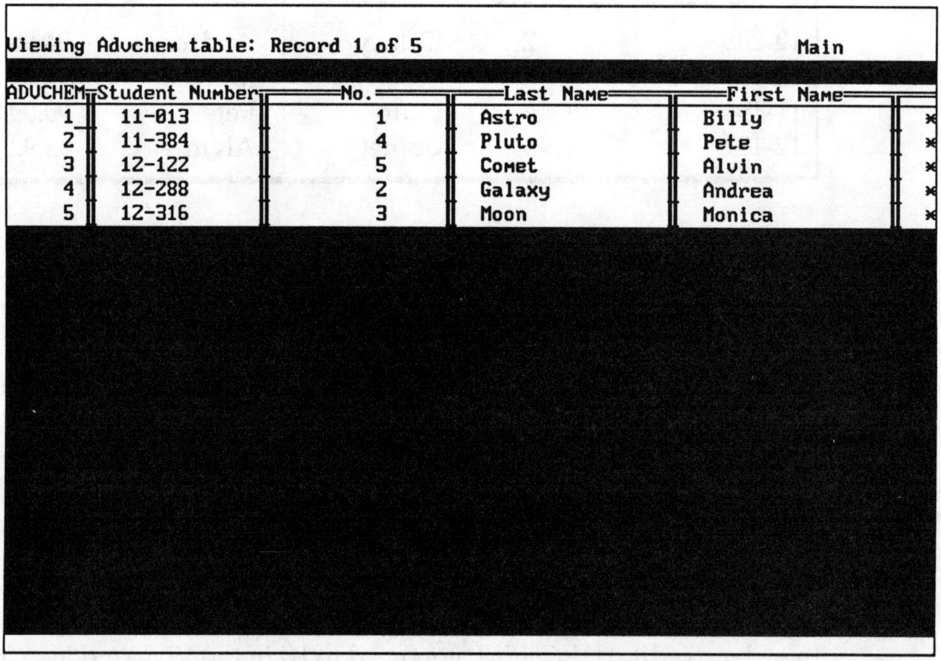

```
Viewing Advchem table: Record 1 of 5                              Main

ADVCHEM Student Number    No.          Last Name      First Name
      1  11-013             1          Astro          Billy        ×
      2  11-384             4          Pluto          Pete         ×
      3  12-122             5          Comet          Alvin        ×
      4  12-288             2          Galaxy         Andrea       ×
      5  12-316             3          Moon           Monica       ×
```

Figure 4.1. The *ADVCHEM* table on screen

Look at Figure 4.2. This is the same table shown after you have pressed F9. The message line now reads "Editing Advchem table: Record 1 of 5." Instead of Main highlighted in the upper right-hand corner, you now see "Edit" highlighted. Paradox informs you of your activity status. Use this information to keep track of the action you intend to take.

The Primary Key Action

Looking again at the figure above, check the No. field. The numbers down the screen are: 1, 4, 5, 2, 3. When you entered this data, you numbered the fields. Paradox has used the primary key to reorder the records.

Look at the Student Number field. This field is defined as the primary key. Those numbers are now in sequential order. Paradox automatically puts these numbers in order when you press F2. This table can be resorted in order to get the numbers back in the original order.

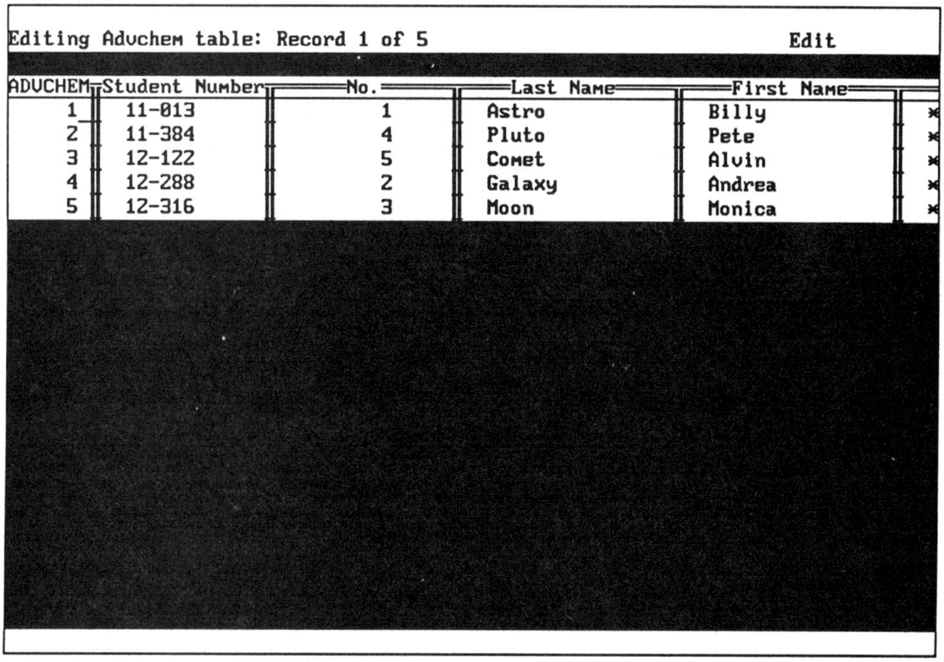

ADVCHEM	Student Number	No.	Last Name	First Name	
1	11-013	1	Astro	Billy	✖
2	11-384	4	Pluto	Pete	✖
3	12-122	5	Comet	Alvin	✖
4	12-288	2	Galaxy	Andrea	✖
5	12-316	3	Moon	Monica	✖

Editing Advchem table: Record 1 of 5   Edit

Figure 4.2. The *ADVCHEM* **Edit** screen

Editing Keys

You are now in basic edit mode. Press the arrow keys a few times to move around in the table. Notice that the blinking cursor is at the end of the data. For example, if the cursor is in the Last Name field with the word "Comet" in it, the blinking cursor is after the "t."

The reason you find the cursor at the end of the entered data is because you cannot type over data that has already been entered into a database table while in the regular editing mode. You can delete letters or numbers and then reenter them. You may also add to the end of the data already entered in a field.

Tip ‖ To type over data, especially in a field that contains a lot of text, use the field edit, described later in this chapter.

Descriptions of the editing keys are listed here. These are used in the basic edit.

Right Arrow or Tab	Move to the next field, moving from left to right and top to bottom. If you are in the last field of a record, press the right arrow key and you move to the first field of the next record.
Left Arrow or Shift-Tab	Moves the blinking cursor to the previous field. If you are in the first field of a record, the left arrow key moves you to the last field of the previous record.
Up Arrow	Moves to the same field in the previous record.
Down Arrow	Moves to the same field in the next record.
Ins Key	Creates a blank field preceding the one the cursor is in.
Del Key	Deletes an entire record.
Backspace	Deletes characters to the left of the blinking cursor.
Home	Moves to the first record in the table with the cursor remaining in the same field.
End	Moves to the last record in the table with the cursor remaining in the same field.

Ctrl-Backspace	This combination deletes all the data in a field.
Ctrl-**Right Arrow**	Moves right an entire screen.
Ctrl-**Left Arrow**	Moves left an entire screen.

1. While in the **Edit** mode, press the **Del** key. What happens?
2. Press the **End** key. What happens?

1. *The record in which the cursor is located is deleted.*
2. *The cursor moves to the last record or row in the table.*

Adding a New Record

Whether you have a list of clients or a list of products in your table, chances are that you are going to add new records to the table. If you enter records in a specific order, you can add new records at the beginning or anywhere in the middle of the table. You can also add records to the end of the table.

Adding a Record to the Top or Middle of a Table

When adding a record to the top or the middle of a table, you must first move the blinking cursor to the record below the location of where you want the new record to appear. In other words, Paradox inserts a new record in the row above the blinking cursor.

STEP 1:

Move the cursor to the record after the location of the new record. In this example, move the cursor to the number one record, "Billy Astro."

STEP 2:

Press: Ins

Figure 4.3 shows how the edited table looks now. One blank row is inserted at the top of the table.

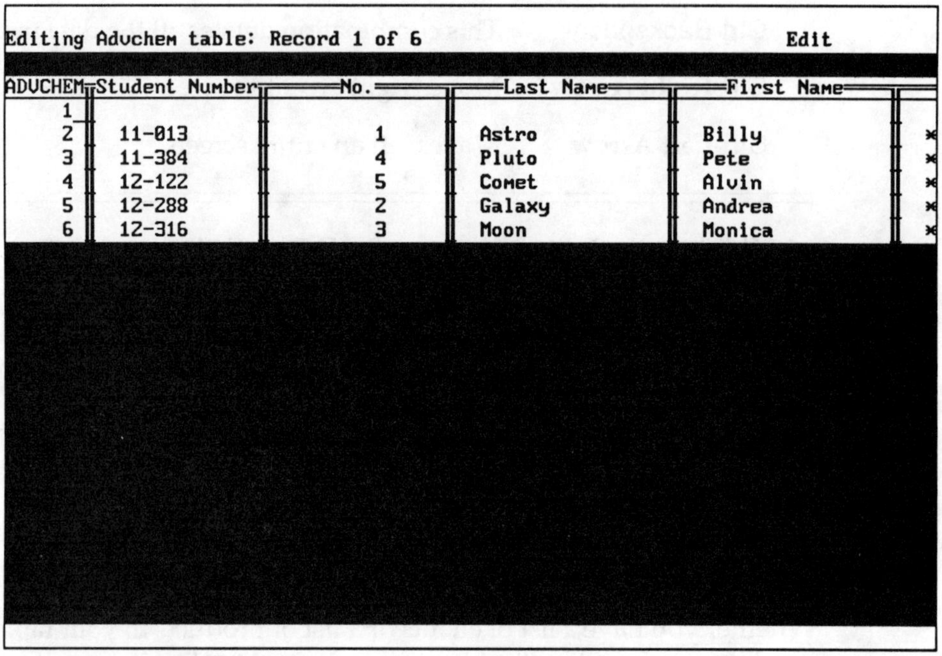

```
Editing Advchem table: Record 1 of 6                          Edit

ADVCHEM┬Student Number┬────No.────┬─────Last Name────┬────First Name────┬──
     1 ║
     2 ║ 11-013           1          Astro             Billy            ║  ×
     3 ║ 11-384           4          Pluto             Pete             ║  ×
     4 ║ 12-122           5          Comet             Alvin            ║  ×
     5 ║ 12-288           2          Galaxy            Andrea           ║  ×
     6 ║ 12-316           3          Moon              Monica           ║  ×
```

Figure 4.3. Blank record inserted

STEP 3:

Type the information for the new record, pressing enter after each field is complete. For this example:

Type: 11-138
Press: Enter
Type: 6
Press: Enter
Type: Beta
Press: Enter
Type: Bart
Press: Enter
Type: 62.45
Press: Enter

A new record is inserted across the top of the table. The last time you press Enter, the cursor moves to the next record. This line is the same line from which you inserted a record. Follow the same procedure above to add a record to the middle of a table. Figure 4.4 shows how the inserted record looks in the *ADVCHEM* table.

Tip

Enter the number 6 in the "No." column because this is the sixth entry into this table. If a table is very long, you can see how many records are in it by looking at the message line above the table. The message line now reads: "Editing Advchem table: Record 2 of 6." This tells you the total number of records in this table.

Adding Records to the End of a Table

Add records to the end of a table simply by pressing the down arrow key beyond the last record. Paradox opens a new blank row seen in the AD-VCHEM column as row 7.

In a longer table, use the **End** key to move to the last record, instead of pressing the down arrow key repeatedly. The **End** key, as stated above,

Editing Advchem table: Record 2 of 6				Edit

ADVCHEM	Student Number	No.	Last Name	First Name	
1	11-138	6	Beta	Bart	✕
2	11-013	1	Astro	Billy	✕
3	11-384	4	Pluto	Pete	✕
4	12-122	5	Comet	Alvin	✕
5	12-288	2	Galaxy	Andrea	✕
6	12-316	3	Moon	Monica	✕

Figure 4.4. A new record inserted in the *ADVCHEM* table

will take you to the end of the table with one keystroke. When you are at the end of the table, press the down arrow key one time to open a new row.

Insert a new record at the end of *ADVCHEM* by following these steps:

STEP 1:

Press: **End**

STEP 2:

Press: Down arrow one time

STEP 3:

Type: 12-306
Press: **Enter**
Type: 7
Press: **Enter**
Type: Mars
Press: **Enter**
Type: Mike
Press: **Enter**
Type: 82.66
Press: **Enter**

A new row is opened after you press **Enter** the last time. With this method, you can add more records at the end of any database table, ad infinitum.

1. Press the **Ins** key. What happens?
2. The cursor is at the end of a table. Press the down arrow key. What happens?

1. *A blank record is inserted in the table.*
2. *A blank row is added to the end of the table.*

Reordering Numbered Fields

Notice how the numbers in the field column "Student Number" are no longer in order. This is the Primary Key field. When you press F2 DO-IT, this field will appear in order. To reorder the Student Number field:

Press: **F2**

Figure 4.5 shows how Paradox reordered the records in the *ADVCHEM* table so that the primary field numbers are in order.

Returning to Edit Mode
Because you pressed the F2 DO-IT key, you have moved out of the **Edit** mode and back in to the **View** mode.

Press: **F9**

You are back to editing the *ADVCHEM* table instead of viewing it.

```
Viewing Advchem table: Record 1 of 7                          Main

ADVCHEM─Student Number─────No.─────────Last Name─────────First Name──
    1 ║ 11-013         ║    1    ║ Astro      ║ Billy     ║   ✳
    2 ║ 11-138         ║    6    ║ Beta       ║ Bart      ║   ✳
    3 ║ 11-384         ║    4    ║ Pluto      ║ Pete      ║   ✳
    4 ║ 12-122         ║    5    ║ Comet      ║ Alvin     ║   ✳
    5 ║ 12-288         ║    2    ║ Galaxy     ║ Andrea    ║   ✳
    6 ║ 12-306         ║    7    ║ Mars       ║ Mike      ║   ✳
    7 ║ 12-316         ║    3    ║ Moon       ║ Monica    ║   ✳
```

Figure 4.5. The Primary field in numerical order

Deleting a Record

Of the advanced chemistry students, Bart Beta is not doing well. After a discussion with the teacher and parents, he decides to drop the class. His record is easily deleted from the *ADVCHEM* table.

STEP 1:

Move the blinking cursor to the row you want deleted.

STEP 2:

Press: **Del**

The record holding data about Bart Beta is removed from the table.

Undoing an Edit

Suppose you make a mistake and delete a record that you didn't want to. Use the **Undo** command to restore the record.

Paradox is taking care of you and you don't even know it. While you are editing a table, Paradox keeps track of every edit you make. The **Ctrl-U** key combination will undo any edits you make in reverse order. You can hit **Ctrl-U** several times and undo editing changes, starting with the most recent change to the first edit you made in this editing session.

Tip   You can only undo edits in reverse order to the last time you pressed the **F2** DO-IT key. In the example you are working on here, you can only undo the record that was deleted. The record additions made earlier cannot be undone because the **F2** DO-IT key has been pressed since the times they were entered to the *ADVCHEM* table.

Recover the record you just deleted:

Press: **Ctrl-U**

A red message appears (if you have a color monitor) in the lower right of the screen telling you that record 2 has been reinserted as seen in Figure 4.6.

Press **Del** again and then press **Ctrl-U** again. See how easily you can delete and then recover lost records. The **Undo** command will be a lifesaver if you delete the wrong record by accident, or make any other editing mistake.

```
Editing Aduchem table: Record 2 of 7                           Edit

ADUCHEM─Student Number┬─────No.═════┬═════Last Name═════┬═════First Name═══┬
      1 ║ 11-013     ║       1      ║  Astro            ║  Billy           ║ ×
      2 ║ 11-138◄    ║       6      ║  Beta             ║  Bart            ║ ×
      3 ║ 11-384     ║       4      ║  Pluto            ║  Pete            ║ ×
      4 ║ 12-122     ║       5      ║  Comet            ║  Alvin           ║ ×
      5 ║ 12-288     ║       2      ║  Galaxy           ║  Andrea          ║ ×
      6 ║ 12-306     ║       7      ║  Mars             ║  Mike            ║ ×
      7 ║ 12-316     ║       3      ║  Moon             ║  Monica          ║ ×




                                                        Record 2 reinserted
```

Figure 4.6. The deleted record is reinserted

Tip

Since the **Undo** command works only before you have pressed F2 DO-IT,
take one precaution. After an editing session, look over a table carefully before you press F2. Make sure the correct records have been changed, added,
or deleted. When you have double checked a table after an editing session,
then press F2.

Bart Beta is going to drop the class, so:

Press: **Del**

The record of Bart Beta is now removed from the table.

1. Press the **Del** key. What happens?
2. Press the **F2 DO-IT** key. What happens?
3. Press **Ctrl-U**. What happens?

1. *A record is deleted from the table.*
2. *The order of records changes to ascending order by primary key.*
3. *The previous edit is returned to its original state. The edit is undone.*

Changing Existing Records

As explained earlier, you cannot type over data that has already been entered into a record. While in an editing session, you want to change data, move to the column or field you want to change, backspace over the incorrect information, and then replace it by typing new information. Correct a few records in *ADVCHEM.*

STEP 1:

Move the cursor to the word "Andrea" in record number 2.

STEP 2:

Press: **Backspace** key, one time

This deletes the letter "a," leaving the name as "Andre" instead of "Andrea."

STEP 3:

Move the cursor to the "Grade-%" column for Billy Astro.

STEP 4:

Press: **Backspace** key, five times
Type: 92.26
Press: **Enter**

Paradox moves you down to the first column in the next record. Press the right arrow key until the "Grade-%" column is visible. The new value you have typed in is visible. You have deleted old information and replaced it with new information in the *ADVCHEM* table.

Tip In the **Edit** mode, you must first backspace over incorrect data and then type the correct data in the field space. Later in this chapter, you will read about a **Field Edit**. Using the **Field Edit**, you may move the cursor to the beginning of a field and type over incorrect data.

Ending an Edit

Before you end an editing session, follow the tip given earlier and check the data entered to make sure there is nothing you want to undo. With the table edited to perfection, tell Paradox to finalize the table, save it, and end the editing session.

There are two ways to end the session. The simplest way is to:

STEP:

Press: **F2** DO-IT

Paradox saves the edited table to disk and returns you to the **View** table mode. The second method involves using the menus:

STEP 1:

Press: **F10** Menu key

The **Edit** menu appears on the screen.

STEP 2:

Select: DO-IT
Press: **Enter**

A note on the lower right of the screen tells you that the edit session is ending. You hear the edited table being saved to disk. You are back in the **View** mode. Remember that the **Undo** command will no longer affect the table just saved; any mistakes have to be corrected with another edit session.

1. Select DO-IT from the **Edit** submenu, or simply press **F2** DO-IT. What happens?
2. With the cursor in a field during an editing session, press the **Backspace** key. What happens?

1. *The editing session is ended. The table is saved to disk.*
2. *The character to the left of the cursor is deleted.*

Canceling an Edit

Instead of pressing the DO-IT key, you may elect to cancel all the edits you have made during an editing session, by canceling an edit before you press the DO-IT key. You are now viewing the ADVCHEM table. Go back to the **Edit** mode in order go through a **Cancel an Edit** procedure.

Press: **F9** Edit

Edit the *ADVCHEM* table as follows:

STEP 1:

Move the cursor to the name "Alvin" in the First Name field.

STEP 2:

Press: **Backspace** key, five times
Type: Alex

The edited table is shown in Figure 4.7.
You decide not to keep this change, so cancel the edit by:

STEP 3:

Press: **F10** Menu

The **Edit** menu appears at the top of the screen.

STEP 4:

Select: **Cancel**

Figure 4.8 shows **Cancel** highlighted on the **Edit** submenu. The line under the menu states "Stop editing, restore all tables to original form and return to workspace."

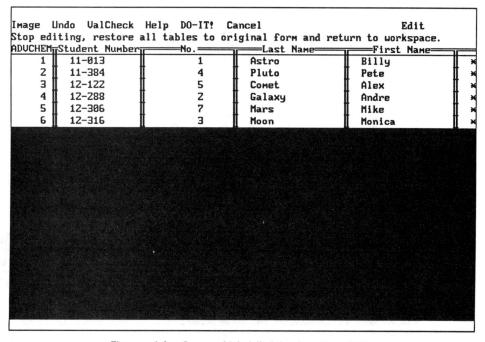

```
Editing Advchem table: Record 3 of 6                        Edit

ADVCHEM┬Student Number┬──────No.═══════════Last Name═══════════First Name═══════╦
      1║  11-013    ║       1       ║ Astro        ║ Billy        ║ ×
      2║  11-384    ║       4       ║ Pluto        ║ Pete         ║ ×
      3║  12-122    ║       5       ║ Comet        ║ Alex        ◄║ ×
      4║  12-288    ║       2       ║ Galaxy       ║ Andre        ║ ×
      5║  12-306    ║       7       ║ Mars         ║ Mike         ║ ×
      6║  12-316    ║       3       ║ Moon         ║ Monica       ║ ×
```

Figure 4.7. Edited *ADVCHEM* table

```
Image   Undo   ValCheck   Help   DO-IT!   Cancel                Edit
Stop editing, restore all tables to original form and return to workspace.
ADVCHEM┬Student Number┬──────No.═══════════Last Name═══════════First Name═══════╦
      1║  11-013    ║       1       ║ Astro        ║ Billy        ║ ×
      2║  11-384    ║       4       ║ Pluto        ║ Pete         ║ ×
      3║  12-122    ║       5       ║ Comet        ║ Alex         ║ ×
      4║  12-288    ║       2       ║ Galaxy       ║ Andre        ║ ×
      5║  12-306    ║       7       ║ Mars         ║ Mike         ║ ×
      6║  12-316    ║       3       ║ Moon         ║ Monica       ║ ×
```

Figure 4.8. **Cancel** highlighted on the **Edit** submenu

STEP 5:

Press **Enter**

Paradox prompts you about whether or not you really want to cancel the edit.

STEP 6:

Press: **Y**

Figure 4.9 shows how the table looks now. The name "Alex" is replaced with "Alvin," the original name in the table.

Tip | If you should select **Cancel** from the **Edit** menu by mistake, select "No" instead of "Yes." This will put you back in the **Edit** mode and keep all the changes you have made. If you want to keep the changes, press F2 DO-IT.

```
Viewing Advchem table: Record 1 of 6                          Main

ADVCHEM┬Student Number┬       No.═        ┬     Last Name═    ┬     First Name═
     1 ║ 11-013       ║       1           ║ Astro            ║ Billy            ║ ×
     2 ║ 11-384       ║       4           ║ Pluto            ║ Pete             ║ ×
     3 ║ 12-122       ║       5           ║ Comet            ║ Alvin            ║ ×
     4 ║ 12-288       ║       2           ║ Galaxy           ║ Andre            ║ ×
     5 ║ 12-306       ║       7           ║ Mars             ║ Mike             ║ ×
     6 ║ 12-316       ║       3           ║ Moon             ║ Monica           ║ ×
```

Figure 4.9. The *ADVCHEM* table with original data

Reordering Columns in a Table Edit

With one keystroke you can change the order in which columns appear on the screen. Press **Ctrl-R** and the column farthest to the right moves one column to the left. At the same time, the column the cursor is in moves to the far right. A circular motion ensues, with the columns moving around as you continue to press **Ctrl-R**.

This can be illustrated by moving the blinking cursor to the "Last Name" column in the *ADVCHEM* table. You should be in the **Edit** mode, with the columns in the same order as you have seen in previous figures in this chapter.

STEP 1:

Move the cursor to the "Last Name" column in *ADVCHEM*.

The columns are in this order:

Student Number   No.   Last Name   First Name   Grade-%

STEP 2:

Press: **Ctrl-R**

The columns are now in this order:

Student Number   No.   First Name   Grade-%   Last Name

STEP 3:

Press: **Ctrl-R**
Press: **Ctrl-R**

The columns are now in their original location. The last three columns have moved in a circular manner.

Resizing Table Images

Shrink or expand the size of the table image on the screen by using the **Edit** menu. During an editing session, press **F10** to see the **Edit** submenu. From the **Image/TableSize** option, choose to expand or shrink a table image.

STEP 1:

> While in the **Edit** mode, press **F10**.
> Select: **Image**
> Select: **TableSize**

The prompt at the top of the screen instructs you to use the up arrow key to decrease the size of the table image by one row. Use the down arrow key to increase the table image by one row.

STEP 2:

> Press: Up arrow four times

The ADVCHEM table image on the screen has two lines, leaving only two records visible on screen, as seen in Figure 4.10.

STEP 3:

> Press: Down arrow four times
> Press: Enter

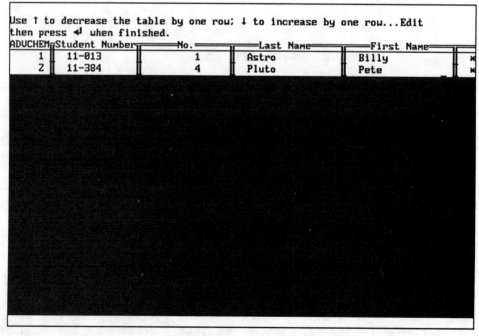

Figure 4.10. A smaller table image

The screen resumes its original size.

1. Press Ctrl-R while in the **Edit** mode. What happens?
2. Choose the TableSize option from the Image submenu. What happens?
3. Press the down arrow key after you have selected **TableSize** from the **Image** submenu. What happens?

1. *The column the cursor is in moves to the far right of the table. Columns between that column and the cursor move to the left. You could say that they circle around.*
2. *Paradox prompts you to press the arrow keys to adjust the size of the table. Press Enter when finished.*
3. *The size of the table image is increased one row each time you press the down arrow key.*

Field Editing

Up to now, the only way to change the contents of a field was to move the cursor to that field, delete the incorrect or old information, and then retype the new information. With a field that holds a great deal of text, using the **Field Edit** option allows you to move the cursor over text to change it.

For example, if you had a field that held lengthy product descriptions and there was an error in the middle of the field, you would not want to delete half the field and then retype it, just to correct the error. Instead, turn **Field Edit** on and move the cursor to the error, correct it, move the cursor to the end, and then end the **Field Edit**.

The **Field Edit** saves time because you don't have to retype large amounts of information. Instead, you move directly to the error and then correct it.

In most word processors, the over write or insert modes are controlled by pressing the Ins key. In the insert mode, new characters are inserted between characters already on the screen. Characters to the right are moved to the right as you type. In the over write mode, the old characters are erased as the new characters take their place.

Tip

In the **Field Edit** mode, you can toggle back and forth between over write and insert modes. While in a normal editing session, press **Ins** and what happens? A blank line for a new record is inserted above the line that the cursor is. During a **Field Edit**, you can toggle between insert and over write just as you would when using a word processing program.

Correct data in a field using the over write mode by first selecting the **Field Edit** function. Use the **Field Edit** in a field:

STEP 1:

Move the cursor to the record and field you want to edit. In the *ADVCHEM* table, move the cursor to "Alvin."

STEP 2:

Press: **Ctrl-F**

The cursor is highlighted to signify that you are in the **Field Edit** function. At this time, try pressing the up and down arrow keys. The computer beeps, and you are not able to move out of the field you are editing.

STEP 3:

Press: Left arrow key five times or until the "A" in "Alvin" is highlighted

STEP 4:

Press: **Insert**
Type: Alfie

This typing over writes the characters that were there previously. The changed field should appear as in Figure 4.11. Again, try to press the right, up, or down arrow keys. You cannot move out of this field.

Before you can continue in the editing session, you must first end the **Field Edit**.

STEP 5:

Press: **Enter**

The **Field Edit** is ended, and the highlighted block cursor is replaced

```
Editing Advchem table: Record 3 of 6                              Edit

ADVCHEM┬Student Number┬──────No.═══╗   ╔═════Last Name══╗   ╔═First Name══╗
    1 ║ 11-013    ║       1          ║   ║ Astro         ║   ║ Billy       ║ ×
    2 ║ 11-384    ║       4          ║   ║ Pluto         ║   ║ Pete        ║ ×
    3 ║ 12-122    ║       5          ║   ║ Comet         ║   ║ Alfie█      ║ ◄  ×
    4 ║ 12-288    ║       2          ║   ║ Galaxy        ║   ║ Andre       ║ ×
    5 ║ 12-306    ║       7          ║   ║ Mars          ║   ║ Mike        ║ ×
    6 ║ 12-316    ║       3          ║   ║ Moon          ║   ║ Monica      ║ ×
```

Figure 4.11. The **Field Edit** mode in a table

with the blinking cursor. Press the up, down, right, or left arrow keys now, and you can move about freely in the *ADVCHEM* table.

While you are in Field view, you will find that the arrow keys and the Home, End, Del, and Ins keys work a little differently. Those differences are outlined here:

Left/Right Arrows	Press either key one time, and the cursor moves one character to the right or left. But the cursor stays within the field. You cannot move between fields when in the **Field Edit** mode.
Home, End	Move to the beginning (Home) or end (End) of a field.
Del	Deletes the character at the cursor.
Ins	Press this key to toggle between over write and insert modes.

Backspace	Deletes the character to the left of the cursor.
Ctrl-Backspace	Deletes the characters in the entire field.
Enter	Ends the **Field Edit**.

1. While in the over write mode, type new characters. What happens?
2. While in the insert mode, type new characters. What happens?
3. While doing a **Field Edit**, press the **Ins** key. What happens?

1. *Characters being typed replace the characters already on the screen.*
2. *Characters are moved to the right as you type new characters.*
3. *You are toggled between the insert and over write mode.*

Restructuring a Table

In the sections above, you learned how to edit data in a Paradox table. The remainder of this chapter discusses changing the structure of the table. This is called restructuring. Use restructuring when you need to add more spaces to a field; add, delete, change, or rename fields; change field types; or change primary keys.

For example, you have an address field defined with 12 spaces. After entering data, you learn that you need at least 20 spaces for the address field. Change this by changing the *STRUCT* table, which is restructuring the table. Perhaps you find that after building a table you need to add a field. Change the *STRUCT* table so that it holds one more field that you define.

While viewing a table, press **F9** to edit the data in the table. Change the table structure by displaying the table structure (shown as "STRUCT" on screen) on screen.

Displaying a Table Structure

Every table created in Paradox has a structure that you have designed. In order to edit the data in a table, you must first be in the **Edit** mode. To restructure a table, you have to have the table structure on screen. Paradox calls this the *STRUCT* table.

If you have been working in Paradox for awhile, start this activity by clearing the screen. (You may have to end the previous editing session by pressing **F2** DO-IT.)

STEP 1:

Press: **Alt-F8**

This clears all the images from the screen.

STEP 2:

Select: **Tools**
Select: **Info**
Select: **Structure**
Type: ADVCHEM
Press: **Enter**

The *ADVCHEM STRUCT* table appears on screen. This *STRUCT* table can be seen in Figure 4.12.

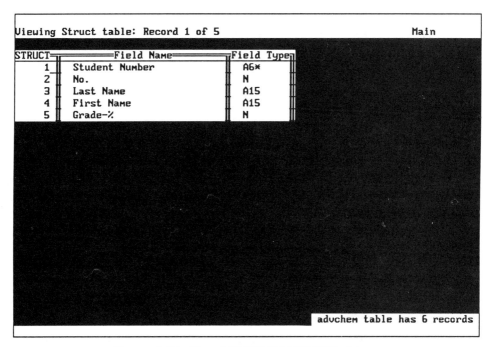

Figure 4.12. The *ADVCHEM STRUCT* table on screen

Viewing and editing a *STRUCT* table is different from viewing and editing a *data* table. The *STRUCT* table defines the data table so any changes to a *STRUCT* table affects the *data* table.

To view the structure of a table, select this menu sequence: **Tools/Info/Structure**. The only way to restructure a table is by the **Modify/Restructure** menu sequence.

Copying a Table

Before you make any changes to the structure of the *ADVCHEM* table, make a duplicate of the table structure. Start by:

Press: **F10**
Select: **Tools**
Select: **Copy**
Select: **Table**
Type: ADVCHEM
Press: **Enter**
Type: ADVCHEM2
Press: **Enter**

You have created an identical table to the first *ADVCHEM* table. With a duplicate table, you can change it, adjust it, and completely mess it up, without losing the original table. The original table is still stored under the name *ADVCHEM*.

Tip

Copy a table before you change the structure of the table. With a copy of the table, you can completely mess it up, but still have the original in another file that is safe from major mistakes. Remember to give the second table a new name because Paradox cannot store two tables on disk with identical names. One of the rules of naming tables is that each must have a unique name. If you try to store two tables with the same name, Paradox will notify you that you already have a table by that name.

Changing the Table Structure

Prepare to change the structure of a table by selecting the table redefinition function.

STEP 1:

> Press: **F10**
> Select: **Modify**
> Select: **Restructure**

This is the only way to get to the restructuring option in Paradox. Paradox prompts you for the name of the table structure you want to change.

STEP 2:

> Type: ADVCHEM2
> Press: **Enter**

Paradox displays the screen, ready for your changes, as seen in Figure 4.13.

While this screen is similar to the screen you saw when you created this table, there are a few differences. The message line at the top tells you that you are in the process of "Restructuring Advchem2 table." The highlighted word in the upper right of the screen tells you that the **Restructure** submenu

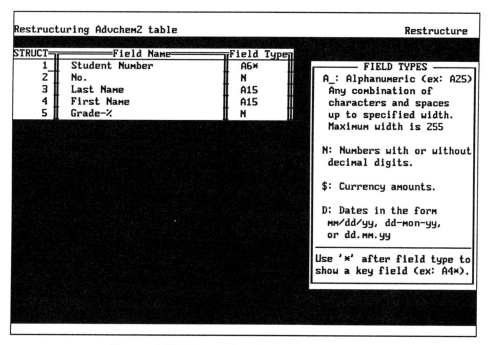

Figure 4.13. The restructure screen

appears if you press **F10**. Paradox is ready to accept your changes.

Inserting a Field

The advanced chemistry teacher decides that she needs the telephone numbers of the students in her class so that she can keep constant communication with their parents. Insert a field to hold the phone number.

STEP 1:

Move the cursor to anywhere in the Grade-% field.
Press: **Ins**

A blank line, numbered 5, appears just above the Grade-% field.

STEP 2:

Press: Right arrow one time or move the cursor to the "Field Name" column.
Type: Phone Number
Press: **Enter**
Type: A8
Press: **Enter**

The Phone Number field is inserted, named, and defined. Figure 4.14 shows how the *STRUCT* table appears now.

Tip | While the Phone Number field holds numbers, you want to define it as an Alphanumeric field. If it is defined as a Number field, you cannot add the dash (-) between the first three and last four numbers. In addition, the telephone number is not going to be used for mathematical functions.

1. Press **Alt-F8**. What happens next?
2. Select **Modify/Restructure** from the menu. Where are you now?
3. Press the **Ins** key during a table restructure and what happens?
4. Why should you define a phone number column as being alphanumeric even though it holds numbers.

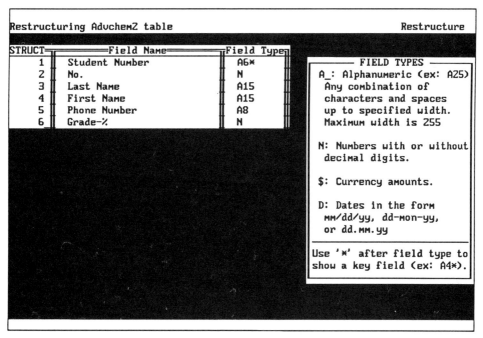

```
Restructuring Advchem2 table                                    Restructure

STRUCT            Field Name            Field Type
    1 ║ Student Number              ║ A6×        ║      ┌──── FIELD TYPES ────
    2 ║ No.                         ║ N          ║      │ A_: Alphanumeric (ex: A25)
    3 ║ Last Name                   ║ A15        ║      │ Any combination of
    4 ║ First Name                  ║ A15        ║      │ characters and spaces
    5 ║ Phone Number                ║ A8         ║      │ up to specified width.
    6 ║ Grade-%                     ║ N          ║      │ Maximum width is 255
                                                        │
                                                        │ N: Numbers with or without
                                                        │ decimal digits.
                                                        │
                                                        │ $: Currency amounts.
                                                        │
                                                        │ D: Dates in the form
                                                        │ mm/dd/yy, dd-mon-yy,
                                                        │ or dd.mm.yy
                                                        │
                                                        │ Use '×' after field type to
                                                        │ show a key field (ex: A4×).
```

Figure 4.14. The *STRUCT* table with inserted field

1. *All images are cleared from the workspace.*
2. *Paradox prompts you to name the table that you want to restructure.*
3. *A row is inserted to hold a new field.*
4. *Because you are not going to use the phone numbers for mathematical functions, and you may want to add other characters like dashes or parentheses to the field.*

Changing the Field Type

With all of the first names of the listed students being less than 15 characters, this field type will be redefined. The "A" remains, but the number of spaces available need be no more than 10.

STEP 1:

Move the cursor to row 4, in the Field Type column in the First Name row.
Press: **Backspace** two times

The "A" remains while the "15" is deleted. With 15 spaces, too many blank spaces are saved on disk. Ten spaces provides plenty of room for the names in the *ADVCHEM* table.

STEP 2:

Type: 10
Press: Enter

The field type stays as Alphanumeric, but the number of spaces changes. If you wanted to change the field type, simply continue the deleting and replace the "A15" with "N," "$," or "D." The new table structure is shown in Figure 4.15.

Tip

Double check the changes made in the table structure. Even if you do make a major error, remember that this is only a copy of the original table. Changing the structure as you have affects only the copy of the *ADVCHEM* table, not the original.

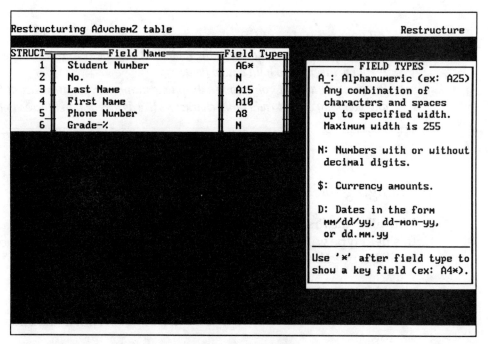

Figure 4.15. Restructured table

STEP 3:

Press: **F2**

Because you have made a field smaller, you are flashed a warning sign: Possible data loss! You knew before you made the structure change that no names were longer than ten characters. From the menu displayed along with this warning, select **Trimming**. You will learn more about this menu in the next section.

Now that you have restructured the *ADVCHEM* table, you can use the *ADVCHEM2* table to work from. You have the option of deleting the original *ADVCHEM* table or keeping both on disk for different uses.

Tip | Remove excess spaces from Alphanumeric fields so that the blank spaces do not take up needed space on the disk.

Responding to Paradox Warning Messages

Paradox flashes a warning stating "Possible data loss for the First Name field." On the menu line are three options.

Tip | This warning is exactly that. It does not mean you will lose data, only that you might. In this example, none of the first names in the *ADVCHEM* table are longer than ten characters. When changing the number of spaces available in field, check the data in the table first and then adjust the *STRUCT* table.

Trimming

Choose this option and Paradox will cut off the last letters in a name so that it fits in the ten spaces available.

No-Trimming

Choose this option and Paradox will create a *PROBLEMS* table to hold all the first names that are longer than ten spaces.

Oops!

Select this option when you have made an error and you want to go back to the *STRUCT* table to restructure the restructure. If you would actually lose data in the First Name field, select this option and go back and change the Field Type column to A12.

Since you checked before making the structure change to make sure that no names were longer than ten spaces, you may proceed with confidence.

Select: **Trimming**

Paradox restructures *ADVCHEM2*, which appears on screen in the **View** mode, as seen in Figure 4.16.

Despite the warning given by Paradox, you did not eliminate any characters from the first name field. In fact, looking at all the blank space in the Last Name field may prompt you to go back and restructure the table again by redefining that field as A8.

```
Viewing Advchem2 table: Record 1 of 6                        Main

ADVCHEM2╥Student Number╥      ╥No. ═      ═      ═Last Name═   ╥First Name═╥Phone N
      1_║ 11-013        ║     ║  1        ║      Astro          ║ Billy     ║
      2 ║ 11-384        ║     ║  4        ║      Pluto          ║ Pete      ║
      3 ║ 12-122        ║     ║  5        ║      Comet          ║ Alfie     ║
      4 ║ 12-288        ║     ║  2        ║      Galaxy         ║ Andre     ║
      5 ║ 12-306        ║     ║  7        ║      Mars           ║ Mike      ║
      6 ║ 12-316        ║     ║  3        ║      Moon           ║ Monica    ║
```

Figure 4.16. The restructured table in **View** mode

Special Restructuring Keys

Additional keys used to change the table structure are as follows:

Ins   As used above, press this key and a new field definition is inserted above the cursor. This field definition is blank. You may define the new field by filling in the blank spaces in the special *STRUCT* table. If you want the blank field definition at the end of the table, press the down arrow key while in the last row of the *STRUCT* table.

Del   Move the cursor to the field definition row and press the **Del** key to remove a field from a table. Paradox will check to make sure that you want to do this when you press the **F2** key. A warning will appear, similar to the example above.

F2   Press the DO-IT key to finalize the table structure. Any changes that might affect data in the table will prompt a warning from Paradox.

1. What happens if you select **No-Trimming** and some fields have too many characters?
2. While in a *STRUCT* table, press the **Del** key. What happens?
3. Which key do you press to finalize and save a table structure?

1. *Paradox creates a special PROBLEMS table so that you have access to and can adjust any information that does not fit in a field.*
2. *An entire field is deleted.*
3. *F2 DO-IT Key.*

Editing the Restructured Table

From the **View** mode, press **F9** to go to the **Edit** mode. Then you can move the cursor to the fields and add the information in the new field.

STEP 1:

Press: **F9**
Move the cursor to the Phone Number field.

STEP 2:

Type: 555-1818
Press: Down arrow
Type: 555-2222
Press: Down arrow
Type: 555-3684
Press: Down arrow
Type: 555-0808
Press: Down arrow
Type: 555-1234
Press: Down arrow
Type: 555-9876

The telephone numbers are added in the new field. Finalize the table:

STEP 3:

Press: **F2**

Effect of Restructuring on Tables

You have seen how Paradox warns you if you try to shorten an Alphanumeric field. The warning encourages you to be sure you want to shorten the field prior to the restructuring action. It also offers you the chance to change the restructuring action by choosing **OOPS!** from the menu.

There is another restructuring action that will produce a warning from Paradox—the action of deleting a field. Should you try to delete a field, Paradox gives you several chances to change your mind. To delete a field and all the data in it, you must be sure that is the action you want to take.

Delete a field while restructuring a table and Paradox displays a menu with the following options.

Delete

Select this option from the menu and you are telling Paradox that you are sure you want to delete the data in the specified field. All data in that field will be lost. This is another reason that restructuring is best done on a copy of a table, not on the original. If you delete hours of work by mistake, the original table is still available on disk.

OOPS!

If you deleted a field in error, select this option from the menu. Paradox moves you back to the *STRUCT* table, where you have to reinsert the deleted field. If you can't remember the name of the deleted field, or exactly how it was worded, cancel the restructuring. Do this by pressing **F10** to display the menu and select **Cancel** from the menu. This cancels all restructuring action and returns you to the original *STRUCT* table.

1. While in the **View** mode, press **F9**. What happens?
2. Which menu option should you choose if you deleted a field in error?

1. *You are in the **Edit Table** mode.*
2. *The **OOPS!** option.*

Effect on the Family of Items

Restructure a table and Paradox automatically goes through any associated items and adjusts the items according the the restructuring. For example, you have a table with an associated custom form. Restructure the table by deleting a field and Paradox will delete the same field from the custom form. In Chapter 9, you will be designing custom forms associated with tables. This Paradox feature will then be more relevant to you.

Summary

Most of the table editing functions have been addressed in this chapter. You have learned how to edit in the tabular format by adding new records, deleting records, undoing edits, changing existing data, ending an edit, and canceling an edit. You have learned to resize and reorder columns in a table. You have learned to use a **Field Edit** in a field with lengthy text to save yourself from deleting and retyping much information.

You have covered many details of restructuring a table, such displaying a table structure, copying a table, and changing a table, including changing the field type and responding to a Paradox warning. How to edit a restructured table and how deleting a field can affect a table and related images is also addressed. The two main headings in this chapter, with included sub-headings, are:

- Editing a table
  - Editing terms
  - Editing a table
  - Editing keys
  - Adding and deleting records
  - Changing existing records
- Restructuring a table
  - Changing a table
  - Inserting a field
  - Special restructuring keys
  - Editing the restructured table

Exercises

What You Should Do	How the Computer Responds
1. Start Paradox by following these steps: Type: CD\PDOX35 Press: **Enter** Type: PDOX35 Press: **Enter**	1. The Paradox screen appears on the screen.
2. Select **Modify** and then **Edit** from the menus. At the prompt, type the name of the table you want to edit, and press **Enter**.	2. Paradox displays a prompt asking you to name the table you want to edit. You type the name of the table, press **Enter**, and that table appears on screen.
3. Move the arrow keys until you are in a data field that you want to change in some way.	3. The blinking cursor moves around the table as you press the arrow keys. The cursor is at the end of data entries in fields.
4. Press the **Backspace** key until the incorrect data is deleted. Type the information in, with the corrections made.	4. Pressing the **Backspace** key deletes characters to the left of the cursor. As you type, the new information is entered into the field.
5. Move the cursor to a line above which you want to insert a new record. Press the **Ins** key.	5. Paradox inserts a blank row above the line in which the cursor is located. This blank row will hold a new record.

6. Move the cursor to the left-most column in the table, and type in the data for the new record, pressing **Enter** as each field is completed.

6. The new data is inserted in a field. When **Enter** is pressed, the cursor moves to the next field to the right, where data can be entered.

7. Move the cursor to a record you no longer want appearing in the table. With the cursor in that record or row, press **Del**.

7. The entire record or row of data is deleted from the table.

8. Press **Ctrl-U** to recover the record you just deleted.

8. Paradox inserts the deleted record back in its original location.

9. If you are happy with the table the way it is now, after you have edited it, press **F2**. If you are not happy with the table, go to Exercise 10.

9. Paradox finishes and saves the edited table to disk.

10. If you are not happy with the way the table is now, go back and edit the table, or cancel the edits. While in the **Edit** mode, cancel the edit by pressing **F10** to see the **Edit** submenu and then select **Cancel**.

10. Paradox disregards any changes made during this editing session and returns you to the **View** mode of the table before changes were made.

11. Edit the table structure by first displaying the table structure. Select **Tools, Info,** and then **Structure** from the menus. At the prompt, type the name of the table you want to restructure and press **Enter**.

11. The menu items are selected. Paradox prompts you to name the table. After you type in the name of the table and press **Enter**, the structure of the table you named appears on the screen.

12. Press **F10**, then select **Modify** and **Restructure** from the menus. At the prompt, name the table you want to modify and press **Enter**.

12. The table structure is now ready for any changes you want to make.

13. Move the cursor to the bottom of the *STRUCT* table. Press the down arrow key to move one line beyond the end of the table.

13. A blank line is created at the bottom of the table.

14. Define a new field by typing the field name, press **Enter**, and then specify the field type.

14. A new field is added to the table and its field type is defined.

15. Press **F2** DO-IT!

15. The restructured table is finished and saved to disk. Paradox moves you to

16. From the **View** mode, press **F9** to edit the table. Move the cursor to the new field and add the data that belongs in this new field.

17. When the data in the new field is as you want it, press **F2** DO-IT!

the **View** mode of the table that has been restructured.

16. New data is entered into the newly created empty field.

17. The restructured and edited table is finished and saved to disk.

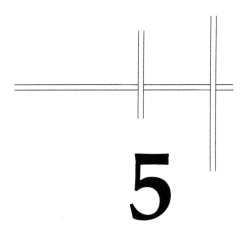

5

Retrieving Information by Query

So far in this book you have created and edited tables. Much of what you have done is not much different than what could be done on paper. In Chapter 5, you are going to dive into the real beauty of an electronic database. Not only is it a convenient way to store your data, but you can retrieve that information in useful ways that will help you make better decisions.

The tool used to retrieve information in a Paradox database is a *query*. Three types of queries will be addressed in this chapter. The first is a single table query, where you look for a record or records meeting one specified condition. The second is a single table query, where you look for records meeting two or more specified conditions. Another term for this is multiple conditions. The third type of query is a query done on multiple tables, where you ask for specific information about two or more related tables. The major components of this chapter are:

- Creating a query
- Multiple conditions in queries
- Querying multiple tables
- Saving queries

Creating a Query

A query can help you pull out specific records in a table, examine certain fields from a table, perform calculations in tables, and combine data from several tables into one answer table. While this may sound like you are doing very complicated activities in Paradox, you will find that Paradox is so well designed that these processes can be done simply and clearly.

What Is a Query?

A query is a question you ask of a database table or tables. Paradox scans through the data you have entered and creates an *answer* table to your question. A query usually creates an *answer* table. This *answer* table can be converted to a report or graph or used on screen to analyze the data you have entered.

Tip | An *answer* table can be empty, which means that no records meet the condition you specify in a query.

The Query Method

When you query Paradox, you create an example of what you want the answer to look like. Paradox does all the work by looking through data tables to find the answer to your question. This is called the Query By Example method (QBE).

For example, in querying a single table that includes a student number, name, phone number, and grade, you ask a question (query) about the student's grade. One question might be, which students have a grade greater than 90 percent. You ask the question, and Paradox displays an *answer* table that lists all the student records in the table with a grade of 90 percent or higher.

Looking at the Query Form

Display a Query form by selecting **Ask** from the Paradox Main menu. First clear the screen by pressing Alt-F8. This removes visible tables so that the workspace is clear.

STEP 1:

Press: Right arrow

This highlights the **Ask** option on the Main menu.

STEP 2:

Press: Enter

Paradox prompts you to name the table for which you want to ask a question.

STEP 3:

Press: Enter

Instead of typing in the name of the table, pressing Enter gives you a list of the tables already created.

STEP 4:

Press: Right arrow until "Salary" is highlighted
Press: Enter

The query form for the *Salary* table is on screen. It appears as the one in Figure 5.1.

This query form looks similar to a *data* table. You will find important differences, however. One difference is that you can type directly into a query form. You do not have to go to the **Edit** mode first. What you type into a query form is not added to a *data* table. It is used only to ask a question of that table. Another difference is that the fields expand to accommodate additional information.

1. Press Alt-F8. What happens?
2. Put a query table on the screen.

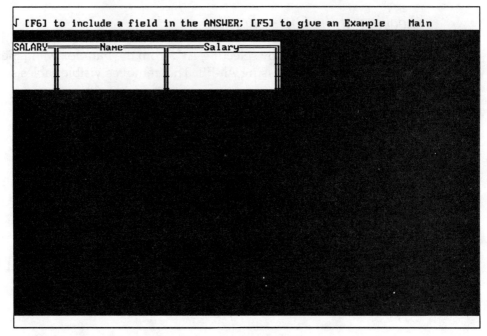

√ [F6] to include a field in the ANSWER; [F5] to give an Example   Main

SALARY════╤═══════Name═══════╤═══════Salary═══╤═╗

Figure 5.1. The salary query form

1. *Clears all images on the workspace.*
2. *Select **Ask** from the Main menu, type the name of the table you want to query, and press **Enter**.*

Viewing the Table

To begin this query, lets look at the *Salary* table. By querying a very small table, you will be able to see how a query works on a very large table. To get to the *Salary* table from the Query form:

STEP 1:

Press: **F10**
Select: **View**

Paradox responds with the "Table:" prompt. Type the name of the table you want to view, or:

STEP 2:

Press: Enter
Move the highlighting to "Salary."
Press: Enter

The *Salary* table appears on screen just below the query form, as you see in Figure 5.2. The two images are on screen, with your blinking cursor in the active image. You can see that the salaries range from $19,900.00 to $38,500.00.

An *answer* table can be empty, which means that no records meet the condtion you specify in a query.

Note   If you prepared this table in the Chapter 2 Exercises, you can see that this version is slightly different. A few names have been added to the table. You can add names to the table by using the **F9** Edit key, or by recreating the table.

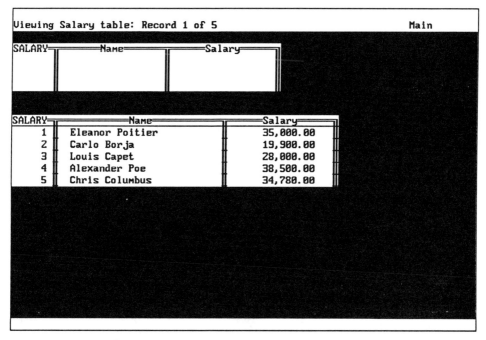

Viewing Salary table: Record 1 of 5   Main

SALARY	Name	Salary
1	Eleanor Poitier	35,000.00
2	Carlo Borja	19,900.00
3	Louis Capet	28,000.00
4	Alexander Poe	38,500.00
5	Chris Columbus	34,780.00

Figure 5.2.   Two images on screen

1. When you press **F10**, what happens?
2. At the "Table:" prompt, what happens when you press **Enter**?

1. *The Main menu is displayed across the top of the screen.*
2. *A list of tables already created is listed across the top of the screen.*

Removing the Table Image

Remove the *Salary* table image:

STEP 3:

Press: **F8**

Your cursor goes immediately to the Query form at the top of the screen.

1. Press **F8**. What happens?
2. Press **Alt-F8**. What happens?

1. *The image where the cursor is located is cleared from the screen.*
2. *All the images in the workspace are cleared.*

A Single Table Query

Get ready to use your imagination. Suppose that you have a list of 300 employees, instead of 5. You are going to query for all employees whose salaries are more than $33,000.00. This is a single table query.

A single table query means you are asking questions of only one table. This is the simplest form a query can take. The query is only going to consider one variable, which also keeps it simple.

Tip || An example of a query using two variables would be to ask for a list of who earns more than $33,000.00 and also whose name begins with the letter A.

The steps in a single table query are:

1. Select the columns you want to include in the answer.
2. Tell Paradox how to select the rows to be put in the *answer* table, by specifying the data Paradox should find.
3. Execute the query.

Selecting Columns

The **F6** Check key is used to select the columns to include in a query. The word check indicates that you will put a "check mark" next to each column that should be included. The **F6** key works as a toggle key. Press the key one time and the column selection is turned on. Press the key again and it is turned off.

In the figure above, you see the Query form for "Salary." The three columns across the top are: SALARY, Name, and Salary. The first time "SALARY" appears in all capital letters, it is indicating the name of the table, which is distinct from "Salary," which indicates the name of the field. If you press the **F6** key while in "SALARY" column, this automatically places a check mark in all of the fields in that table.

Tip || Toggle all of the checks in a query on and off by pressing **F6** while the cursor is in the first column of the query form.

For example, if you want a simple count of all the people listed in the table who earn more than $33,000.00 per year, you would toggle the "Salary" column on by pressing **F6**, the Check key. If you want to list the names and salaries of all the people listed in the table who earn more than $33,000.00 per year, check the "SALARY" column. In a larger table, this saves the step of going through the table to check each column.

For this example, get a list of the name and salary. With the cursor in the "SALARY" column:

STEP:

Press: **F6**

Check marks are placed in each column as you see in Figure 5.3.

Tip ‖ The answer table will list only the fields you check. If you want the answer table to list names and salaries, you will want both columns checked.

1. Press the **F6** key one time. What happens?
2. Press the **F6** key again from the same location. What happens?
3. In the query table above, what action would you take to check every column in the table with one keystroke?

1. *A check mark is placed in the column you select.*
2. *The check mark is removed.*
3. *Press **F6** while in the "SALARY" column.*

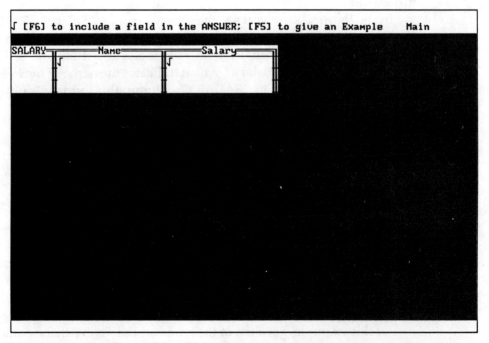

Figure 5.3. Query form with check marks

Specifying the Data in Columns

The next step is to specify data. In the name column, no data needs to be specified since you want to list every name. In the salary column, however, data must be specified to get a list of those who earn more than $33,000.00.

STEP 1:

Press: Right arrow, two times

The blinking cursor moves to the "Salary" column.

STEP 2:

Type: >33000

Figure 5.4 shows how the Query form looks now. By typing >33000, you are asking Paradox to find all records where the salary is greater than (>) $33,000.00.

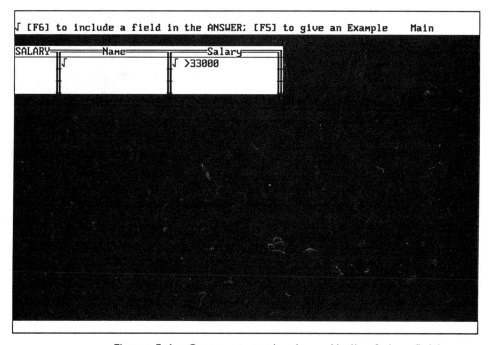

Figure 5.4. Query example placed in the Salary field

Executing the Query

Tell Paradox to execute the query.

STEP:

Press: **F2** DO-IT!

The Answer Table

The answer table appears on screen, directly below the query form. Three names are listed from the *Salary* table. These are the names of the three people listed who earn more than $33,000.00. The *answer* table is shown in Figure 5.5.

1. Type the command for finding all the salaries greater than $50,000.
2. Type the command for finding all salaries less than $50,000.
3. When you have completed the input in the *query* table, press **F2**. What happens?

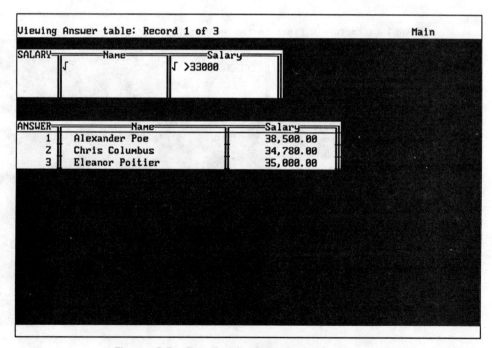

Figure 5.5. The *Salary Answer* table

1. *>50000.*
2. *<50000.*
3. *Paradox searches through the data in the table you have specified. Matching data is displayed in an answer table.*

Using Query Operators

In the example above, the greater than (>) operator was used. With Paradox, you can use other range operators. A range operator gives you an answer to your query in the specified range. In the example above, that range was all salaries greater than $33,000.00. Table 5.1 lists the Paradox range operators, describes them, and gives an example of each.

1. Type a command to specify salaries equal to $33,000.
2. Type a command to specify salaries greater than or equal to $33,000.
3. Type a command to specify salaries less than or equal to $33,000.

1. *=33000.*
2. *>=33000.*
3. *<=33000.*

Multiple Conditions in Queries

The query done in the beginning of this chapter was a single condition query of a single table. You specified a range of data for only one condition, which was greater than $33,000.00. The query was done in a single table, *Salary.*

In this section, expand on the single condition concept by doing a multiple condition query. You will look for records in a table that meet two or more specified conditions. Later in this chapter, you will work with queries of multiple tables.

Table 5.1 Paradox Range Operators

Symbol	Description	Example
=x	Selects the records whose values equal x. This is an optional operator. When no operator is specified, it is assumed that the operator is equal (=).	To list all records with the last name Poe, put this in the Last Name column: =Poe.
> x	Selects records with a value greater than x.	To list all orders received after December 31, 1990, put this in the date column: >12/31/90.
< x	Selects records with a value less than x.	To list all orders for less than $10.00, put this in the amount column: <10.
>= x	Selects records with a value greater than or equal to x.	To list all orders equal to $10.00 and larger, put this in the amount column: >=10.
<= x	Selects records with a value less than or equal to x.	To list all orders equal to $10.00 and less, put this in the amount column: <=10.

Planning the Query

The more conditions you want to find in a query, the more complicated the query becomes. Practice writing down exactly what you want to know from a query. This will help you clarify which range operators belong in which field columns.

Some examples of queries and how they would be recorded are given below:

Example 1: In a table with a customer number, date of sale, and item number, you want to list all orders with the item number equaling three. In the Item Number field in the Query form, you would type 3. You could type =3, but, as you recall, the equal sign is assumed when no operator is included.

Example 2: In a table with a customer number, customer name, date of sale, and item number, you want to list all orders with the item number equaling three, and the customers numbers exceeding 13545. In the Item Number field in the Query form, you would type 3. In the Customer Number field, you would type >13545.

Using 'AND' for Record Selection

Part of the ability of selecting records based on more than one criteria is the ability to use **AND** options in queries. If a query is to meet two criteria, you are asking a question using **AND**. Both criteria must be met for a record to be selected.

For example, you are looking for all the records that have an item number of three AND a customer number that is greater than 13545. In order for any one record to be selected, it must meet both criteria.

Another example is all products with the number A8088 AND that were purchased after December 31, 1991. The selected records will have the specified product number and be purchased after the specified date.

The concept of AND can be extended to three criteria. If you have five fields in a table and you specify that in order for a record to be selected it has to equal three criteria, you are asking an additional AND question. For example, all products with the number A8088 AND that were purchased after December 31, 1991 AND that were purchased by customer number 38.

These examples show how selective a query can be. You can get a list of the total number of products ordered by a specific customer in a specific time frame.

Practice using an **AND** query by specifying two criteria in the *Salary* table.

STEP 1:

Select: Ask

Type: SALARY
Press: Enter

You have selected the **Ask** option from the menu and specified that you want to query the *Salary* table. The SALARY query appears on screen, with the blinking cursor in the "SALARY" column.

STEP 2:

Press: **F6** Check

Check marks are entered into each field column. Each one should be checked, since you want both fields included in the answer table.

STEP 3:

Press: **Tab**
Type: A . .

You are telling Paradox to select any record with a name beginning with A.

STEP 4:

Press: **Tab**
Type: >33000

You are telling Paradox to select any record with a salary greater than $33,000.00.

STEP 5:

Press: **F2** DO-IT

The answer table appears just below the query form as you see in Figure 5.6. To put this query in English, you are asking the following:

Paradox, tell me all of the records in the *Salary* table where the name field begins with the letter A AND the salary is more than $33,000.00.

Paradox answers this query with one record, with the name Alexander Poe. Of the five records in the *Salary* table, only one meets both of the criteria specified in the query form.

1. What happens when you press **F6** while in the "SALARY" column?
2. Press **Tab** while in the query form and what happens?

1. A check mark is placed in each column in the query form.
2. The blinking cursor moves to the next field.

Using a Wildcard Operator

In the example above, you used a wildcard indicator to ask for all the records in the *SALARY* table where the name field begins with A. In a table with hundreds of names, placing "A.." in the query, under the Name field, would find Alexander, Alicia, Algernon, and Abernathy.

The ".." operator will match any group of characters in a field. Typing A . . will find any data in the name field that begins with the letter A, followed by any other numbers or characters of any length.

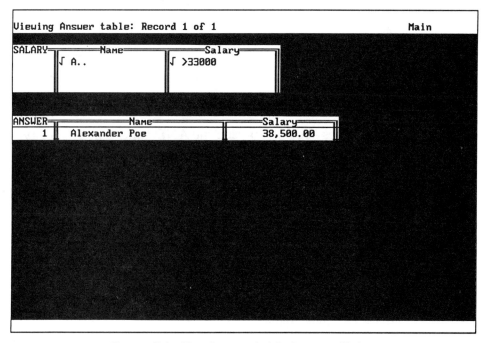

Figure 5.6. The *Answer* table to a multiple query

The wildcard can be used to find any type of data that begins with a certain character. For example, your companies product numbers are listed here:

A203	B308	C809
A444	B286	C943
A562	B789	C966

You want to find out how many products have sold with an item number beginning with B. In the item number field, in the query form, you would type B...

This would find all the products sold with the item numbers beginning with B. The numerals following the letter B would not matter. From the list above, only B308, B286, and B789 would be selected.

1. In the query table, type Mac.. in the last name field and execute the query. What happens?
2. Type the command that finds all product numbers beginning with A8.

1. *You will get an answer table listing all last names that begin with Mac. This includes MacPherson, and Mack.*
2. *A8..*

Using the AND Condition in the Same Field

In the examples above, you used the **AND** condition by specifying criteria in two separate fields. A record is selected if it meets both of the criteria that you have specified in the Query form. You can also use the **AND** condition in the same field. For example, in the *Salary* table, you want to find all the records where the salary is less than $33,000.00 AND greater than $20,000.00.

Both of the criteria specified will be identified in the same field. Use a comma to separate the two criteria in the Salary field. The process would be as follows:

STEP 1:

Press: **F8** Clear Image

Paradox puts you back in the query form in the Salary field.

STEP 2:

Press: Up arrow, one time
Press: **Ctrl-Backspace**

You move to the criteria previously specified in the Salary field. Pressing **Ctrl-Backspace** removes the criteria previously specified in that field, and the cursor remains in the Salary field.

STEP 3:

Press: **Shift-Tab**
Press: **Ctrl-Backspace**
Press: **Tab**

The cursor moves to the Name field. Pressing **Ctrl-Backspace** removes the criteria previously specified in that field. The **Tab** key moves the cursor back to the Salary field.

STEP 4:

Type: >20000,<33000

You are asking for a list of records where the salary is above $20,000.00 AND where the salary is below $33,000.00. You will get an answer table that shows the middle range of salaries from this table.

STEP 5:

Press: **F2** DO-IT

The answer table, with the query form above, is seen in Figure 5.7. One record meets the specified criteria.

Enter as many conditions in a single field as you want to when doing a query. Each **AND** condition must be separated by a comma. The query field columns will stretch to accommodate the amount of conditions you specify.

1. In the last name field, type this command: A..,B.. Execute the query and what happens?
2. Press **F8**. What happens?
3. Type a command in a Patient Number field to get a list of patient numbers greater than 10 and less than 50.

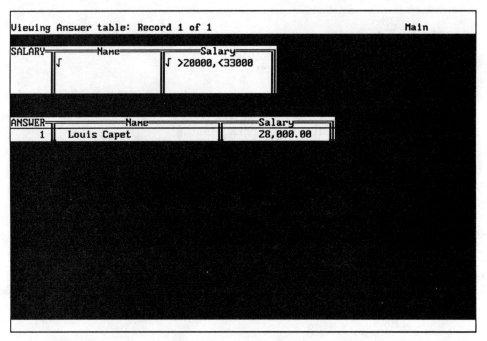

Figure 5.7. Table with the **AND** condition in the same field

1. *An answer table is created that lists last names beginning with A and B. (This answer table will be empty because no last name can begin with both an A and a B.)*
2. *The image the cursor is in is removed from the screen.*
3. *>10,<50.*

Using OR Conditions in a Query

Using the **AND** condition means you want to include two or more kinds of data. In order for a record to be selected, it must meet both conditions specified. Contrast that with the **OR** condition. The **OR** condition will select all the records that meet one of the criteria you specify OR the other criteria.

Here is an example. In the *Salary* table you want to select all the people with salaries less than $20,000.00 OR greater than $33,000.00. In contrast to the exercise above, you want to select the high and low salaries instead of the middle range.

STEP 1:

Press: **F8** Clear Image

This removes the answer table from the previous query and moves the cursor back to the query form. The cursor moves to the Name field.

STEP 2:

Press: **Tab**
Press: **Ctrl-Backspace**

The **Tab** key moves you to the Salary field. Press **Ctrl-Backspace** and the previous data is removed.

STEP 3:

Type: <20000 or >33000

Instead of using a comma like you did to separate the **AND** conditions, you type the word or to separate the **OR** conditions.

STEP 4:

Press: **F2** DO-IT

Figure 5.8 shows the query form and the answer table you see after you press **F2**. Four records are listed where the salaries are below $20,000.00 OR above $33,000.00. The query has again worked.

Tip

You can get an instant report of the information in the data table with one keystroke. After the answer table has been created:

Press: **Alt-F7** Instant Report

A report displaying the answer table is printed provided your printer is connected. The Query form is not shown on the report. You can quickly get a printout of the results of your query.

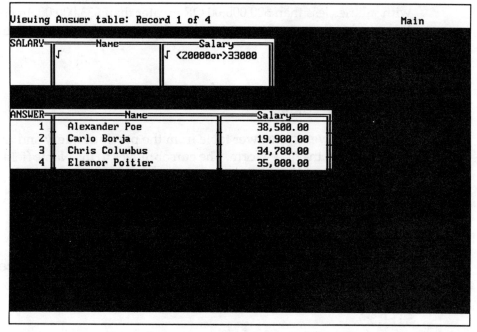

Figure 5.8. *Answer* Table with **OR** condition specified

1. While in a *query* table, press **Ctrl-Backspace**. What happens?
2. Type A . . or B . . in the last name field. Execute the query. What happens?
3. Type <10 or >50 in a patient number field. Execute the query. What happens?

---

1. *The condition in that field is deleted.*
2. *An answer table lists all the last names in the database that begin with A or B.*
3. *An answer table lists all the patient numbers less than 10 or greater than 50.*

Using OR Conditions in Different Fields

The method for using the **OR** conditions in different fields is a little different than the methods you have used so far. In the *Salary* table, you can ask an

OR question by specifying the data to be selected in the two fields. An example is to query for the names that begin with A OR the salaries less than $33,000.00.

Start by selecting the records in a query where the name field begins with A.

STEP 1:

Press: **F8**

Paradox clears the previous answer table and moves the cursor to the Salary field in the query form.

STEP 2:

Press: **Ctrl-Backspace**

The data in the Salary field is deleted.

STEP 3:

Press: **Shift-Tab**

The blinking cursor moves to the Name field.

STEP 4:

Type: A . .

You have asked for any records that begin with the letter A, in the Name field.

STEP 5:

Press: **F2** DO-IT

The answer table appears with the query form above it. One name meets the criteria of having the name beginning with the letter A. The screen appears, as in Figure 5.9.

---

1. Press **Shift-Tab**. What happens?
2. When you type A . ., you are asking Paradox to select which records?

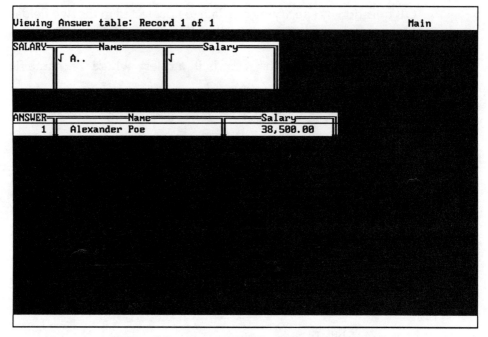

Figure 5.9. *Answer* table with one condition

1. *The blinking cursor moves left, one field.*
2. *Those records where A is the first character, followed by any other characters.*

Adding the Second OR Condition

The next step is to add the second criteria. To make this an **OR** condition, another line has to be added to the Query form.

STEP 1:

Press: **F8**

This clears the *answer* table image and moves the cursor back to the Name field in the Query form.

STEP 2:

Press: Down arrow

This step creates a new row in the Query form.

STEP 3:

Press: **F6** Check
Press: **Tab**
Press: **F6** Check

The Name field is checked in the second line of the query form. The blinking cursor moves to the Salary field, and this field is checked.

STEP 4:

Type: <33000

You are telling Paradox to look for records where the name begins with A or the salaries are less than $33,000.00.

STEP 5:

Press: **F2** DO-IT

The *answer* table and query for these **OR** conditions appears as in Figure 5.10. The records listed include one where the name begins with the letter A and two more where the salary is less than the amount specified.

In a query form where you are using **OR** conditions for more than one field, you can have up to 22 lines. This means you can ask 22 OR questions. Paradox will select records that match any line in the query.

Tip | When you enter multiple lines in a query, you must check each line in each column, as well as the same fields in each line. If you do not check the same fields in each line, Paradox will beep you when you press the **F2** DO-IT key, because it cannot understand the query entered.

Tip | If your query gets to be 22 lines long, use the **Ctrl-Home** key to move to the first column of the query form. Use **Ctrl-End** to move to the last line of the query column.

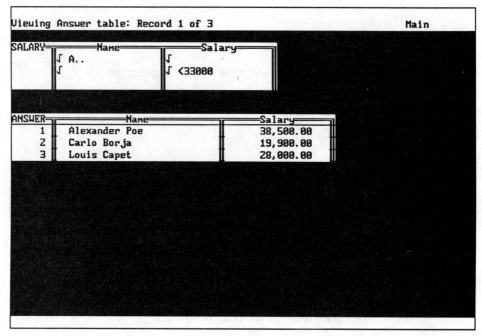

Figure 5.10. *Answer* table with second **OR** condition

1. While in the name field of the query form, press down arrow. What happens?
2. With <33000 in the Salary field, Paradox will find what records?
3. What is the maximum number of OR questions you can ask in one query?

1. *A new row is created in the query form.*
2. *Salaries less than $33,000.*
3. *22.*

Changing the Order of Records in an Answer Table

Any time you have a set of records in an *answer* table, they are listed in a specific order. If the primary field has numbers, the *answer* table will display the records in ascending numerical order. The lowest number will be at the top of the table, with the numbers getting larger as you move down the table.

Paradox provides a way for you to reverse that order. You can check a column to appear in the *answer* table in descending order. The largest number will then be at the top, with the numbers getting smaller as you move down the table. When no numbers are involved, this concept will work with alphabetical order.

You can practice changing the order in any table with a number column to see its effect. For this example, the *ADVCHEM* table is on the screen, with the query form above the data table. Figure 5.11 shows the Student Number, Last Name, and Grade-% fields checked. These were checked using the F6 key, so all should appear on the *answer* table in ascending order. In the Grade-% field, all grades greater than 80 percent are specified to appear in the *answer* table.

At the top of the screen is the Query form, followed by the *data* table. At the bottom is the *answer* table. The numbers in the "Student Number" column in the *answer* table appear in ascending order.

Press: **F8** to clear the answer table.
Press: **F3** to move up to the Query form.

```
Viewing Answer table: Record 1 of 5                          Main

=Student Number=        =No. =        =Last Name=        =First Name=
  √                                     √                                   √ >



ADUCHEM Student Number      No. =              Last Name       First Name
   1  ║ 11-013  ║         1           Astro            Billy           ×
   2  ║ 11-384  ║         4           Pluto            Pete            ×
   3  ║ 12-122  ║         5           Comet            Alfie           ×
   4  ║ 12-288  ║         2           Galaxy           Andre           ×
   5  ║ 12-306  ║         7           Mars             Mike            ×
   6  ║ 12-316  ║         3           Moon             Monica          ×


ANSWER Student Number    =Last Name=      =Grade-%=
   1  ║ 11-013  ║ Astro            92.26
   2  ║ 11-384  ║ Pluto            90.09
   3  ║ 12-122  ║ Comet            98.92
   4  ║ 12-288  ║ Galaxy           94.88
   5  ║ 12-306  ║ Mars             82.66
```

Figure 5.11. Query form, *Data* table, and *Answer* table in ascending order

Checking Descending Order

Change the order of the numbers in the *answer* table by moving the cursor to the check already placed in the "Student Number" column.

STEP 1:

Press: **F6** Check

This toggles the check, which has already been made to the off position.

STEP 2:

Press: **Ctrl-F6** Check Descending

A new check is inserted, this time a down arrow appearing with it, symbolizing descending order.

STEP 3:

Press: **F2** DO-IT

With all other query information remaining the same, check the results of this query in Figure 5.12. The *answer* table appears at the bottom of the screen, with the records appearing in descending order by student number.

Descending Alphabetical Order

In one more example, seen in Figure 5.13, the student number check has been removed in the query. A descending order check is placed in the Last Name field. The Grade-% criteria remains the same as in the previous two queries. The answer table at the bottom of the screen lists the last names of the students, in descending alphabetical order.

1. Press **F3**. What happens?
2. Press **F6** one time while in a field column in the query table. What happens?
3. With the cursor in the same field, press **F6** again. What happens?
4. Press **Ctrl-F6**, with the cursor in a field column in the query table. What happens?

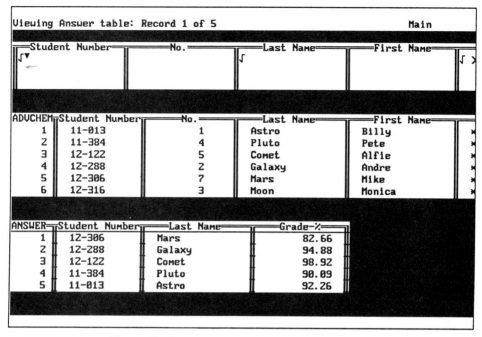

Figure 5.12. Query form, *Data* table, and *Answer* table in descending order

1. *The blinking cursor moves up one image.*
2. *The field is checked.*
3. *The check is removed from the field.*
4. *The field is checked, and descending order is specified.*

Editing Query Forms

As you move the cursor around in the Query form, you see that it is placed at the end of the data in the column. Just as you did while editing a table, you delete and retype incorrect characters in the query form.

The query editing keys are listed here:

Right Arrow or Tab   Move to the next column, moving from left to right, top to bottom. If you are in the last column of a row, press the right arrow key and you move to the first column of the next row.

```
Viewing Answer table: Record 1 of 5                              Main

 Student Number         No.              Last Name          First Name
                                         √▼                                 √ >



ADVCHEM Student Number  No.              Last Name          First Name
   1    11-013           1               Astro              Billy          ×
   2    11-384           4               Pluto              Pete           ×
   3    12-122           5               Comet              Alfie          ×
   4    12-288           2               Galaxy             Andre          ×
   5    12-306           7               Mars               Mike           ×
   6    12-316           3               Moon               Monica         ×


ANSWER      Last Name        Grade-%
   1    Pluto                 90.09
   2    Mars                  82.66
   3    Galaxy                94.88
   4    Comet                 98.92
   5    Astro                 92.26
```

Figure 5.13. Query form, *Data* table, and *Answer* table in descending alphabetical order

Left Arrow or Shift-Tab	Moves the blinking cursor to the previous column. If you are in the first column of a row, the left arrow key moves you to the last column of the previous row.
Up Arrow	Moves to the same column in the previous row.
Down Arrow	Moves to the same column in the next row.
Del Key	Deletes an entire row in the query, including checks.
Backspace	Deletes characters to the left of the blinking cursor.
Ctrl-Backspace	This combination deletes all the data in a column.
Ctrl-Right Arrow	Moves right an entire screen.

Ctrl-Left Arrow	Moves left an entire screen.
Ctrl-Home	Moves the cursor to the first row in the left column of the table.
Ctrl-End	Moves the cursor to the last row in the right column of the table.
F6 Check	Toggles the check mark in the query on and off. Only checked fields will appear in the *answer* table. This is the normal check where the *answer* table will display records in ascending order.
Ctrl-F6 Check Descending	Fields marked with the **Ctrl-F6** key will display in descending order by number or by alphabet.
Alt-F6 Check Plus	By default, Paradox eliminates duplicate records from the *answer* table. Use **Alt-F6** to display duplicate records in the *answer* table, providing these records answer the question being asked.

Tip   If you press **Home** or **End** while in a query, instead of **Ctrl-End** or **Ctrl-Home**, nothing happens. Control must precede these keys in order to move the cursor.

1. In the Query form, press the **Tab** key. What happens?
2. Press the **Del** key. What happens?
3. Press the **Home** key. What happens?

1. *The cursor moves to the next field to the right.*
2. *Deletes an entire row in the query, including checks.*
3. *Nothing happens. The cursor does not move.* **Ctrl-Home** *must be pressed.*

Querying from Multiple Tables

Paradox is built on relations between tables of data. In Chapter 3, when you planned and designed a Paradox table, the important concept was to keep tables simple. Later, you would pull the data you need from the related tables. That is what you will learn to do in this section.

Querying from multiple tables brings together related data from more than one table. The related data will appear in one *answer* table.

Defining the Answer

Two tables have been created for this exercise of querying multiple tables. Both tables are displayed in Figure 5.14. Each table has ten records.

The table at the top of the screen is the *Customer Sales* table, called CUSTSALS in this example. The *CUSTSALS* table has two fields. The first, defined as the Primary Key field, is the Customer Number (Cust #) field. The second field lists the annual sales for each customer. (Not all of the records in this table are visible on screen. Paradox has scrolled the first records up because there is not room to display all the records.)

The second table is called *CUSTID* since it contains the customer number and the name and address of each customer. The Cust # field is defined as the primary key in this table as well.

Create these or similar tables by following the steps in Chapter 3.

The answer wanted by the sales manager of an organization is a list of all the customers who purchased more than $10,000 worth of products in the previous year. This question alone could be answered by a single table query of the *CUSTSALS* table. However, the sales manager also wants to know the names and addresses of these same customers in order to send them a special promotional mailing.

The answer table should give the name and address of the customers who purchased more than $10,000 worth of products in the previous year. This will be accomplished by using the related data in the two tables.

Listing the Steps for a Multiple Table Query

There are four steps to a multiple table query after the tables are created. The steps are listed here:

```
Viewing Custid table: Record 1 of 10                          Main   =

CUSTSALS    Cust #          Annual Sales
   2          124            3,142.88
   3          125           12,365.52
   4          126           13,471.12
   5          127           15,022.24
   6          128            4,948.18
   7          129            8,336.99
   8          130           10,082.65
   9          131           11,667.22
  10          132            9,455.38



CUSTID     Cust #       Last Name        First Name         Address
   1         123        Mousse           Mickey          987 Holly Wood
   2         124        Goofie           Glen            876 Peaches Lane
   3         125        Placid           Pluto           765 Bucolic Plac
   4         126        Duck             Daphne          654 Tauny Pond
   5         127        Ferdie           Fred            543 15th Street
   6         128        Mortie           Montey          432 Montivideo A
   7         129        Dilly            Daisy           321 Piccadilly S
   8         130        Menace           Minnie          210 Mystery Crt.
   9         131        Jerry            Tom             109 Egg Nog Cent
  10         132        Doodle           Dipsy           909 Topsy Turvy
```

Figure 5.14. Two tables for multiple table query

1. Display a Query form on screen for each table in the multiple table query.
2. Define the example elements.
3. Check the fields that should appear in the *answer* table.
4. Execute the query and create the *answer* table.

Displaying the Query Forms on Screen

In a multiple table query, a Query form for each table involved must be displayed on screen at the same time. In this example, place two Query forms on screen.

STEP 1:

Press: Alt-F8 Clear All

The workspace is cleared of all tables and queries.

STEP 2:

Select: **Ask**
Type: CUSTSALS
Press: **Enter**

The CUSTSALS Query form appears on screen.

STEP 3:

Press: **F10** Menu

The Paradox Main menu appears across the top of the screen.

STEP 4:

Select: **Ask**
Type: CUSTID
Press: **Enter**

Both Query forms are now on screen. The blinking cursor is in the CUSTID Query form. CUSTID is the active Query form. The screen looks like the one in Figure 5.15.

1. Create a multiple table query.
2. Press **Alt-F8**. What happens?
3. How can you tell which Query form is the active Query form?

1. *Display a Query form on screen, one for each table. Define the example elements and then check the fields to appear in the answer table. Execute the query.*
2. *All images are cleared from the workspace.*
3. *The blinking cursor is in the active Query form.*

Defining Example Elements

An example element is a special name you identify to type into a query form. The example element is placed in the field you want to link to another

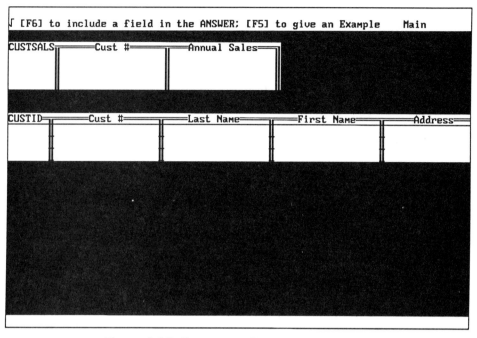

Figure 5.15. Two query forms on screen

table. In this example, the field that will link the two tables is the Cust # field. The Cust # field in each query form will hold the example element.

Each query form will hold an example element. The example element in each query form must be identical so that Paradox can match these fields.

It does not matter what characters you choose to be an example element. For example, you could have an example element be "bob." The characters "bob" must appear in the Cust # field in both Query forms on screen. If you had more than two Query forms on screen, the example element "bob" would have to appear at least once in one field column for each query form.

Example elements are entered in a query form using the F5 Example key. With the cursor in a query form, you press F5, indicating that the next word you type will be the example element. Paradox flashes a highlighted message that you will be typing the example element. The word typed after you press F5 is highlighted on screen, indicating that this is the example element.

Put the example elements in the two tables you have on screen. With the blinking cursor in the CUSTID Query form:

STEP 1:

Press: Right arrow

The cursor is moved to the Cust # field. This field is identified as the Primary Key field in both tables to be queried. It is the field used to link the two tables in the multiple table query.

STEP 2:

Press: **F5** Example

At the point of the blinking cursor, a block-shaped cursor flashes as you press **F5**.

STEP 3:

Type: bob

The highlighted example element "bob" is inserted in the Cust # field.

STEP 4:

Press: **F3**

The blinking cursor moves up one image to the CUSTSALS Query form.

STEP 5:

Press: Right arrow

The cursor is moved to the Cust # field.

STEP 6:

Press: **F5** Example
Type: bob

Tip   Pressing **Enter** or the arrow keys will stop the example element. When you have entered the example element, press **Enter** or any key other than an alphanumeric key to end the example element.

Figure 5.16 shows how the two defined example elements appear in the Query forms on screen.

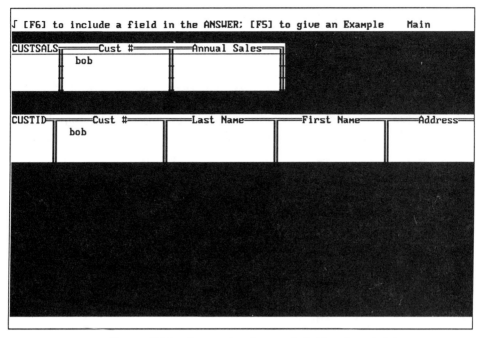

√ [F6] to include a field in the ANSWER: [F5] to give an Example   Main

CUSTSALS━━━━━Cust #━━━━━━Annual Sales━━━
            bob

CUSTID━━━━━Cust #━━━━━━Last Name━━━━━First Name━━━━Address━━
          bob

Figure 5.16. Example elements linking two tables

Creating example elements is really quite simple. You have done it!

Tip There is no significance to using "bob" as the example element. You can use any set of alphanumeric symbols you want to link tables. What is important is to make sure the example elements in each query form are identical.

1. Place the example element in the last name field. What happens to that field?
2. After you have placed an example element in one Query form, what do you do next?
3. What happens when you press F5?

1. *It becomes the field that will be linked to another table.*
2. *Place the same example element in the linked field in the second query form.*
3. *You tell Paradox that the next word you type is the example element for that query form.*

Checking the Fields to Appear in the Answer Table

Earlier in this section, the *answer* table was defined. This step involves checking those fields you want to appear in the *answer* table.

According to the definition already written for this query, the *answer* table should have the following fields in it: Last Name, First Name, Address, City, State, Zip Code, and Annual Sales. These are the fields that should be checked. With the cursor in the CUSTSALS Query form under the Cust # field:

STEP 1:

> Press: Right arrow
> Press: **F6** Check

The check selects this field to appear in the *answer* table. But not just this field needs to appear. It is also a specified field that is to display records exceeding $10,000.

STEP 2:

> Type: >10000

STEP 3:

> Press: **F4** Down Image

The blinking cursor moves down to the next Query form on screen.

STEP 4:

> Press: Right arrow
> Press: **F6** Check

Repeat step four until Last Name, First Name, Address, City, State, and Zip are all checked.

The two Query forms appear as you see in Figure 5.17.

Executing the Query

The final and simplest step is to execute the query.

STEP:

> Press **F2** DO-IT

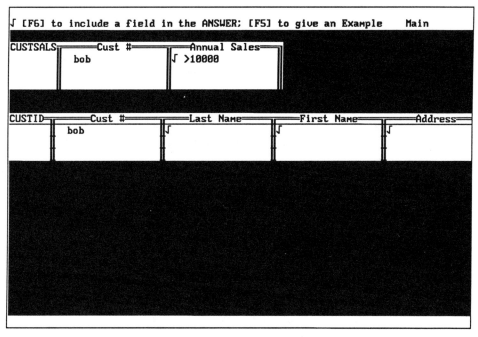

Figure 5.17. Multiple table query on screen

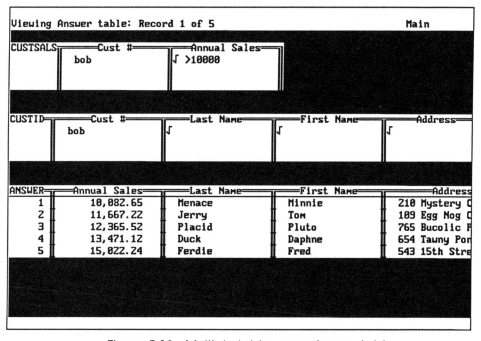

Figure 5.18. Multiple table query *Answer* table

The *answer* table is shown below the two Query forms in Figure 5.18. Of the original ten records, five meet the criteria of the multiple table query. Five have annual sales exceeding $10,000. The names and addresses for those five customers are listed in the *answer* table. Paradox has even put the five records in ascending order.

Notice that the Cust # field does not appear in the *answer* table. This field was used to link the tables by holding the example element, but it was not checked; therefore, it does not appear in the answer table.

Tip ‖ Get an instant report of this *answer* table by pressing **Alt-F7**. Only the *answer* table will be printed.

1. Place a check mark in a field. What are you achieving?
2. With two query forms on screen, press **F2**. What happens?
3. With the cursor in the *answer* table, press **Alt-F7**. What happens?

1. *You are selecting that field to appear in the answer table.*
2. *Paradox searches through the two tables to find the records that match the conditions specified in both Query forms. Paradox displays an answer table.*
3. *You get an instant report of the answer table, printed on the printer.*

Adjusting the Multiple Table Query

Now that you know that Paradox will do what you tell it to do, try a simple adjustment to the query. The sales manager who defines this query decides that the Annual Sales total does not need to be in the *answer* table. These steps will adjust the query accordingly:

STEP 1:

Press: **F3** Up Image, two times

The cursor is now in the "Annual Sales" column.

STEP 2:

Press: **F6** Check

This removes the check in this column, telling Paradox that this field does not need to appear in the *answer* table. Even though this field is not checked, Paradox will still use this data to create the *answer* table.

STEP 3:

> Press: **F2** DO-IT

Paradox displays the adjusted *answer* table, which lists the five records that meet the criteria specified in the multiple table query. This time they are listed in alphabetical order by last name, as shown in Figure 5.19. Both queries and the *answer* table are displayed. The Annual Sales field is not included in this *answer* table since the check was removed.

All of the elements of a single table query can be used in a multiple table query. Review the use of **AND** and **OR** operators, as well as other operators listed in Table 5.1.

1. Press **F6**. What happens?
2. Press **F3**. What happens?
3. Press **F2**. What happens?

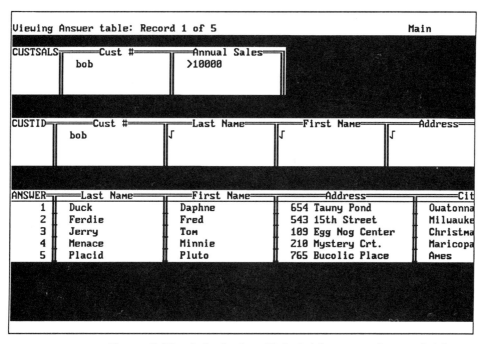

Viewing Answer table: Record 1 of 5				Main

CUSTSALS	Cust #	Annual Sales
	bob	>10000

CUSTID	Cust #	Last Name	First Name	Address
	bob	√	√	√

ANSWER	Last Name	First Name	Address	Cit
1	Duck	Daphne	654 Tawny Pond	Owatonna
2	Ferdie	Fred	543 15th Street	Milwauke
3	Jerry	Tom	109 Egg Nog Center	Christma
4	Menace	Minnie	210 Mystery Crt.	Maricopa
5	Placid	Pluto	765 Bucolic Place	Ames

Figure 5.19. Adjusted multiple table query *Answer* table

1. *The field is checked, which means it is selected to appear in the answer table.*
2. *The cursor moves up one image on the screen.*
3. *Paradox searches through the two tables to find the records that match the conditions specified in both Query forms. Paradox displays an answer table.*

Saving Queries

Saving queries is important, if, for example, a query gives you a specific month-end report. This saves time by assuring that you don't have to retype the query every time you want to duplicate it. You can then retrieve the saved query and apply it to the new data at the end of the month.

The steps to saving a query are:

1. Create the query.
2. Execute the query and then verify that Paradox answers with the correct information.
3. Save the query.

In this chapter you have already completed steps one and two. In fact, you have a query on screen now. With CUSTSALS and CUSTID queries on screen, practice saving this query.

STEP 1:

Press: F10 Menu

The Main menu appears on screen.

STEP 2:

Select: **Script**
Select: **QuerySave**

Paradox prompts you to name the query to be saved. Select a name that will give you a hint to what answer the query will produce.

Tip ‖ Name a query, using up to eight alphanumeric characters.

STEP 3:

> Type: OVER10K
> Press: **Enter**

This query is now saved to disk. You can use this same query at the end of the next year to answer to the same question.

Retrieving a Query

Once you have saved a query and you are ready to see the same query at a later date, follow these steps:

STEP 1:

> Press: **Alt-F8**

All images are cleared from the Paradox workspace.

STEP 2:

> Select: **Script**
> Select: **Play**
> Press: **Enter**

Paradox prompts you to name the query you want to retrieve. Press **Enter** and the names of all saved queries appear on screen.

STEP 3:

> Select: OVER10K

The query you saved appears on screen. You can modify and/or execute this query. Any changes in data from the previous execution will be taken into consideration, and a new *answer* table is created.

1. Select **QuerySave** from the **Script** submenu. What happens?
2. Select **Play** from the **Script** submenu. What happens?

1. *Paradox prompts you for a name for the query on screen, which is also the query to be saved.*
2. *You are asked to name the query you want to retrieve.*

Summary

In Chapter 5, the elements of retrieving specific data by means of a query is encapsulated. You have defined, created, and executed a single table query. You have planned, created, and executed a more complicated multiple table query. Finally, you have saved and retrieved a query. What appears to be a very complicated process has been simplified. Consider yourself successful at the Paradox query process.

The subjects covered in this chapter are:

- Creating a query
  - A single table query
  - Using query operators
- Multiple queries
  - Planning the query
  - Using **AND** and **OR** conditions
  - Using wildcards in queries
  - Ascending and descending order
  - Editing query forms
- Querying multiple tables
  - Displaying query forms
  - Defining example elements
  - Executing the query
- Saving queries
  - Retrieving queries

Exercises

What You Should Do	How the Computer Responds
1. View the table you want to query. Select: **View** Type: The name of the table you want to view. Press: **Enter**	1. When you select **View**, Paradox prompts you to name the table you want to view. Press **Enter** and Paradox displays the table on screen.

2. Display a Query form on screen for the table you are viewing.
Press: **F10**
Select: **Ask**
Type: The name of the table you want to query.
Press: **Enter**

3. Select the columns you want to appear in the *answer* table. If you want all the columns to appear in the *answer* table, leave the cursor in the left-most column.
Press: **F6**
If you want only a few fields to appear in the *answer* table, move the cursor to those fields by pressing the right arrow key or **Tab** key. In those fields you want to appear in the *answer* table:
Press: **F6**

4. Select the records to appear in the *answer* column. For this example, in the Last Name field, select names beginning with M.
Type: M..

5. In a field holding numerical data, specify records holding more than a certain amount. For this example, move the cursor to the numerical field.
Type: >70

6. Execute the query:
Press: **F2**

7. Go back and adjust the query. Start by clearing the *answer* table you just created.
Press: **F8**

2. The table you were viewing moves down on the screen. The Query form is inserted at the top of the screen. The Query form is active.

3. Paradox places check marks in the fields you want to appear in the *answer* table.

4. The Last Name field now contains a check mark and "M.."

5. In the numerical field you see a check mark and ">70."

6. Paradox searches through the table to find the records that match the conditions specified in the Query form. Paradox displays an *answer* table. The *answer* table holds all the records where the last name begins with M, and the numerical field holds numbers greater than 70.

7. The *answer* table is removed from the screen.

8. Move up to the query form.
Press: **F3**

8. The blinking cursor moves up one image on the screen.

9. Move the cursor to the Last Name field.
Press: Right arrow

9. The cursor moves to the right until it is under the Last Name field.

10. Adjust the conditions in this field by adding an **OR** condition and asking to list the names in descending order.
Type: or G..
Press: **F6**
Press: **Ctrl-F6**

10. Paradox adds the conditions "or G.." to the Last Name field. Pressing **F6** removes the check mark. Pressing **Ctrl-F6** adds a check mark, indicating that these records are to be displayed in descending order.

11. Execute the adjusted query.
Press: **F2**

11. Paradox searches through the table to find the records that match the conditions specified in the Query form. Paradox displays an *answer* table where last names begin with M or G and the numerical value exceeds 70.

12. Save the query by:
Press: **F10**
Select: **Script**
Select: **QuerySave**

12. When you press **F10**, the Main menu appears. After making the two menu selections, Paradox prompts you to name the query you want to save.

13. At the prompt, type the name of the query.
Type: Over70
Press: **Enter**

13. Paradox saves the query to disk under the name OVER70.

14. Retrieve the query by following these steps:
Press: **F10**
Select: **Scripts**
Select: Play
Press: **Enter**

14. Pressing **F10** displays the Main menu. You selected the menu options and Paradox prompts you to name the query you want to retrieve.

15. Press: **Enter**.

15. Paradox displays all of the queries that have been saved to disk.

16. Select the query you want to retrieve from those listed.

16. Paradox displays the query form for the query you have retrieved. You can now execute that query on the same table.

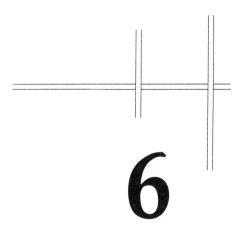

6

Creating Paradox Reports

The Paradox report function can produce more than the instant reports you have already created. Paradox will customize reports to meet your needs. You will learn the basics of report creation in this chapter under these topics:

- Instant reports
- Custom reports

Instant Reports

Paradox is as friendly and powerful in its ability to create reports as it is in creating tables and queries. As in many previous topics in this book, you had to learn guidelines for using Paradox tools. Along the same line, we start this chapter with learning the limitations of the Paradox report.

While these limitations are not rules, they will give you a framework of what you can and cannot do with a Paradox report. The limitations listed here will increase your understanding of Paradox. As you look at the limitations, you will realize that rarely will you butt your head against any one of them.

Paradox Report Limitations

Following are Paradox report limitations

Maximum number of report characters per record: 2000. For every record in a report, there can be no more than 2000 characters printed about that record.

Maximum number of fields: 255. A single report can hold no more than 255 fields.

Maximum number of groupings: 16. Groupings can be based on field values, ranges, or numbers of records.

Maximum number of pages in a report: No Limit.

Minimum number of lines in a report: 2.

Maximum number of lines in a report: 2000. Depending on how the report is designed, this would be approximately 40 pages.

Maximum number of reports per table: 15. If you have a long table with a great deal of information, you can create up to 15 separate reports that organize and reorganize the information.

You can link tables together and gather as much information into one report, until 255 fields are included or a maximum of five tables are linked. This is as large as a multiple table report can be.

Tabular and free-form reports cannot be mixed together in one report. Both styles of report will be described later.

As you can see, these limitations provide plenty of room for creative reporting.

Tabular Reports

One type of report printed by Paradox is the tabular report. This is the kind of report you have seen up to this point. When you press Alt-F7 for an instant report, you are getting a tabular report.

A tabular report is printed like a spreadsheet. The records are listed down the page, with the fields across the page. You can group records, make subtotals, and keep running totals in a tabular report. This type of report is similar to a Paradox table.

Free-Form Reports

With the free-form report you have freedom in setting up the printed page. Use this type of report to print mailing labels, create form letters, create invoices, or print checks. Instead of listing data, you can put table fields anywhere on the page. The free-form report is similar to the Form view in Paradox. Free form reports will be covered in Chapter 10.

1. Press **Alt-F7**. What happens?
2. Create a mailing label. Which form do you select?

1. *You get an instant tabular report.*
2. *Free-form reports.*

Report Concepts

One important concept in understanding Paradox reports is to know that reports are generated one record at a time. For example, if you were printing a free-form report that was designed to print checks, Paradox would look at the first record, print the corresponding check, then move to the next record, and so on.

Paradox reads the record, acts on the record in the way you have designed in the report definition, and then goes on to the next record. This is how a report is generated.

Report Bands

Report bands are used in Paradox to define and control what is being printed at different locations in the report. Every custom report has four bands, described below.

Table Band—This section of the report tells Paradox what to do with every record in the table. This band holds the body of the report. You can put comments, field values, and the results of calculations in the table band. A report can be printed with or without a table band.

Group Band—This band is used to divide records into logical groups. For example, you may want to group a list of patients by the first letter of their last name. You may want to group the scores of students on an exam by their percentage. Students who got 90 percent and above would be in one group, students with 80 percent to 90 percent would be in the next group, and so on. You can calculate the sum of values in a report group. Groups can have headers and footers.

Page Band—A page band includes information you want included on every page. Report titles, page number, headers, and footers are some of the things you might want to include in the page band.

Report Band—Information included at the beginning of each report is placed in the report band. A report header is printed once at the beginning of a report, and a report footer is printed once at the end of a report. A report header and a report footer are both placed in the report band. A report footer can hold totals calculated at the end of a report.

Creating an Instant Report

The most basic Paradox report is the instant report. With the cursor in the *ADVCHEM data* table:

STEP:

Press: Alt-F7 Instant Report

Figure 6.1 shows the printed instant report of the *ADVCHEM* table.

The instant report holds the date and page number at the top of the page, along with the words "Standard Report." Each field name is printed as a column heading.

Only two table bands appear in this report. The page band holds the date and page number along with the words "Standard Report." The table band holds definitions for each of the fields listed.

12/07/90		Standard Report		Page 1
Student Number	No.	Last Name	First Name	Grade–%
11–013	1	Astro	Billy	92
11–384	4	Pluto	Pete	90
12–122	5	Comet	Alfie	99
12–288	2	Galaxy	Andre	95
12–306	7	Mars	Mike	83
12–316	3	Moon	Monica	72

Figure 6.1. Instant report

Custom Reports

When a standard report is not enough and you want to add more detail or remove some fields from a report, you create a custom report. Choose the type of report you wish to create, either a tabular report or a free-form report. A tabular report looks similar to the standard report except for some embellishments. The free-form report is more like a Form view of a database. In the following sections, you will find information about creating the tabular report first. Creating a free-form report can be found in Chapter 10.

Creating a Tabular Report

Paradox provides you with a report design screen in which you place the verbiage in the proper report bands. The process of creating a tabular report starts with getting to the report design screen.

In this example, we will create a report where two columns are removed from the table seen on screen. Column headings will be enhanced via the report design screen.

Getting to the Report Design Screen

If you have been working in Paradox for awhile, start this process by clearing the workspace.

STEP 1:

Press: **Alt-F8** Clear All

From the Main menu at the top of the screen:

STEP 2:

Select: **Report**
Select: **Design**

Paradox prompts you to name the table for which you want to design a report. The *ADVCHEM* table created in Chapter 3 will be used in the example below, but you can use any table you choose.

STEP 3:

Type: ADVCHEM
Press: **Enter**

Across the top you see "R 1 2 3 4," and so on. This is a list of report numbers. Choose one of these numbers to assign to the report you are creating. One table can have 14 reports assigned to it. For this example, select one. In Figure 6.2, you can see what happens when you move the cursor to the number 1. Paradox tells you that this is an "unused report."

STEP 4:

Select: 1

Paradox prompts you to describe the report. Later, when you print this report, the description is displayed.

Tip ‖ The description you type will be inserted as the name for the report.

STEP 5:

Type: Student Names and Grades
Press: **Enter**

Paradox displays the two types of reports available.

STEP 6:

Select: **Tabular**

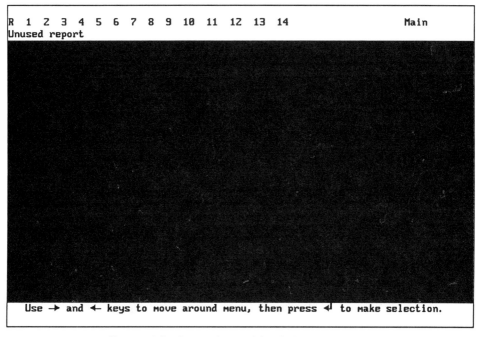

R 1 2 3 4 5 6 7 8 9 10 11 12 13 14   Main
Unused report

Use → and ← keys to move around menu, then press ◄┘ to make selection.

Figure 6.2. Report one highlighted

The report design screen is now on screen and should match the screen you see in Figure 6.3.

1. Press Alt-F7 and what do you get?
2. Press Alt-F8. What happens?
3. Select **Report/Design.** Type the name of the table. Select the number of the report. What will you accomplish?

1. An instant report.
2. All images are cleared from the workspace.
3. You will select a new report to design.

Describing the Report Design Screen

Unlike the *STRUCT* table or the *Query* table, the design screen does not start out empty. The components of the report design screen, seen in Figure 6.4, will be described here.

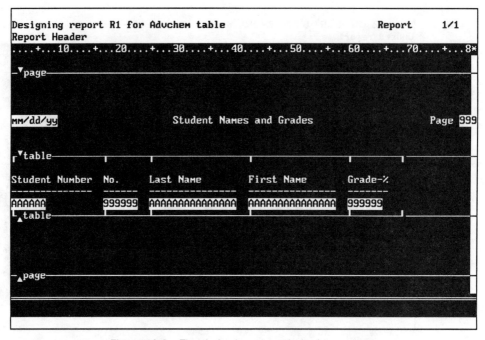

Figure 6.3. The tabular report design screen

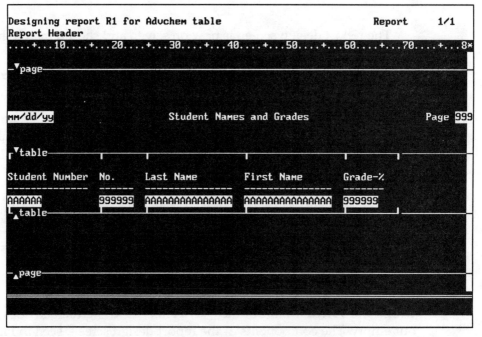

Figure 6.4. The report design screen

At the very top of the screen, you see the message: "Designing report R1 for ADVCHEM table." Paradox reminds you that what you are doing is designing the first report for the data found in *ADVCHEM*. As you move across the top of the screen, you see the word "Report" highlighted, which indicates that the **Report** submenu will appear if you press the **F10** Menu key.

The second line holds the words "Report Header." You are being told where your cursor is located. Notice that the blinking cursor is just above and to the left of the word "page." Press the down arrow key one time. The cursor moves to the "Page Header." Press the up arrow key to go back to the "Report Header."

Move your eye to the top line of the workspace. You see a series of dots, plus signs, and numbers that show you the column numbers across the screen. This line is called the horizontal ruler line. Your cursor should be just below this line.

Below the blinking cursor is the word page, preceded by an arrow pointing down. The page band begins at this line and extends down to the word page, preceded by an arrow pointing up.

Continue down the page to find "mm/dd/yy" highlighted in the page header area. This is a preset item that prints the current month, day, and year according to the setting in your computer. Centered on this line is the description you gave for this table: "Student Names and Grades." At the right is the word "Page 999." Paradox will automatically print the correct page number at this location. Items in the page header are printed once per page.

The table band is next, indicated by a down arrow and the word "table." Just as with the page indicator, this is the top of the table band and it continues down to where you see the up arrow preceding the word "table." The field names found in the *ADVCHEM* table are listed horizontally across the page within the table band.

Dashes separate the field headers from the field data. Below the dashes are a series of A's and 9's, which are called field masks. These characters reserve space for the values from the table. When you print the report, data from the table replaces the A's and 9's. A's indicate that the data in that field is alphanumeric. The 9's indicate that numbers are placed in the field.

1. While in the report design screen, press **F10**. What happens?
2. Look at the page header area. What information will you find there?
3. What do the series of A's or 9's represent on the screen?

1. *The **Report** submenu appears.*
2. *The date, title, and page number for the report.*
3. *The field masks for alphanumeric characters or numerals.*

Moving the Cursor in the Report Design Screen

The descriptions below tell how the cursor moves in the report design screen.

Up Arrow	Moves the cursor up one line.
Down Arrow	Moves the cursor down one line.
Right Arrow	Moves the cursor to the right one character.
Left Arrow	Moves the cursor to the left one character.
Ctrl-Right Arrow	Moves the cursor one half screen to the right.
Ctrl-Left Arrow	Moves the cursor one half screen to the left.
Home	Moves the cursor to the first line of the report design screen.
Ctrl-Home	Moves the cursor to the beginning of the current line.
End	Moves the cursor to the last line of the report design screen.
Ctrl-End	Moves the cursor to the end of the current line.
PgUp	Moves the cursor up one page.
PgDn	Moves the cursor down one page.
Tab	Moves the cursor to the next report column when in the tabular report screen.
Shift-Tab	Moves the cursor to the previous report column when in the tabular report screen.
Backspace key	Deletes the character to the left of the cursor.

Use the keys as described above to move around in the report design screen. Just as you made edits in the *STRUCT* table and the *data* table, you can make changes in the report design screen. Use the *Backspace* key to delete characters to the left of the cursor and then retype the correct characters.

1. Press the **End** key. What happens?
2. Press the **Tab** key. What happens?

1. *The cursor moves to the last line of the report design screen.*
2. *The cursor moves from field column to field column.*

Using the Insert Mode

In the report design screen, you can toggle between the insert and over write modes. The default mode is the over write mode. In over write mode, characters you type in will replace those characters already on the screen.

Toggle to insert mode by pressing the **Ins** key. When in insert mode, an "Ins" indicator appears to the right of the highlighted report in the upper right corner of the screen. In insert mode, characters are inserted at the cursor position. Characters that have already been entered on the screen move to the right, instead of being replaced. Press the **Ins** key again and you switch back to the over write mode.

Removing Fields from the Report

For this report, we do not need all of the fields named in the table band. Of the five fields listed, only Last Name, First Name, and Grade-% are necessary in the report. Start by removing the Student Number and No. field names.

STEP 1:

Press: Down arrow 10 times

The cursor should be under the "S" in "Student Number" in the table band.

STEP 2:

Press: **F10** Menu key

The **Report** menu appears across the top of the screen.

STEP 3:

Select: **TableBand**

The **TableBand** submenu appears with five options. The options describe the actions you can take with a field column in the table band.

STEP 4:

Select: **Erase**

The screen appears as in Figure 6.5. Paradox tells you to use the right and left arrow keys to move to the column you want to erase. You then press Enter to delete it. You do not need to move the cursor because the field column you want to delete is Student Number.

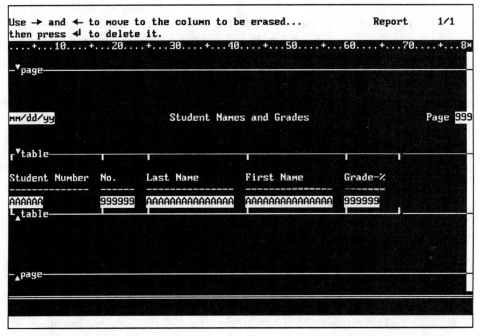

Figure 6.5. The erase screen of the report design screen

STEP 5:

Press: **Enter**

The Student Number field column is removed from the report design screen.
Repeat the process above to delete the No. field column.

STEP:

Press: **F10** Menu key
Select: **TableBand**
Select: **Erase**
Press: **Enter**

The No. field column is erased. The three remaining fields are: Last Name, First Name, and Grade-%, as you see in Figure 6.6.

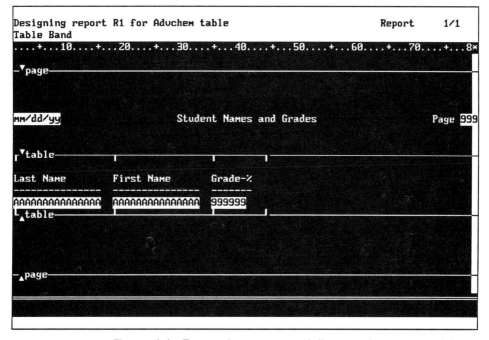

Figure 6.6. Two columns erased, three columns remaining

1. With your cursor in a field column, select **TableBand/Erase** from the menu and press **Enter**. What happens?
2. Press **F10**, select **TableBand/Erase,** and press **Enter**. What will you accomplish?

   1. *The field column is deleted.*
   2. *You will erase a field.*

Modifying Column Headings

Instead of having the report list Last Name and First Name, to clarify the report the name of the first column will be changed to "Student's." The name of the second column will be changed to "Name." Start with the cursor under the "L" in "Last Name."

STEP 1:

Type: Student's

The word "Student's" over writes the words "Last Name."

STEP 2:

Press: **Tab**

Now the cursor is under the "F" in "First Name."

STEP 3:

Type: Name
Press: Delete until the remaining letters are deleted.

The screen has been adjusted to match the screen in Figure 6.7.

Inserting Literals in a Report

Literals are characters printed in a report, just as you see them on screen, (that is, literally). An example is when at the top of a report, the report header, you insert "TOP SECRET." Another way a literal might be used is to

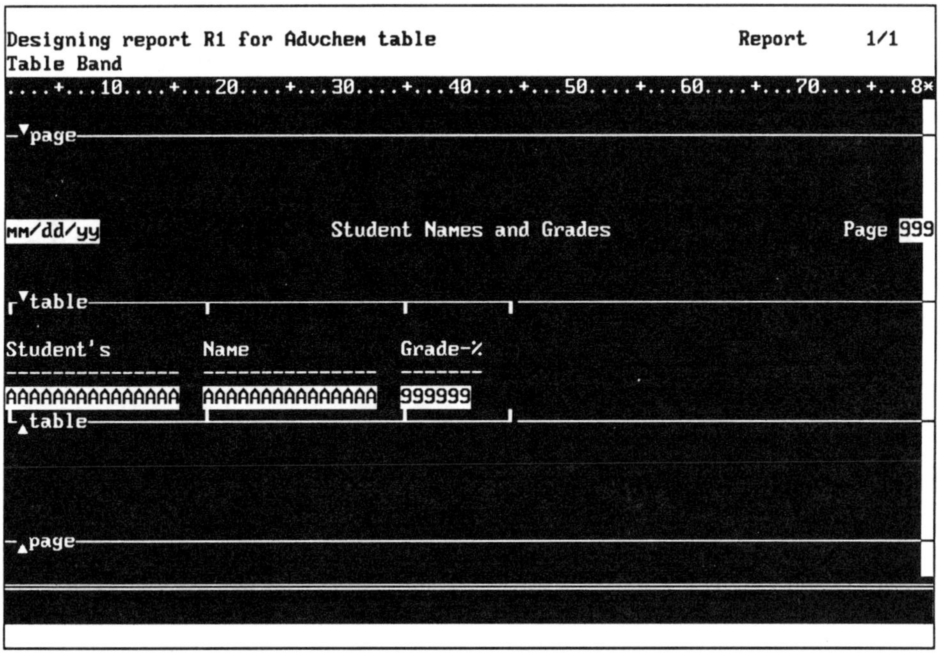

```
Designing report R1 for Advchem table                  Report    1/1
Table Band
....+...10....+...20....+...30....+...40....+...50....+...60....+...70....+...8×

─▼page────────────────────────────────────────────────────────────────────


MM/dd/yy                      Student  Names  and  Grades             Page 999


┌▼table──────────┬──────────────┬──────────────┐
Student's         Name           Grade-%
───────────────   ───────────────   ───────
AAAAAAAAAAAAAAA   AAAAAAAAAAAAAAA   999999
└▲table──────────┴──────────────┴──────────────┘



─▲page────────────────────────────────────────────────────────────────────
```

Figure 6.7. Modified column headings

describe a sum. Suppose you total all the sales per month. You would add a literal that labels the sum, such as "Total Monthly Sales."

Where the literals are printed on the report depends on where you enter them on the report design screen. As you move the cursor down the page, the following areas are found. From top to bottom, they are:

Report header

Page header

Table band

Page footer

Report footer

When you enter literals in each of these areas, you get a different result, which is described here:

Report Header	Literals entered in this area are printed on the first page of the report, only.
Page Header	Literals entered in this area are printed at the top of each page in the report.
Table Band	Literals typed above the field names will appear above the field names on the printed report. Literals typed between the field masks (the string of A's and 9's) and the bottom of the table band are printed after each record.
Page Footer	Literals typed in this area are printed at the bottom of each page in the report.
Report Footer	Literals typed in this area are printed at the end of the report.

Adding a Report Header

The page header has already been added to this report for you. It includes the date at the left margin, the description of the report centered at the top, and the page number at the far right. Move the cursor to the area that holds the report header.

STEP 1:

Press: **Home**

Report header appears on the message line above the workspace.

STEP 2:

Move the cursor to the left margin.
Type: Angstrom's Advanced Chemistry Class

This is a literal typed in the report header area and will be printed at the top of the first page of the report.

1. Create a literal to appear at the bottom of each page. Where do you place it?
2. Press **Home**. What happens?

1. *In the page footer.*
2. *The cursor moves to the top line in the report design screen.*

Adding a Report Footer

Another literal added to the report footer will appear at the end of the report.

STEP 1:

> Press: **Ctrl-Home**
> Press: **End**

The cursor moves to the left margin and then to the report footer area of the report design screen.

STEP 2:

> Type: `First Semester, 1992`

This literal, placed in the report footer, will be printed at the end of the report.

Tip | The same steps as above can be taken to add page headers and footers. When the message line above the workspace reads "Page Header" or "Page Footer," you know you are adding the literal to the correct area. Page headers and footers are printed at the top and bottom of every page, respectively.

The screen matches the one in Figure 6.8. Notice the location of literals in the report header and footer.

1. Press **End**. What happens?
2. Look on the screen. Where do you see an indicator that tells you if the literal is in the right place?

1. *The cursor moves to the report footer area.*
2. *The message line indicates which area you are in.*

```
Designing report R1 for Aduchem table                          Report      1/1
Report Footer
....+...10....+...20....+...30....+...40....+...50....+...60....+...70....+...8×
Angstrom's Advanced Chemistry Class
─▼page─────────────────────────────────────────────────────────────────────



MM/dd/yy                        Student Names and Grades              Page 999

 ┌▼table─────────────────┬─────────────────┬───────────────────
 │
Student's              Name              Grade-%
─────────────          ─────────────────  ───────
AAAAAAAAAAAAAAAA       AAAAAAAAAAAAAAAA    999999
 └▲table─────────────────────────────────────────────────────



─▲page─────────────────────────────────────────────────────────
First Semester, 1992
```

Figure 6.8. Report header and footer added

Grouping Data in the Report

When preparing a more sophisticated custom report, one feature you will want to take advantage of is grouping data. Perhaps you want a list of names and addresses grouped by zip code. You may want data grouped by amount sold or in alphabetical order. Grouping can help make reports more legible.

The group menu has five options:

Insert	Create a new group in the report.
Delete	Remove a group created by the **Insert** option.
Headings	Specify headings printed at the beginning of each group.
SortDirection	Used to select the printing of items within a group, in either ascending or descending order.
Regroup	Changes the current setup of a group.

Create a new group in the report.

STEP 1:

Press: **F10** Menu key
Select: **Group**

The **Group** submenu appears with the options described above.

STEP 2:

Select: **Insert**

The three options on the **Insert** submenu are: **Field, Range,** and **NumberRecords. Select Field** and Paradox will group records together by their field value. **Select Range** and Paradox will group records by a range that you specify. **Select NumberRecords** and Paradox will group a specified number of records—for example, if you wanted every ten records to be grouped.
For this example, group the records in alphabetical order by last name.

STEP 3:

Select: **Range**

The **Field** submenu appears, which is actually a list of the fields available in this table. You can sort by fields that will or will not appear in the report.

STEP 4:

Select: Last Name

Paradox prompts you to enter the number of initial characters in a range. If you enter "1," Paradox will group the names alphabetically by the first letter in the name; if you enter "2," Paradox will group the names alphabetically by the first two letters in the name; and so on.

STEP 5:

Type: 1
Press: **Enter**

Paradox prompts you to place the group where you want it to be inserted. If you try to insert it in the table band, you will get a warning message: "Cursor must be within the Page band or a Group band to insert a new group."

STEP 6:

Move the cursor above the word table with the down arrow.
Press: **Enter**

The grouping indicator is inserted above and below the table band: "group Last Name, range=1."

1. Name one way to group data.
2. In the steps above, which menu appears the first time you press **F10** Menu key?
3. Select **NumberRecords**. How will Paradox group records?

1. *Alphabetically.*
2. *The **Report** submenu.*
3. *By a specified number of records.*

Grouping By More Than One Criteria

Beyond grouping by only one criteria, if you remember the report limitations specified at the beginning of the chapter, you can group by up to 16 criteria. This means that, if you want to, you can group first alphabetically, then group by 10 records, and then group by amount sold.

For each grouping, you would create a group band like the one in the steps above. The group band that surrounds the others is considered the primary group. For example, if the group band that surrounds the others says to group by alphabet, then that is the primary group.

The primary grouping is done first. First, all of the names would be listed alphabetically by the first letter. If the next group band was amount sold, and ascending was selected, the names would appear in alphabetical order, but the names would appear in the ascending order of amount sold. In other words, all the M's would be in one group. Within the M's, the records would be listed by amount sold in ascending order.

If the third grouping was to group by ten records, you might see a list like this:

Marvin	10,000
Muggsy	11,000
Mertz	12,000
McBeth	13,000
Melvin	14,000
Mertz	15,000
McAllen	16,000
Mick	17,000
Moby	18,000
Maxine	19,000

In the Exercises at the end of the chapter, an example report will be created, where two groupings are placed on the data in a table.

Printing the Report

With the changes made above, print the report to see how it looks on paper.

STEP 1:

Press: **F10** Menu key
Select: **Output**

The **Output** submenu has three options. You can send the file to the printer, the screen, or a file.

Tip | With a very complicated and long custom report, send it to the screen first. That way you can view the results. If you don't like the way the report looks, make changes before printing it.

STEP 2:

Select: **Printer**

Figure 6.9 shows how Paradox printed the custom report.
Only two last names in this report begin with the same letter. Those two

Angstrom's Advanced Chemistry Class

12/07/90   Student Names and Grades   Page 1

Student's	Name	Grade-%
Astro	Billy	92
Comet	Alfie	99
Galaxy	Andre	95
Mars	Mike	83
Moon	Monica	72
Pluto	Pete	90

First Semester, 1992

Figure 6.9. Student names and grades report

names, Mars and Moon, appear in the same group, within the alphabetical list of names.

Tip With a list of hundreds or thousands of names, group by the first two letters or first three letters. This will give you smaller groups, which helps make the report more legible.

1. After you press the **F10** Menu key, which menu item do you select to print the report?
2. From the **Output** submenu, what item should you select to see your report on screen, before you print it?

1. *Output.*
2. *Screen.*

Changing a Report Design Screen

Make changes you need to the report design screen by accessing the **Report** submenu.

STEP 1:

Press: **F10** Menu key

The Main menu appears across the top of the screen.

STEP 2:

Select: **Report**

The **Report** submenu appears. Previously, when you created a custom report, you used the **Design** option from the **Report** submenu. The task now is to change the report design screen.

STEP 3:

Select: **Change**
Type: ADVCHEM (or the name of the table you want to change)

Paradox will list the reports created for the table.

STEP 4:

Select: 1

At the top of the screen, you will see "Report description: Student Names and Grades." At this time, you can change the report description by deleting old or incorrect characters and typing in a new description. Keep the report description the same for this example.

STEP 5:

Press: **Enter**

The report description screen appears. Make any changes or additions you want in this screen.

These special keys may be used in designing or changing a report.

Ctrl-Y Deletes all characters and field markers from the cursor to the end of the current line.

| Ctrl-V | Displays a vertical ruler on the report design screen. Press **Ctrl-V** and the vertical ruler is turned off. The vertical ruler is especially helpful if you are planning to print the report on a form. |
| Ctrl-R | Rotates the order of the columns on the report screen. |

1. Change the report design. What menu item do you select from the **Report** submenu?
2. Press **Ctrl-V** while in the report design screen. What happens?
3. Press **Ctrl-V** again. What happens?

1. *Change.*
2. *A vertical ruler is displayed on screen.*
3. *The vertical ruler is removed.*

Reformatting Fields

Already, you have controlled the fields that appear in the report, the headers, the footers, and how the records are grouped. You can also control how the fields are formatted.

While creating or changing a report design, reformat one of the fields on screen.

STEP 1:

Press: **F10** Menu key

Paradox displays the **Report** submenu.

STEP 2:

Select: **Field**
Select: **Reformat**

Paradox asks you to use the arrow keys to move to the field you want to reformat.

STEP 3:

Move the cursor to the Grade-% field in *ADVCHEM*, or choose a field in a table you want to change.

STEP 4:

Press: **Enter**

Paradox prompts you to decide how you want to adjust the number.

STEP 5:

Select: **Digits**

Paradox instructs you to use the right and left arrow keys to adjust the number of digits.

STEP 6:

Press: Left arrow until two nines are left in the field.

Tip | One of the 9's has the block cursor directly over it. The other 9 is highlighted.

STEP 7:

Press: **Enter**

Again, you are instructed to move the right and left arrow keys to adjust the number of decimal places. If you try to press the left arrow key, Paradox emits a beep.

STEP 8:

Press: Right arrow, one time and the decimal point appears.
Press: Right arrow, two more times to show two decimal places.
Press: **Enter**

Figure 6.10 shows how the reformatted field looks on screen.

The printed report would show the student grades as two digits and two decimal places, which is identical to the way they were entered in the original *ADVCHEM* table.

When reformatting fields, you are limited by the type of field with

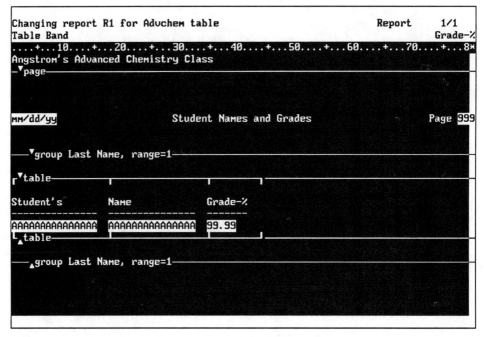

```
Changing report R1 for Aduchem table                    Report    1/1
Table Band                                                        Grade-%
....+...10....+...20....+...30....+...40....+...50....+...60....+...70....+...8*
Angstrom's Advanced Chemistry Class
—▼page—



MM/dd/yy                    Student Names and Grades              Page 999


        —▼group Last Name, range=1—

┌▼table—           ┬           ┬           ┬
Student's          Name        Grade-%
───────────        ──────────  ───────
AAAAAAAAAAAAAAAA   AAAAAAAAAAAAAAAA  99.99
└▲table—

        —▲group Last Name, range=1—
```

Figure 6.10. Reformatted fields

which you are working. The only format change you can make to an *alphanumeric* field is to decrease or increase the number of characters allowed in the field.

With a Number field (one where you see 9's on the report design screen), you can change the number of digits used to display a number. In addition, you can alter how negative numbers are printed, whether commas appear in the number, and whether commas or periods are used to break large numbers.

1. Press **F10**, Select **Field/Reformat.** What will you accomplish?
2. Reformat a number. What two things do you adjust?
3. Reformat an *alphanumeric* field. What one thing can you adjust?

1. *You will be able to reformat a field.*
2. *The number of digits displayed and the decimal location.*
3. *You can change the number of characters displayed in the field.*

Using Summary Functions in a Report

There will be times when you want to use a summary function when working with Paradox reports. A summary function will give you a total, an average, a count, a minimum, or a maximum number. These are especially useful when working with groups. For example, a report listing sales, grouped by month, could calculate total sales at the end of each month grouping.

The summary functions are described in more detail in the list below.

Sum   Shows the total for a group, calculated by adding all of the values together.

Average   Shows the average for a group, calculated by adding all of the values and dividing by the number of values.

Count   Shows the number of records in each group.

Maximum   Shows the highest value found in a group.

Minimum   Shows the lowest value found in a group.

The teacher creating the *ADVCHEM* report wants to create two reports. One will give an average grade for each grouping of students. Another report will give an average grade for all the students in the advanced chemistry class.

Tip The summary function "average" will be used in these examples, but remember that you can substitute any summary function in its place.

1. Choose the summary function that will show the total number of records in a group.
2. Choose the summary function that will show the lowest number in a field.

1. *Count.*
2. *Minimum.*

Placing Summary Functions in Groups

With the cursor in the report design screen, place a summary function at the end of every group.

STEP 1:

> Press: **F10** Menu key
> Select: **Field**

> The **field** submenu appears.

STEP 2:

> Select: **Place**
> Select: **Summary**

> At this point, you are given two choices. You can summarize a regular field, or summarize a calculation from fields in a record.

STEP 3:

> Select: **Regular**

> Paradox asks you to select the field you want to summarize.

STEP 4:

> Select: **Grade-%**

> Paradox asks you to select the summary function you wish to use in the group.

STEP 5:

> Select: **Average**

> Select between a per group calculation or an overall calculation. In this chapter, you will eventually do both, but they have to be done one at a time.

STEP 6:

> Select: **PerGroup**

> You are instructed to use the arrow keys to indicate where the field should begin. You decide where you want the summary function to appear.

If you place the field above the table band, the summary function will appear before the data itself. Place the field below the table band, and the summary function will appear after the data. In this example, place the summary function just below the Grade-% field.

STEP 7:

> Move the cursor under the Grade-% field. The cursor should be below the line for the table band, but above the line for the group band, as you see in Figure 6.11.

Press: Enter

> A series of 9's appears where you inserted the summary function.

> Paradox instructs you to adjust the number of digits. Make this field identical to the Grade-% field.

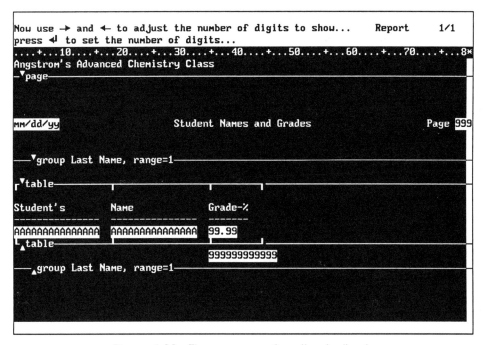

Figure 6.11. The summary function indicator on screen

STEP 8:

> Press: Left Arrow, ten times
> Press: **Enter**
> Press: Right Arrow, three times
> Press: **Enter**

The grouping is completed, and the summary function is placed in the report design screen to be calculated for the group.

---

1. Follow this menu selection: **Field/Place/Summary/Regular/Grade-%/Average/PerGroup.** What do you accomplish?
2. Insert a summary function in the Grade-% field. Do you get 9's or A's.

1. *You place summary functions in groups.*
2. *9's.*

Printing the Report

Print this report again, to compare the result of the different formatting changes.

STEP 1:

> Press: **F2 DO-IT**

The workspace is cleared. The custom report is saved. The Main menu is on screen.

STEP 2:

> Select: **Report**
> Select: **Output**
> Press: **Enter**

Paradox lists the tables.

STEP 3:

> Select: *ADVCHEM*

Select: 1
Select: **Printer**

The adjusted report will be printed. Now go back to the report design screen to place a summary function in the report, this time to get an average of all the scores combined.

Placing Summary Functions for the Entire Report

The steps to get back to the report design screen are listed here:

STEP:

Select: **Report**
Select: **Change**
Press: Enter
Select: *ADVCHEM*
Select: 1
Press: Enter

The report design screen is displayed. The message at the top of the screen informs you that you are changing the report. Add one more summary function which will give the teacher an average of all the scores for the first semester, 1992.

STEP 1:

Press: F10 Menu key
Select: **Field**
Select: **Place**
Select: **Summary**
Select: **Regular**

Paradox lists the fields to be summarized.

STEP 2:

Select: **Grade-%**

Paradox lists the summary functions from which you can choose.

STEP 3:

Select: **Average**

The options of **PerGroup** and **Overall** are presented.

STEP 4:

Select: **Overall**

You are instructed to move the cursor where you want the summary function in the report.

STEP 5:

Move the cursor below the group band, below the Grade-% field.
Press: Enter

The series of 9's appear on screen. Format the number.

STEP 6:

Press: Left arrow, ten times
Press: Enter
Press: Right arrow, three times
Press: Enter

The **Overall** summary function is added to the custom report.

1. Press F2 DO-IT. What happens?
2. Press F10 Menu key, select **Summary/Regular/Place/Field.** What will you accomplish?

1. *The workspace is cleared, the custom report is saved, and the Main menu appears on screen.*
2. *You place a summary function for the entire report.*

Adding a Comment

You might want to add a comment (literal) to the report that describes the summary function. Right now, the report will just display the number that is the average of all the grades. Since you plan to share this report, put a comment before the summary function that describes what the number represents.

STEP 1:

Move the cursor to the left of the overall summary function. (Under the "N" in "Name" is a good place.)

STEP 2:

Type: Average

A comment can be longer if you like, but "Average" gives a brief description of the number displayed. The report design screen should look like the one in Figure 6.12.

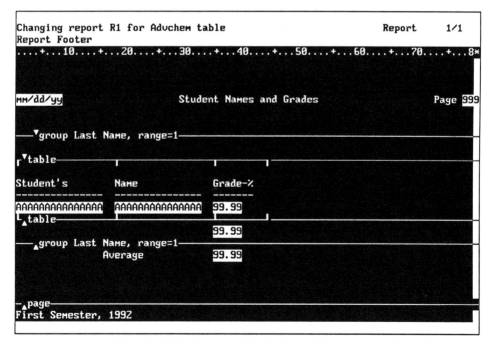

Figure 6.12. The report design with summary functions

Saving and Finalizing the Report

When you are done creating a customized report, finalize the report and save it to disk. Paradox saves the report format so that you can recall it any time you want to reproduce it. You may want to apply the same report to a new set of data or a new time period.

STEP:

Press: **F2** DO-IT

The report design screen disappears from the screen. You are returned to either a clear workspace or whatever you were working on previously.

Printing a Saved Custom Report

Now that the report has been saved, you can print by accessing the **Report** submenu.

STEP 1:

Press: **F10** Menu key

The Main menu appears across the top of the screen.

STEP 2:

Select: **Report**
Select: **Output**

Paradox prompts you for the name of the table for which you want to print a report.

STEP 3:

Press: **Enter**
Select: The report for which you want to print a report.

Paradox will list the reports that have been created for the table you have selected. For this example, *ADVCHEM* was selected. Only one report has been created for this table, so R and 1 are displayed at the top of the screen.

STEP 4:

Select: The number of the report you want to print.

In Figure 6.13, you see the highlighting on the number 1. Below the number, the message line displays the description of the report.

After you select the report number you want to print, Paradox displays the **Output** submenu.

STEP 5:

Select: **Printer**

Paradox prints the report without displaying the report design screen. This makes printing a report on a repetitive basis quite simple.

The final printed custom report appears in Figure 6.14. Notice that for four out of five "groups," the average and the score are identical. This is to be expected, since the average of one number will equal that number.

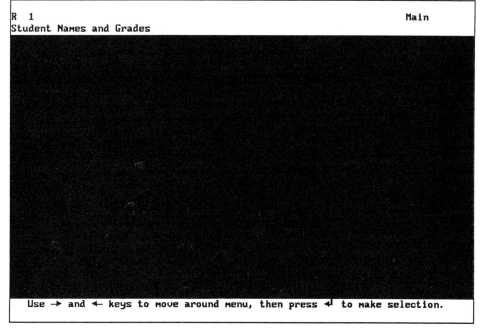

Figure 6.13. The Number 1 highlighted

For the grouping of the names that begin with M, you see the average 77.50. Also, the average of all the scores at the bottom of the page is 88.53. Paradox has automatically calculated the values and placed them where the summary functions are located in the report design screen.

Tip

The first time this report was printed, it took the entire page. If you would like to leave margins at the top and bottom of a page to make your look neater, follow these steps:

STEP 1:

Press: **F10** Menu key (to get the **Report** submenu)
Select: **Setting**
Select: **PageLayout**
Select: **Length**

Paradox is set at a page of 66 lines. The standard page may vary depending on your printer. A standard page on the printer used for this figure is 60

Angstrom's Advanced Chemistry Class		
12/07/90	Student Names and Grades	Page 1
Student's	Name	Grade–%
– – – – – – – – – – – –	– – – – – – – – –	– – – – – –
Astro	Billy	92.26
		92.26
Comet	Alfie	98.92
		98.92
Galaxy	Andre	94.88
		94.88
Mars	Mike	82.66
Moon	Monica	72.34
		77.50
Pluto	Pete	90.09
		90.09
First Semester, 1992		
	Average	88.53

Figure 6.14. Final printed custom report

lines long. The page length should be set to 60 lines so that the report prints correctly.

STEP 2:

Delete: 66
Type: 60
Press: **Enter**
Press: **F2** DO-IT

This saves the report with the new setting for page length.

1. Select what items from the **Report** submenu are needed to print a custom report.
2. Select the report number you want to print. Select **Printer** from the **Output** submenu. What happens?

1. **Output.**
2. Paradox prints the report without displaying the report design screen.

Summary

Creating instant and custom reports from any Paradox image is now at your fingertips. You have explored the steps of creating custom Paradox reports, including getting to the report design screen, moving the cursor around in the report design screen, removing fields, modifying column headings, inserting literals, adding headers and footers, and grouping report data.

Printing options are covered in the latter part of the chapter. Saving a report is done in a similar way to finalizing and saving all Paradox objects. Changing a report and reformatting fields are the final topics covered. Some of the topics covered in this chapter are listed here:

- Instant reports
  - Report limitations
  - Report concepts
- Custom reports
  - Tabular reports
  - The report design screen
  - Moving the cursor in the report design screen
  - Inserting literals in a report
  - Adding headers and footers
  - Grouping data in the report
  - Printing the report
  - Changing a report design screen
  - Reformatting fields
  - Using summary functions in a report
  - Adding a comment
  - Saving and finalizing the report
  - Printing a custom report once it is created

Exercises

What You Should Do	How the Computer Responds
1. Display a report design screen by taking these steps: Press: F10 Menu key Select: **Report** Select: **Design** Type: The name of the table for which you want to create a report (in this example, use: SALARY). Press: Enter	1. Paradox displays the Main menu and the **Report** submenu and then prompts you for the name of the table for which you want to create a report. After you type the name and press Enter, the line below appears: disp = R 1 2 3 4 5...

2. Select: 1
   Type: 1992 Salaries for Mid-Age, Inc.
   Press: Enter
   Select: **Tabular**

2. Paradox prompts you for a report description, which it will insert in the page header. The report design screen appears for a tabular report.

3. Move the cursor to the line above the table band.

3. The message indicator tells you that you are in the page header area.

4. Press: F10 Menu key
   Select: **Group**
   Select: **Insert**
   Select: **Range**
   Select: **Name**
   Select: 1
   Press: Enter

4. The **Report** submenu appears. From there you select the menu items stated. After you press Enter, the group band is placed around the table band. The group band reads: "group Name, range=1." This will be the primary grouping.

5. Move the cursor to the single line between the top group band line named "group Name" and the table band line.
   Press: F10 Menu key
   Select: **Group**
   Select: **Insert**
   Select: **Field**
   Select: **Salary**
   Press: Enter

5. The **Report** submenu appears. You select the items stated. After you press Enter, the group band is placed around the table band. The group band reads: "group Salary." Because this band is inside the first band, it is the secondary grouping.

6. Press: F10 Menu key
   Select: **Setting**
   Select: **PageLayout**
   Select: **Length**

6. Paradox displays the message, "New page length: 66." This tells you that the report is printed for a page that is 66 lines long. The standard 8 1/2 by 11 inch paper is 64 lines long.

7. Press: Backspace key, two times
   Type: 64
   Press: Enter

7. The number 66 is erased. The number 64 is entered. Paradox displays an indicator in the lower right corner that the new page length is set. With 64 lines you have a nice margin, instead of having records printed on the last line of the paper.

8. Move the cursor to a line where the message indicator shows that you are in the page footer.
   Type: Confidential Information-TOP SECRET

8. "Confidential Information—TOP SECRET" is added as a literal comment in the page footer area.

9. Move the cursor to the line just below the "(up arrow) page" line.
   Type: Total
   Move the cursor, in the same line, under the first 9 in the Salary field. (The cursor is in the report footer area.)
   Press: **F10** Menu key
   Select: **Field**
   Select: **Place**
   Select: **Summary**
   Select: **Regular**
   Select: **Salary**
   Select: **Sum**
   Select: **Overall**
   Determine the digits and decimal spaces you want.

9. A summary function that will total all the salaries in the report is created. A series of 9's indicates the location of the function.

10. Press: **F2** DO-IT

10. Paradox finalizes and saves the report to disk. The workspace is cleared.

11. From the Main menu:
    Select: **Report**
    Select: **Output**
    Type: Salary
    Select: 1
    Select: **Printer**

11. Paradox prints the Salary report you just created. The names are grouped alphabetically by the first letter and then they are listed in ascending order by the amount of salary earned in 1992.

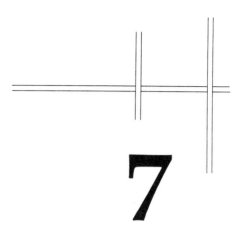

7

Creating Graphs

The Paradox graphing feature allows you to make a picture of your data. While reports have their place, graphs can simplify the presentation of some data. Like the report generator, graphing with Paradox is a matter of collecting the data and making the correct menu selections. Paradox gives you several graphing options. The instant graph will be covered first, which gives you a bar graph of the data. Custom graphs are covered later in the chapter with bar graphs and pie graphs.

- Instant graphs
- Custom graphs

Instant Graphs

Getting a picture of data with Paradox is as easy as one keystroke. Figure 7.1 shows a table that holds five names and the corresponding salaries of these people. You can either reproduce this table or use one of your own. (This table was created in Chapter 2 Exercises.)

Move the cursor to the Name field column. Press **Ctrl-F7**. You get a

```
┌────────────────────────────────────────────────────────────────────┐
│Viewing Salary table: Record 1 of 5                          Main     │
├────────────────────────────────────────────────────────────────────┤
│SALARY══════════════Name═══════════╦══════Salary═══════╗              │
│     1 ║  Eleanor Poitier           ║    35,000.00      ║              │
│     2 ║  Carlo Borja               ║    19,900.00      ║              │
│     3 ║  Louis Capet               ║    28,000.00      ║              │
│     4 ║  Alexander Poe             ║    38,500.00      ║              │
│     5 ║  Chris Columbus            ║    34,780.00      ║              │
│                                                                      │
└────────────────────────────────────────────────────────────────────┘
```

Figure 7.1. *Salary* table

warning in the bottom right corner of the screen: "Active field not numeric." Paradox can only graph the numeric fields. Paradox will graph the numeric field in which the cursor is located.

Creating an Instant Graph on Screen

Press the right arrow key, placing the cursor in the Salary field column.

STEP:

Press: **Ctrl-F7**

Paradox creates a graph on screen, as you see in Figure 7.2. The five salaries are illustrated in a bar graph. Instantly, you can see that Carlo Borja is the lowest paid and Alexander Poe is the highest paid in the table.

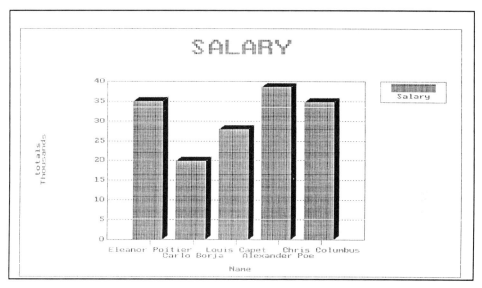

Figure 7.2. Instant graph of *Salary* table on screen

Removing the Instant Graph

To go back to the table you were viewing:

STEP:

Press: Any key

Paradox removes the graph from the screen and puts you back in the *Salary* table view.

1. Press **Ctrl-F7**. What happens?
2. With the cursor in the Name field, press **Ctrl-F7**. What happens?
3. What is the next step after the situation in 2?

1. *A graph appears on screen.*
2. *Paradox displays a warning message in the lower right corner of the screen that says: "Active field not numeric."*
3. *Press* **F9** *Edit key. With the cursor back in the table, move the cursor to a numeric field. Now, press* **Ctrl-F7**.

Printing the Instant Graph

You can print the instant graph to your printer. You will get a standard bar graph, identical to the one you see on the screen. Start by viewing the table for which you want to print a graph. The cursor should be in a numerical field column that you want to be graphed.

STEP:

> Press: **F10** Menu key
> Select: **Image**
> Select: **Graph**
> Select: **ViewGraph**
> Select: **Printer**

The screen tells you that the graph is being sent to a printer. The computer should be set up to work with the kind of printer you have. The mode of printing is stated, in most cases 150 x 150 dpi Med. If you want to stop the printing process, press **Esc**. Paradox sends the graph to the printer.

The bar graph shows the salary information for each employee. The employee names become the labels along the bottom of the graph (the horizontal or x axis). The amount of the salary in thousands appears along the left vertical (y) axis. Each person's salary is displayed as a bar, where the top of the bar shows their salary amount. The printed bar graph appears in Figure 7.3.

Note | The first time you print you may get a warning message on the bottom right of the screen that tells you to play a custom script. This means you have not set up the printer for printing graphs. Follow these steps if that happens.

> Press: **F10** Menu key
> Select: **Scripts**
> Select: **Play**

Paradox asks you to name the script you want to play.

> Press: **Enter**
> Select: **Custom**

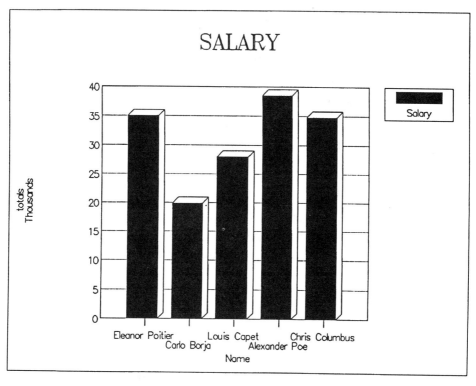

Figure 7.3. Printed bar graph

The Borland opening screen appears. A new menu appears across the top of the page.

Select: **Graphs**
Select: **Printers**
Select: **1stPrinter**

You are going to set up the printer to print graphs. The first printer should be your default printer.

Select: **Type of Printer**

Paradox loads a list of printer manufacturers.

Select: The manufacturer of your printer.
Select: The model of your printer.

Select: 150 x 150 dpi Med. for 8 1/2 by 11 inch paper
Select: **Return**
Select: **Return**
Select: **Return**
Select: DO-IT
Select: **HardDisk**

Paradox saves the configuration settings and returns you to the DOS prompt, with the Paradox directory named.

Type: Paradox
Press: **Enter**

Paradox is loaded to the screen.

After you complete this process, the graph should print. If not, refer to the Paradox manual on presenting information.

Creating a Pie Graph

The bar graph is the default graph used in Paradox. This means that unless you specify something different, bar graphs will be used to display information. You can specify a standard pie graph by using the menu system. View the table that you want to graph with the cursor in a numerical or currency field.

STEP 1:

Press: **F10** Menu key
Select: **Image**
Select: **Graph**

The **Graph** submenu is displayed on screen.

STEP 2:

Select: **Modify**

The Customize Graph Type screen is displayed, as shown in Figure 7.4. The cursor is located in the Graph Type field, where *stacked bar* is the current type of graph.

On the right of the screen are the different types of graphs available with Paradox. Each type of graph has a single letter in parentheses that is used to select that type of graph. Select any type of graph by pressing that letter. Change the graph type from stacked bar to *pie graph*.

STEP 3:

Type: P

Pie is inserted in the Graph Type field.

STEP 4:

Press: F2 DO-IT

You are returned to the Paradox screen, with the cursor in the table you were viewing before changing the graph type.

STEP 5:

Press: Ctrl-F7 Graph

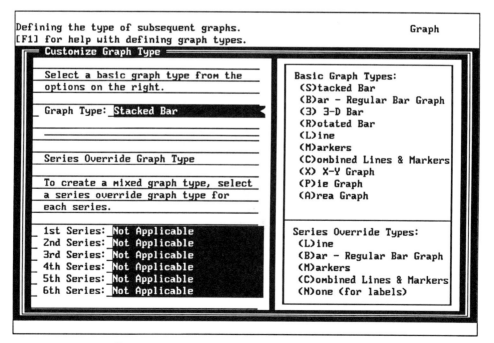

Figure 7.4. The Customize Graph Type screen

The pie chart is displayed on screen as in Figure 7.5. It is not as easy to compare salaries with the pie graph as it is with the bar graph.

Remove the pie graph from the screen by pressing any key.

1. Press **F10**, select **Image, Graph, ViewGraph,** and **Printer**. What happens?
2. Select **Image** from the Main menu and then **Graph/Modify**. What happens?
3. What do you press after selecting the graph type?

1. *A graph will be printed.*
2. *The Customize Graph Type screen is displayed.*
3. *Press* **F2** *DO-IT.*

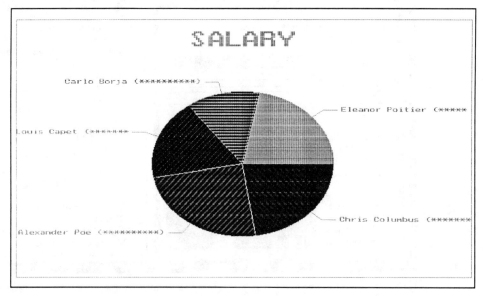

Figure 7.5. The pie graph on screen

Printing the Pie Graph

As quickly as the bar graph was printed, you can also print the pie graph.

STEP 1:

> Press: **F10** Menu key
> Select: **Image**
> Select: **Graph**
> Select: **ViewGraph**

> You can send the graph to the screen, the printer, or a file.

STEP 2:

> Select: **Printer**

> Paradox displays messages telling you that the graph is being sent to the printer. You can press **Esc** to cancel the printing.

Tip | Be patient. There is a lot of information in a graph, so it takes a while for it to be sent to the printer.

> The graph is printed as you see in Figure 7.6. As you can see, there are some problems with the graph. For example, the dollar amount of the salaries do not appear. Instead, you see a series of asterisks. It would be more ideal if one of the salaries were set apart from the others. These changes will be covered in the next section, on custom graphs.

Custom Graphs

You have put two types of graphs on screen and sent them to the printer. These are standard types of graphs. As with reports, you can make changes to the graph, making a custom graph, so that your information is presented in a better way.

Modifying a Graph

Using the pie graph you created earlier, modify the labels and display so that it provides more information.

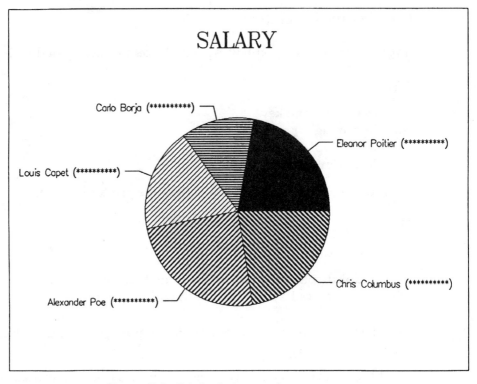

SALARY

Carlo Borja (**********)

Eleanor Poitier (**********)

Louis Capet (**********)

Chris Columbus (**********)

Alexander Poe (**********)

Figure 7.6. Printed pie graph

STEP 1:

Press: **F10** Menu key
Select: **Image**
Select: **Graph**
Select: **Modify**

The Customize Graph Type screen appears. Tell Paradox to display the pie graph labels in a different format.

STEP 2:

Press: **F10** Menu key
Select: **Pies**

The Customize Pie Graph screen appears. This screen is shown in Figure 7.7.

The cursor is located in the Label Format field. The word "Value" appears in this field. As with the Customize Graph Type screen, the options for

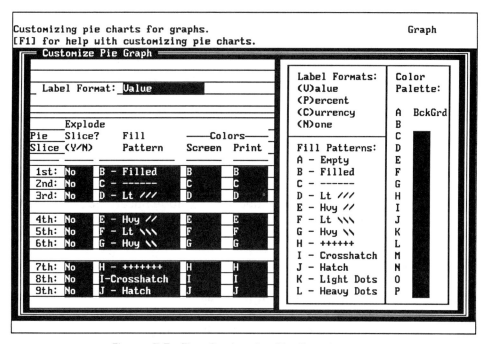

Figure 7.7. The Customize Pie Graph screen

the Label Format are listed on the right of the screen. To get a better idea of the relative salaries, select the percent option for the label format.

STEP 3:

Type: P

The word "Percent" is inserted in the Label Format field. The next step is to explode a slice of the pie.

1. From the **Graph** submenu, you select **Modify**. What do you see?
2. With the Customize Graph Type screen displayed and pie graph selected, you press **F10** Menu key. What do you see?

1. *The Customize Graph Type screen.*
2. *The Customize Pie Graph screen.*

Exploding a Slice of the Pie

On the Customize Pie Graph screen, below the Label Format field, you see the question: "Explode Slice?" Move the cursor under that area and explode one of the slices.

STEP 1:

Press: **Tab**

The cursor moves under the "Explode Slice?" question for the first pie slice.

STEP 2:

Press: Down arrow, three times

The cursor moves to the fourth pie slice.

STEP 3:

Type: Y

This tells Paradox to explode the fourth slice of pie, which is the slice for Alexander Poe. His salary is the greatest of the five salaries.

STEP 4:

Press: **F2** DO-IT

Paradox brings you back to the view of the *Salary* table. With the cursor in the Salary field, create the new graph.

STEP 5:

Press: **Ctrl-F7** Graph

The Salary graph appears on screen with the salaries listed as a percent and with one pie slice exploded. Figure 7.8 shows how the graph looks now.

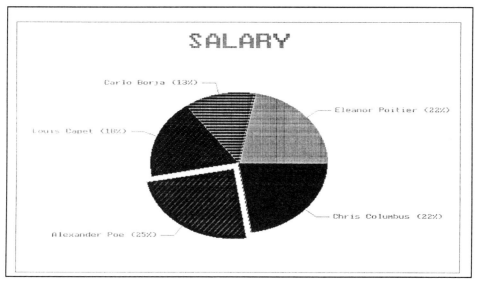

Figure 7.8. The modified salary pie graph

Saving a Custom Graph

Unlike other members of a family of images, the graph image will be discarded unless you save it. Graph settings are saved with their own names. Now that this graph is customized, save it.

STEP 1:

> Press: Any key to remove graph from screen
> Press: **F10** Menu key
> From the Main menu, make the following selections.

STEP 2:

> Select: **Image**
> Select: **Graph**
> Select: **Save**

Paradox prompts you to name the graph.

STEP 3:

> Type: SALPIE
> Press: **Enter**

You can use these same graphic settings on this or any other table. As the table expands with more names and more salaries, these same settings can be applied to it.

1. Press **F10** and select **Image, Graph,** and **Save**. What happens?
2. Select the piece of pie to be exploded. What do you press next?

1. *The graph you have created is saved.*
2. *F2 DO-IT.*

Recalling a Saved Graph

Apply the graph setting created above to a different graph. Start by clearing all images.

STEP 1:

> Press: **Alt-F8** Clear All
> Press: **F10** Menu key
> Select: **View**

Select a table to view other than the *SALARY* table used in the example above. In this example, view *SALARY2*. (*SALARY2* is another table with the same fields, but with 15 records instead of 5.)

STEP 2:

> Type: SALARY2
> Press: **Enter**

STEP 3:

> Move the cursor to the Salary field in the table.

STEP 4:

> Press: **F10** Menu key
> Select: **Image**

Select: Graph
Select: **Load**

Paradox prompts you to name the graph you want to apply to this table.

STEP 5:

Type: SALPIE
Press: **Enter**
Press: **Ctrl-F7 Graph**

You have recalled the saved graph settings and applied them to a different table. As you can see in the graph, the pie is divided into 15 sections. The Alexander Poe slice is still exploded, and the salary amounts appear as a percentage of the whole. Figure 7.9 shows this graph when printed.

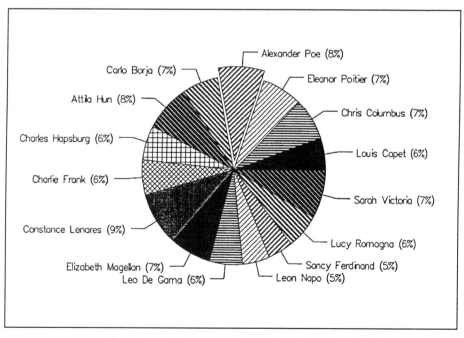

Figure 7.9a. SALARY2 as a Pie Graph, Printed

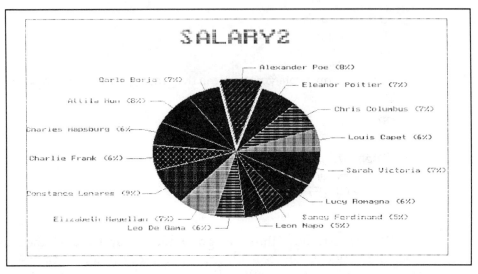

Figure 7.9b. SALARY2 as a Pie Graph, as Shown on Screen

Using a Graph Cross Tabulation

Up to this point you have graphed two pieces of information. This is most clearly seen in the bar graph. You graphed salary amount on the vertical y axis and the names of individuals on the horizontal x axis. With Paradox, you can add a third element to make a different type of graph.

Before graphing with three elements, you need to create a cross tabulation. A cross tabulation arranges the table data into a spreadsheet. This spreadsheet can then be graphed.

Start by creating a table, with an additional numerical field. Use the same data in the *SALARY* table but add an additional field. Or use any table you like, with at least two numerical fields. In this example, the table *SALARY3* was created with three fields, as shown in Figure 7.10. Instead of showing a salary with a single field, this table contains a salary history for the five individuals, for the years 1992, 1993, and 1994.

For the graph you will make in this section, the fields have to be in a certain order on screen. You would have no way of knowing this beforehand. By trial and error you would find that the graph would not turn out as you predicted, unless the fields are in a specific order. In order to prepare the cross tabulation, the order of the fields has to be changed.

```
┌────────────────────────────────────────────────────────────────────────┐
│ Viewing Salary3 table: Record 1 of 15                            Main    │
│ ╔═══════╤══════════════════╤══════════════════╤══════════════════╗      │
│ ║SALARY3│      Name        │     Salary       │     Year         ║      │
│ ║   1   │ Eleanor Poitier  │    35,000.00     │     1992         ║      │
│ ║   2   │ Carlo Borja      │    19,500.00     │     1992         ║      │
│ ║   3   │ Louis Capet      │    28,000.00     │     1992         ║      │
│ ║   4   │ Alexander Poe    │    38,500.00     │     1992         ║      │
│ ║   5   │ Chris Columbus   │    34,780.00     │     1992         ║      │
│ ║   6   │ Eleanor Poitier  │    38,000.00     │     1993         ║      │
│ ║   7   │ Carlo Borja      │    21,000.00     │     1993         ║      │
│ ║   8   │ Louis Capet      │    31,000.00     │     1993         ║      │
│ ║   9   │ Alexander Poe    │    42,000.00     │     1993         ║      │
│ ║  10   │ Chris Columbus   │    39,000.00     │     1993         ║      │
│ ║  11   │ Eleanor Poitier  │    44,000.00     │     1994         ║      │
│ ║  12   │ Carlo Borja      │    36,000.00     │     1994         ║      │
│ ║  13   │ Louis Capet      │    35,000.00     │     1994         ║      │
│ ║  14   │ Alexander Poe    │    50,000.00     │     1994         ║      │
│ ║  15   │ Chris Columbus   │    40,000.00     │     1994         ║      │
│ ╚═══════╧══════════════════╧══════════════════╧══════════════════╝      │
└────────────────────────────────────────────────────────────────────────┘
```

Figure 7.10. The *SALARY3* table

Changing the Order of the Fields

Change the order of the fields with a simple keystroke. You want to adjust them so that the Year field is first, followed by the Name, and then the Salary. Start with the cursor in the **View** mode in the *SALARY3* table.

STEP:

Press: **Ctrl-R**, two times

Tip | The cursor must be in the *SALARY3* column or the first field on screen for rotating to work.

The fields rotate until Year is the leftmost field, followed by Name, and then Salary.

1. Press **F10** and select **Image, Graph,** and **Load**. What happens?
2. What form does a cross tabulation take?
3. Press **Ctrl-R**. What happens?

1. *You are prompted to name the graph you want to recall.*
2. *The form of a spreadsheet.*
3. *The fields rotate in the table, changing their order.*

Creating the Cross Tabulation

Create the spreadsheet table for the new graph.

STEP 1:

Move the cursor to the Year field.

STEP 2:

Press: **F10** Menu key
Select: **Image**
Select: **Graph**
Select: **CrossTab**
Select: **Sum**

Paradox prompts you to select the field to contain the row labels.

STEP 3:

Move the cursor to "Year."
Press: **Enter**

Now Paradox wants you to select the field to contain column labels.

STEP 4:

Move the cursor to "Name."
Press: **Enter**

Paradox asks you to select the field column that will contain the cross tab values.

STEP 5:

Move the cursor to "Salary."
Press: Enter

The *cross tab* table lists the years down the left side, lists the names of people across the top of the table, and has a salary inserted for each person for the appropriate year. The *SALARY3* table and the *cross tab* table are shown in Figure 7.11.

Print the cross tab graph. Start with the cursor in the *cross tab* table.

Tip

The cursor must be in the column under the name Eleanor Poitier. If the cursor is in the Year column or Louis Capet column, the results will be far different from the graph you see in the next figure.

```
Viewing Crosstab table: Record 1 of 3                    Main

SALARY3    Year           Name              Salary
   1       1992    Eleanor Poitier       35,000.00
   2       1992    Carlo Borja           19,500.00
   3       1992    Louis Capet           28,000.00
   4       1992    Alexander Poe         38,500.00
   5       1992    Chris Columbus        34,780.00
   6       1993    Eleanor Poitier       38,000.00
   7       1993    Carlo Borja           21,000.00
   8       1993    Louis Capet           31,000.00
   9       1993    Alexander Poe         42,000.00
  10       1993    Chris Columbus        39,000.00
  11       1994    Eleanor Poitier       44,000.00
  12       1994    Carlo Borja           36,000.00
  13       1994    Louis Capet           35,000.00
  14       1994    Alexander Poe         50,000.00
  15       1994    Chris Columbus        40,000.00


CROSSTAB   Year     Eleanor Poitier    Carlo Borja    Louis Capet
   1       1992      35,000.00          19,500.00      28,000.00
   2       1993      38,000.00          21,000.00      31,000.00
   3       1994      44,000.00          36,000.00      35,000.00
```

Figure 7.11. The *SALARY3* table and the *cross tab* table

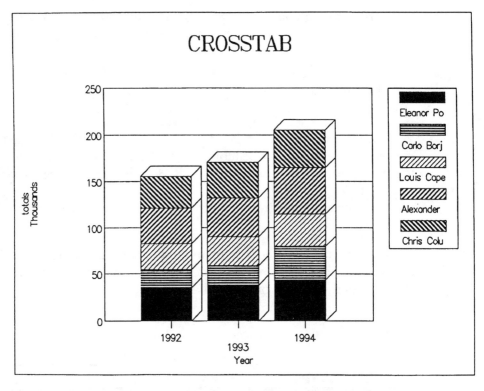

Figure 7.12. The SALARY3 stacked bar graph

STEP 6:

> Press: **F10** Menu key
> Select: **Image**
> Select: **Graph**
> Select: **ViewGraph**
> Select: **Printer**

The *cross tab* table is converted to a graph, with the years on the x axis, the total salary on the y axis, and the bars divided by person earning the salary. The stacked bar graph is seen in Figure 7.12.

The relative contribution of each person's salary to the total salaries paid can be seen quite readily. The key on the right of the graph shows that each person is assigned a pattern that indicates their salary.

Tip If the first time you tried to view this graph, you got a pie graph instead of a stacked bar, follow these steps:

Press: **F10** Menu key
Select: **Image**
Select: **Graph**
Select: **Modify**

The Customize Graph Type screen appears, with the cursor in the Graph Type field. If you got a pie graph, it should say "Pie Graph" in this field.

Press: **S**

"Stacked Bar" is entered in the Graph Type field.

Press: **F2** DO-IT

Paradox returns you to the cross tabulation table. Print the graph again, and you will get a stacked bar graph instead of a pie graph.

1. Press **F10** select **Image, Graph, CrossTab,** and **Sum.** What are you getting ready to do?
2. Change the graph type. What screen do you have to access?

1. *Begin a cross tabulation.*
2. *The Customize Graph Type screen.*

Using the Same Data to Create a Different Graph Type

The stacked bar graph shows how each person's salary contributed to the total salaries paid for each year. A *lines and markers graph* will show how each person's salary progressed over the three years. To view the same data in a different type of graph, you access the Customize Graph Type screen. Start with the cursor in the *cross tab* table.

STEP 1:

Press: **F10** Menu key
Select: **Image**
Select: **Graph**
Select: **Modify**

The Customize Graph Type screen appears. The cursor is in the Graph Type field. The type of graph selected at this point should be the stacked bar graph.

STEP 2:

Type: C

The words "Combined Lines & Markers" appear in the Graph Type field. The Customize Graph Type screen should look like the one in Figure 7.13.

STEP 3:

Press: F2 DO-IT

With the cursor returned to the *cross tab* table, print the new graph type or view it to screen.

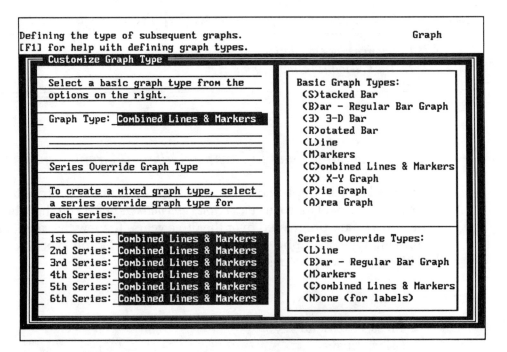

Figure 7.13. Customize Graph Type screen with Combined Lines & Markers selected

STEP 4:

Press: **F10** Menu key
Select: **Image**
Select: **Graph**
Select: **ViewGraph**
Select: **Screen** or **Printer**

The new graph type is seen in Figure 7.14. The salaries for each year are plotted independently. Each person's salary is connected with a line. On screen, each person's line is a different color.

Tip

The location of the cursor influences the graph result. For example, with your cursor in the third field of the *cross tab* table (in this case, Carlo Borja) you print the graph. The data for the previous field will not be printed (in this case, Eleanor Poitier). If the cursor is in the Year field, only the year will be graphed, excluding all the salary data. In order to complete graphs of the cross tab for the examples above, place the cursor in the field after the Year field, starting with Eleanor Poitier, in this example.

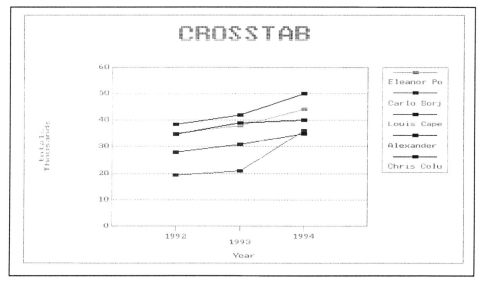

Figure 7.14a. CROSSTAB Graphed with Lines and Markers, as Shown on Screen

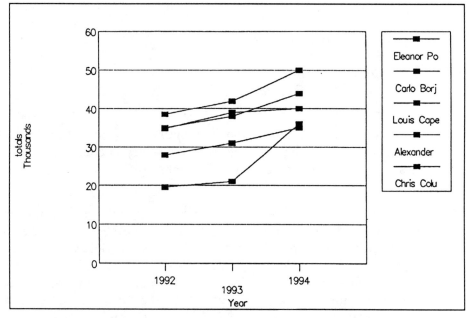

Figure 7.14b. CROSSTAB Graphed with Lines and Markers, as Printed

1. What command do you select from the **Graph** submenu to access the Customize Graph Type screen.
2. Select C. What graph type are you selecting?
3. Look at the graph on screen. How can you tell the salary lines apart?

1. *Modify.*
2. *Combined lines and markers.*
3. *Each line is a different color if you have a color monitor.*

Customize Fills and Markers

If you printed the graph in the example above, you found that each line was represented as a solid line with a solid marker. Maybe you can tell which line is which. Even if you can, no one else will be able to. On screen you can see the difference because each line appears in a different color, providing you have a color monitor. In order to distinguish the lines when printed, you will have to customize the fills or the markers.

You will have to access the Customize Fills and Markers screen. Start with the cursor in the a numerical field; or in a cross tabulation, start with the cursor in first data field.

STEP 1:

Press: **F10** Menu key
Select: **Image**
Select: **Graph**
Select: **Modify**

The Customize Graph Type screen appears.

STEP 2:

Press: **F10** Menu key
Select: **Series**
Select: **MarkersAndFills**

The Customize Fills and Markers screen appears as you see in Figure 7.15. At the top of the screen you see the Fill Pattern series. This does not affect the Lines and Markers type graph.

Instead, move the cursor down the screen to the Marker Symbol area. You can distinguish one line from the other in the graph by changing the marker symbols. As you can see in the figure above, each marker symbol is a filled square.

STEP 3:

Move the cursor down the screen so it is in the first series under Marker Symbol.
Leave the first symbol as a filled square.

STEP 4:

Press: Down arrow, one time

Now, look at the right side of the screen. The various marker symbols are listed. As in the previous screens, type the letter that indicates a different marker symbol for each series in the graph.

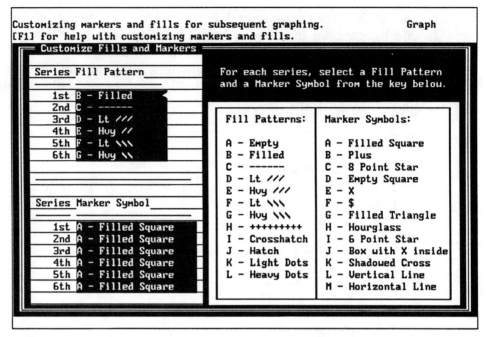

Figure 7.15. Customize fills and markers screen

STEP 5:

Type: **B**
Press: Down arrow, one time
Type: **C**
Press: Down arrow, one time
Type: **D**
Press: Down arrow, one time
Type: **E**
Press: Down arrow, one time
Type: **F**

Now each series on the screen has a different marker. This allows you to distinguish between each line on the graph because it is marked by a different marker. The Customize Fills and Markers screen should look like the one in Figure 7.16.

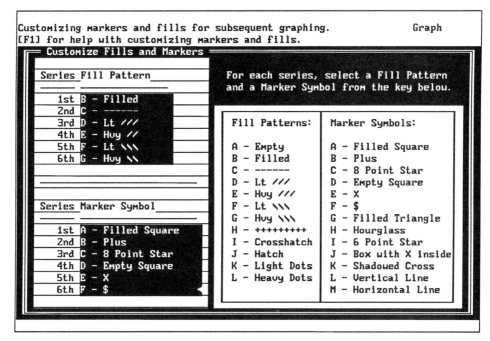

```
Customizing markers and fills for subsequent graphing.          Graph
[F1] for help with customizing markers and fills.
╔═ Customize Fills and Markers ═
║
║   Series Fill Pattern_____        For each series, select a Fill Pattern
║   _____ _____              and a Marker Symbol from the key below.
║      1st B - Filled
║      2nd C - ------
║      3rd D - Lt ///           ┌─────────────────┬───────────────────────┐
║      4th E - Hvy //           │ Fill Patterns:  │ Marker Symbols:       │
║      5th F - Lt \\\           │                 │                       │
║      6th G - Hvy \\           │ A - Empty       │ A - Filled Square     │
║                               │ B - Filled      │ B - Plus              │
║                               │ C - ------      │ C - 8 Point Star      │
║                               │ D - Lt ///      │ D - Empty Square      │
║   Series Marker Symbol_____   │ E - Hvy ///     │ E - X                 │
║   _____ _____      │ F - Lt \\\      │ F - $                 │
║                               │ G - Hvy \\\     │ G - Filled Triangle   │
║      1st A - Filled Square    │ H - +++++++++   │ H - Hourglass         │
║      2nd B - Plus             │ I - Crosshatch  │ I - 6 Point Star      │
║      3rd C - 8 Point Star     │ J - Hatch       │ J - Box with X inside │
║      4th D - Empty Square     │ K - Light Dots  │ K - Shadowed Cross    │
║      5th E - X                │ L - Heavy Dots  │ L - Vertical Line     │
║      6th F - $                │                 │ M - Horizontal Line   │
║                               └─────────────────┴───────────────────────┘
```

Figure 7.16. Modified customize fills and markers screen

STEP 6:

Press: **F2** DO-IT

The modified line and marker graph appears printed like the one in Figure 7.17. Notice the various markers that distinguish the salary of one person compared to the others.

1. When in the Customize Graph Type screen, press **F10** Menu key. What happens?
2. Select **Series** from the **Graph** submenu. What are the three options?
3. Select **MarkersAndFills**. What happens?

1. *The* **Graph** *submenu appears.*
2. *LegendsAndLabels, MarkersAndFills, and Colors.*
3. *The Customize Fills and Markers screen is displayed.*

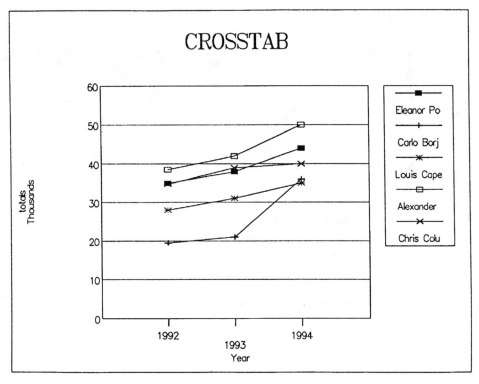

Figure 7.17. Printed modified lines and markers graph

Summary

More than just a pretty picture, a graph puts your data in an appealing, clear format. You have created instant bar and pie graphs. In Chapter 7 you modified graphs, including exploding pieces of a pie graph. You learned how to save and recall graphs for later use. The complex task of graphing more than two items in a cross tabulation was taken step-by-step. You can now present your data in a variety of formats for easy viewing.

- Instant graphs
  - Creating an instant graph on screen
  - Printing an instant graph
  - Creating a pie graph
- Custom graphs
  - Modifying a graph
  - Exploding a slice of the pie

- Saving and recalling graphs
- Using a graph cross tabulation

Exercises

What You Should Do	How the Computer Responds
1. Place the cursor in a Numeric or Currency field in any table, and press **Ctrl-F7**.	1. Paradox responds by displaying a graph of the Numeric or Currency field on screen.
2. With the cursor in a Numeric or Currency field in a table: Select: **Image** Select: **Graph** Select: **ViewGraph** Select: **Printer**	2. Paradox sends the graph to the printer to be printed.
3. Modify a graph type by accessing the Main menu. Select: **Image** Select: **Graph** Select: **Modify**	3. The Customize Graph Type screen is displayed. The cursor is located in the Graph Type field.
4. Type the highlighted letter that indicates the different kind of graph type you want to create. Press: **F2 DO-IT**	4. You are returned to the workspace and the table for which you are creating a graph.
5. With the cursor in a numeric or currency field in the table: Select: **Image** Select: **Graph** Select: **ViewGraph** Select: **Printer**	5. Paradox sends the graph to the printer to be printed.
6. From the Main menu: Select: **Image** Select: **Graph** Select: **Save**	6. Paradox prompts you to name the graph you want to save.
7. Type the name of the graph and press Enter.	7. The graph is saved to disk and can be recalled later and applied to the same table.

8. In a table where at least two items can be graphed, create a cross tabulation. With the cursor in the left-most field:
   Press: F10 Menu key
   Select: **Image**
   Select: **Graph**
   Select: **CrossTab**
   Select: **Sum**

8. Paradox prompts you to select the field to contain the row labels.

9. Select the field to contain the row and press Enter. Select the field to contain the column labels as prompted, and select the field that will contain the cross tab values, as prompted.

9. A *cross tab* table is created that places the components of the fields in a spreadsheet-like format.

10. With the cursor in the second data field:
    Press: F10 Menu key
    Select: **Image**
    Select: **Graph**
    Select: **ViewGraph**
    Select: **Printer**
    Or, Press: Ctrl-F7

10. If you go through the menus and select **Printer**, the graph of the cross tabulation will be printed. If you press Ctrl-F7, the graph will appear on screen. The printed graph should compare two items in a stacked bar graph (for example) to one item on the vertical y axis.

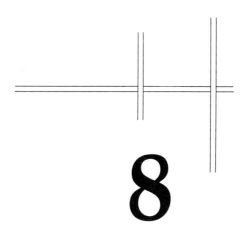

8

Performing a Lookup and Sorting Data

A lookup is used to find corresponding field amounts in related tables and to verify the accuracy of other data. Only a true relational database can perform this function.

When you need to find information in a hurry, the **Zoom** command lets you find a name or value in a few seconds, even in a large database. Later in this chapter you will read about sorting data to make it more manageable and easier to understand.

- Performing a lookup
- Sorting a table by a single field
- Sorting a table by multiple fields

Performing a Lookup

Looking for specific data in Paradox can involve looking for a single piece of information in one table, or comparing data from two tables, which is a lookup.

The first type of lookup allows you to move to a specific record out of many. In Chapter 5, you created queries that pulled out specific records that matched certain criteria. Perhaps you are working in a large database of several hundred names and you want to check the information stored in one particular record.

Using the Zoom Command

Use the **Zoom** command from the **Image** submenu to locate a specific field, or record by record number, or the value in the record. With the cursor in a table image, follow the steps below.

STEP 1:

> Press: F10 Menu key
> Select: **Image**
> Select: **Zoom**
> Select: **Value**

Paradox asks you to move the cursor to the field column you wish to search. In this example, search for a specific name.

STEP 2:

> Move the cursor to the "Name" column.
> Press: Enter

Paradox leaves a space for you to type the name for the record you would like to find.

STEP 3:

> Type: Sarah Victoria
> Press: Enter

The cursor moves to the matching record in the field you have selected.

Tip The name you type in step 3 must match the record you are looking for exactly, including symbols and spaces. For example, if you typed "Sara Victoria," Paradox would display a message that no matches were found.

In the same way, with your cursor in a numerical field, you could select **Value** from the menu, and type a certain number. Paradox would put the cursor in the field that matched the number you were looking for.

If you were to select **Record** from the **Zoom** submenu, you would type in the record number you were looking for. Press Enter and Paradox moves the cursor to that record number. The record number used is the number seen in the field headed by the table name that is the left-most column on the screen.

Select **Field** from the **Zoom** submenu and Paradox prompts you for the name of the field you want to move to. You can move very quickly around a

Tip   While the action of zooming to a specific piece of data may not seem important with 15 records in a table, imagine 1500 records in a table. The **Zoom** feature can take you to any record almost instantly.

large database, using the **Zoom** command.

1. Select **Zoom** from the **Image** submenu. What happens next?
2. Select **Value** from the **Zoom** submenu. What will you be able to match?
3. After you type the data you are looking for, press Enter. What happens to the cursor?

1. *Paradox prompts you to select a **Field, Record,** or **Value.***
2. *A number or a name.*
3. *The cursor is in the field with the data for which you are searching.*

Using Lookups in Related Tables

The idea of a relational database is that tables can be kept fairly simple with small amounts of related data in one table. A correctly designed database table should have all the fields in that table related to each other.

For example, in a table that lists names and salaries, the salary is related to the name. We could say that there is one, and only one, salary for each name in the table. If you had a table that listed the salary only, without a corresponding name, the table would mean very little.

The multiple table query was used to pull data together from related tables. In a little different way, a lookup is used to establish relationships between tables.

In this example, we create two tables. One holds the product number and a product description. The other table, an *INVOICE* table, holds an invoice number, customer number, product number, quantity ordered, and price.

With the lookup, you will be able to enter the product number in the invoice table. While you enter the number, Paradox will check the *product description* table to make sure that you actually have that product on the list. With the lookup feature, a data entry person who enters PPM1 instead of POM1 will get a message from Paradox that the PPM1 product is not available. The person entering the data can immediately correct the entry.

In one table, you describe the products in relation to their product numbers. When you enter data into the invoice table, Paradox checks the entry to make sure it is valid.

Figure 8.1 shows the *product description* table created for this example. There are five products listed. Each has an assigned product number.

```
Viewing Prodscrp table: Record 1 of 5                         Main

PRODSCRP═Product No.═╦══════════════Product Description══════════
     1  ║  COM1    ║ Contour Map of Scandinavia
     2  ║  COM2    ║ Contour Map of the Grand Canyon
     3  ║  PHM1    ║ Physical Map of the Early Dutch Empire (1556-1663)
     4  ║  POM1    ║ Political Map of Medieval Europe
     5  ║  POM2    ║ Political Map of Modern Europe (1990)
```

Figure 8.1. The *product description* table

Recording the Table Lookup

The related *invoice* table can be created with the following fields: Invoice No., Product, Quantity, and Price. Add some records to the *invoice* table to experience a relational table lookup. In the **Edit** mode of the *invoice* table, follow the steps below to tell Paradox that you want the product number checked every time you enter a value in that field.

STEP 1:

> Press: **F10** Menu key
> Select: **ValCheck**
> Select: **Define**

Paradox asks you to move the cursor to the field for which you want to set a check.

STEP 2:

> Move the cursor to the Product Number field.
> Press: **Enter**
>
> A **ValCheck** menu is displayed.

STEP 3:

> Select: **TableLookup**

Paradox prompts you for the name of the table that, in this example, holds the descriptions you want to check.

STEP 4:

> Type: PRODSCRP
> Press: **Enter**
> Select: **JustCurrentField**
> Select: **HelpAndFill**

A note appears at the lower right side of the screen, informing you that Paradox has recorded the table lookup shown in Figure 8.2.

1. While in the **Edit** mode, press **F10**, and select **ValCheck**. What process are you starting?
2. Start a value check. What option do you select from the **ValCheck** submenu?
3. After you select **TableLookup,** you type the name of the table and press **Enter**. What two menu selections are next?

1. *The value check process.*
2. *Define.*
3. *JustCurrentField/HelpAndFill.*

Testing the Table Lookup

Enter new invoices to the *INVOICE* table and test the table lookup. With the cursor in the *INVOICE* table in the **Edit** mode, enter the data listed here.

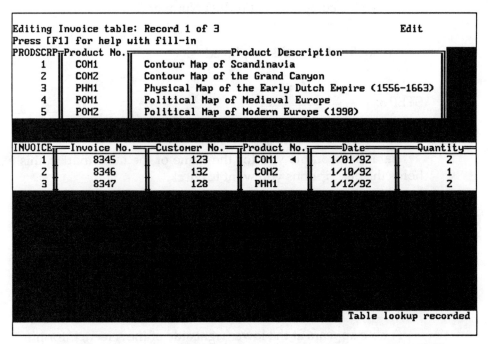

Figure 8.2. Table lookup recorded message on screen

STEP 1:

Move the cursor to a blank record in the Invoice No. field.

STEP 2:

Type: 8348
Press: Enter
Type: 129
Press: Enter

The invoice number and customer number are added to the fields.

STEP 3:

Type: CHM1
Press: Enter

Immediately, the CHM1 is highlighted and a warning message appears on the screen shown in Figure 8.3. Paradox has checked the value of this data, and it is not one of the possible values you have listed for the Product No. field.

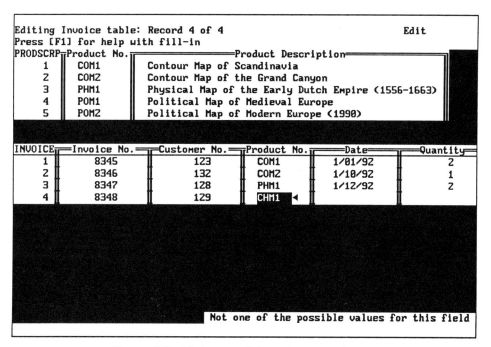

Figure 8.3. Not a possible value warning

STEP 4:

Press the **Backspace** key to delete the incorrect entry.

STEP 5:

Type: COM2
Press: **Enter**

Continue editing the table now that the correct product number has been added.

1. Type CHM1 in the Product No. field and press **Enter**. What happens?
2. Type COM2 in the Product No. field and press **Enter**. What happens?

1. *A warning message is displayed: "Not a Possible Value."*
2. *Paradox checks to make sure it is an acceptable value. It finds that it is acceptable and accepts the entry.*

Using HelpAndFill to Check Values

You could memorize all the products listed in the *PRODSCRP* table, or you could print a report of that table to check which product number you would enter in the *INVOICE* table, or you can use the **HelpAndFill** option to check the values that can be entered into a table.

The **HelpAndFill** option is set up to prevent you from having to memorize tables and to prevent you from having 30 table reports laying all over your desk. Use the **HelpAndFill** option by clearing all tables from the screen. (Press **Alt-F8** Clear All).

STEP 1:

Press: **F10** Menu key
Select: **View**
Type: INVOICE
Press: **Enter**

The *Invoice* table is on screen in the **View** mode.

STEP 2:

Press: **F9** Edit

You are now in the **Edit** mode.

STEP 3:

Press: Down arrow, until a blank record is created

This creates a blank record.

STEP 4:

Move the cursor to the Product No. field.
Press: **F10** Menu key
Select: **ValCheck**
Select: **Define**

Paradox prompts you to move to the field you want to check. Keep the cursor in the Product No. field.

STEP 5:

Press: **Enter**
Select: **TableLookup**

Paradox prompts for the name of the table. The correct name is already filled in (*PRODSCRP*).

STEP 6:

Press: **Enter**
Select: **AllCorrespondingFields**
Select: **HelpAndFill**

The screen is shown in Figure 8.4. Paradox informs you of your action— "Editing *Invoice* table." The message line tells you to press **F1** for help with the fill-in.

STEP 7:

Press: **F1**

The *PRODSCRP* table appears on screen. Move the cursor to the product number you want to insert in the *INVOICE* table.

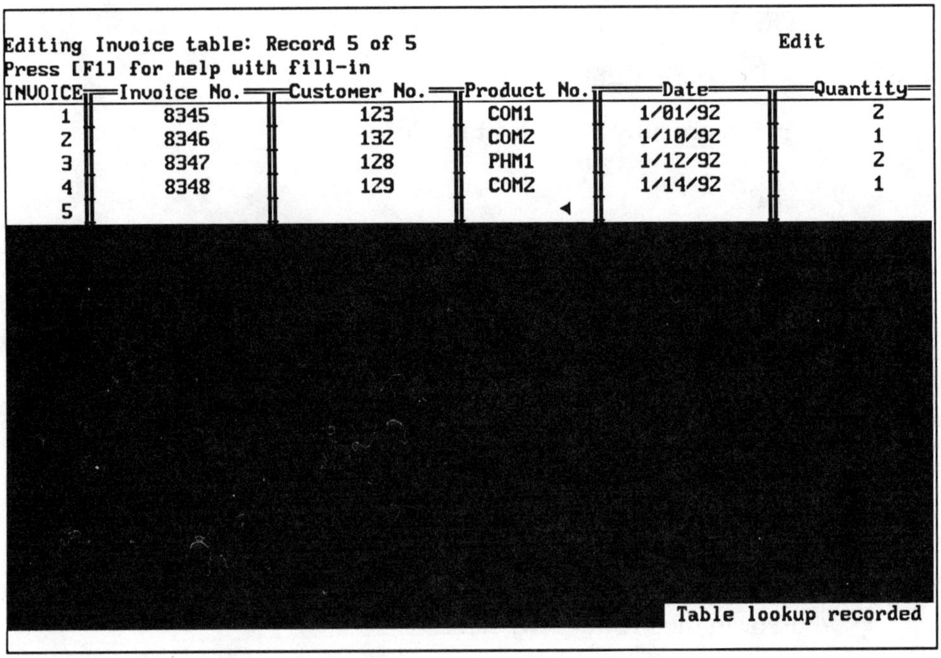

```
Editing Invoice table: Record 5 of 5                        Edit
Press [F1] for help with fill-in
INVOICE==Invoice No.===Customer No.==Product No.======Date====Quantity==
     1 ||     8345  ||      123   || COM1  ||  1/01/92  ||     2
     2 ||     8346  ||      132   || COM2  ||  1/10/92  ||     1
     3 ||     8347  ||      128   || PHM1  ||  1/12/92  ||     2
     4 ||     8348  ||      129   || COM2  ||  1/14/92  ||     1
     5 ||                               ◄
```

Table lookup recorded

Figure 8.4. HelpAndFill Prompt

STEP 8:

Move the cursor to "POM2."
Press: **F2**

Paradox inserts "POM2" into the empty record for the product number. Once a number is inserted (filled) from one table to another the
"Press" [F1] prompt stays on screen. The next time you want to insert or
fill a product number from the *PRODSCRP* table, you simply press **F1** to
get the list of products available. Then select the product number by
pressing **F2**.

Figure 8.5 shows how the *INVOICE* table appears after three product
numbers have been inserted using the **HelpAndFill** option.

End the edit session just as you would any other. When the *INVOICE*
table is filled in to your liking, press **F2** DO-IT. You now understand the basics of a Paradox lookup and can use this information to make your tables
more accurate and take advantage of the relational database.

```
Editing Invoice table: Record 7 of 7                              Edit
Press [F1] for help with fill-in
INVOICE╥══Invoice No.══╤══Customer No.══╤══Product No.══╤══════Date══════╤══Quantity══
   1 ║     8345       │      123       │    COM1       │    1/01/92     │       2
   2 ║     8346       │      132       │    COM2       │    1/10/92     │       1
   3 ║     8347       │      128       │    PHM1       │    1/12/92     │       2
   4 ║     8348       │      129       │    COM2       │    1/14/92     │       1
   5 ║                │                │    POM2       │                │
   6 ║                │                │    COM1       │                │
   7 ║                │                │    POM1   ◄   │                │
```

Figure 8.5. The *INVOICE* table with inserted product
numbers

1. Press **F9**. What happens?
2. What menu option do you select after selecting **AllCorresponding-Fields**?
3. After you select **HelpAndFill**, press **F1**. What happens?
4. You move the cursor to a selected spot and then press **F2**. What happens?

1. *Paradox puts you in the **Edit** mode.*
2. *HelpAndFill.*
3. *You get a list of the data in the related table.*
4. *You select the data to fill the empty field.*

Sorting a Table by a Single Field

When you are working with Paradox tables, you begin to notice a few patterns. When a primary field is defined, Paradox will display the records in that field based on the primary field. You saw this in the *ADVCHEM* file when the students were displayed according to their student number, which is the primary field.

If a table has no primary fields defined, the records are displayed in the order in which they were added to the table. You can view the records in a table in any order you want. The Paradox **Sort** option will arrange the records in the order you specify.

The **Sort** option allows you to arrange the records based on the content of any field in a table. Sorting in ascending order places records from lowest to highest values. Sorting in descending order places records from the highest to the lowest values.

A major difference is seen when sorting a table with no primary key compared to a table with a designated primary key. In a table with a key, records are displayed in ascending order by the primary key field. The records in this table can only be sorted into a new table. The new table created to hold the sorted data will have no keys defined.

In a table where no key fields are defined, you can sort the table in any order you wish. When you sort records, the records will continue to be displayed in that order until you sort the table in a different way. If you like, you can sort the table one way in one table and a difficult way in another table, in case you need to see a table in more than one way.

1. What kind of field determines the order of records in a table?
2. Select ascending order for the sort. What happens?
3. Sort the records in a table with no primary key. The next time you view that table, what do you see?

1. *The Primary Key field.*
2. *Records will be sorted from lowest to highest.*
3. *The records are in the same order as the last sort.*

Sorting a Table in Ascending Order

View a table with no key fields defined on screen. For this example, *SAL-ARY2* is on screen. As you can see in Figure 8.6, this is a list of 15 names, with their corresponding salaries. The names are listed in the order in which they were added to the table.

STEP 1:

> Move the cursor to the Name field.
> Press: **F10** Menu key
> Select: **Modify**
> Select: **Sort**
> Type: SALARY2
> Press: Enter

Paradox asks you if you want to place the results of the sort in the same table or create a new table.

```
Viewing Salary2 table: Record 1 of 15                         Main

SALARY2          Name                    Salary
    1    Louis Capet                    28,000.00
    2    Chris Columbus                 34,780.00
    3    Eleanor Poitier                35,000.00
    4    Alexander Poe                  38,500.00
    5    Carlo Borja                    32,000.00
    6    Attila Hun                     38,500.00
    7    Charles Hapsburg               28,800.00
    8    Charlie Frank                  29,900.00
    9    Constance Lenares              44,000.00
   10    Elizabeth Magellan             35,000.00
   11    Leo De Gama                    28,000.00
   12    Leon Napo                      22,800.00
   13    Sancy Ferdinand                22,400.00
   14    Lucy Romagna                   28,000.00
   15    Sarah Victoria                 39,900.00
```

Figure 8.6. The *SALARY2* table

STEP 2:

> Select: **New**
> Type: SAL2A
> Press: **Enter**

The Sort screen appears and is shown in Figure 8.7. The instructions are written at the top of the screen. The field names for the table are listed in the workspace. The cursor is across from the Name field.

STEP 3:

> Type: 1
> Press: **F2 DO-IT**

SAL2A is displayed on screen in alphabetical order, starting with Alexander and ending with Sarah. There were three steps to the new record order displayed in Figure 8.8. Notice that the salary amounts do not appear in any particular order.

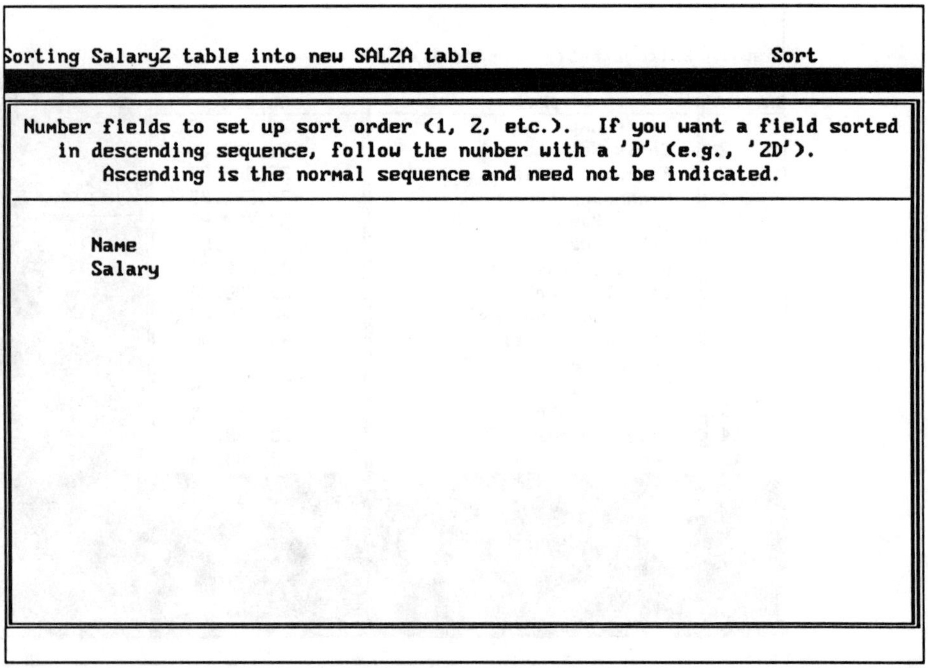

Sorting Salary2 table into new SAL2A table   Sort

Number fields to set up sort order (1, 2, etc.). If you want a field sorted
in descending sequence, follow the number with a 'D' (e.g., '2D').
Ascending is the normal sequence and need not be indicated.

Name
Salary

Figure 8.7. The sort screen

Sorting a Table in Descending Order

Using the *SALARY2* table, sort the Salary field in descending order. View the *SALARY2* table, with the cursor in the Salary field.

STEP 1:

Press: **F10** Menu key
Select: **Modify**
Select: **Sort**
Type: SALARY2
Select: **New**
Type: DESCSAL
Press: **Enter**

The Sort screen appears.

STEP 2:

Press: **Enter**

```
Viewing Sal2a table: Record 1 of 15                      Main  ═

SALARY2┌─────────Name──────────┬────────Salary───────┐
    12 ║   Leon Napo           ║   22,800.00         ║
    13 ║   Sancy Ferdinand     ║   22,400.00         ║
    14 ║   Lucy Romagna        ║   28,000.00         ║
    15 ║   Sarah Victoria      ║   39,900.00         ║


SAL2A──┬─────────Name──────────┬────────Salary───────┐
     1 ║   Alexander Poe       ║   38,500.00         ║
     2 ║   Attila Hun          ║   38,500.00         ║
     3 ║   Carlo Borja         ║   32,000.00         ║
     4 ║   Charles Hapsburg    ║   28,800.00         ║
     5 ║   Charlie Frank       ║   29,900.00         ║
     6 ║   Chris Columbus      ║   34,780.00         ║
     7 ║   Constance Lenares   ║   44,000.00         ║
     8 ║   Eleanor Poitier     ║   35,000.00         ║
     9 ║   Elizabeth Magellan  ║   35,000.00         ║
    10 ║   Leo De Gama         ║   28,000.00         ║
    11 ║   Leon Napo           ║   22,800.00         ║
    12 ║   Louis Capet         ║   28,000.00         ║
    13 ║   Lucy Romagna        ║   28,000.00         ║
    14 ║   Sancy Ferdinand     ║   22,400.00         ║
    15 ║   Sarah Victoria      ║   39,900.00         ║
```

Figure 8.8.   *SAL2A* with name field in alphabetical order

This moves the cursor to the Salary field.

STEP 3:

Type: 1D
Press: **F2** DO-IT

The *DESCSAL* table, which lists the salaries in descending order, appears on screen. The *DESCSAL* table sorted in descending salary order is shown in Figure 8.9.

1. Place sorted records in a separate table. You name the table at the prompt and press **Enter**. What happens next?
2. Place a D after the number of the sort. What are you indicating?

1. *The Sort screen is displayed.*
2. *Descending order.*

```
Viewing Descsal table: Record 1 of 15                          Main  ═

SALARY2┌──────────Name──────────┬────────Salary────────┐
    12 │ Leon Napo              │        22,800.00      │
    13 │ Sancy Ferdinand        │        22,400.00      │
    14 │ Lucy Romagna           │        28,000.00      │
    15 │ Sarah Victoria         │        39,900.00      │


DESCSAL┌──────────Name──────────┬────────Salary────────┐
     1 │ Constance Lenares      │        44,000.00      │
     2 │ Sarah Victoria         │        39,900.00      │
     3 │ Alexander Poe          │        38,500.00      │
     4 │ Attila Hun             │        38,500.00      │
     5 │ Eleanor Poitier        │        35,000.00      │
     6 │ Elizabeth Magellan     │        35,000.00      │
     7 │ Chris Columbus         │        34,780.00      │
     8 │ Carlo Borja            │        32,000.00      │
     9 │ Charlie Frank          │        29,900.00      │
    10 │ Charles Hapsburg       │        28,800.00      │
    11 │ Leo De Gama            │        28,000.00      │
    12 │ Louis Capet            │        28,000.00      │
    13 │ Lucy Romagna           │        28,000.00      │
    14 │ Leon Napo              │        22,800.00      │
    15 │ Sancy Ferdinand        │        22,400.00      │
```

Figure 8.9. *SALARY2* sorted in descending salary order

Sorting a Keyed Table

The *ADVCHEM* table is a keyed table where the student number is the primary key field. Place the cursor in that table or any table with a primary key defined, to do a sort.

STEP 1:

> Press: **F10** Menu key
> Select: **Modify**
> Select: **Sort**

Paradox asks you to name the table to sort.

STEP 2:

> Type: *ADVCHEM*
> Press: **Enter**

Since the *ADVCHEM* table has a primary key defined, Paradox asks you to name the new sorted table.

STEP 3:

> Type: SORT
> Press: **Enter**

The Sort screen, which lists the fields in *SORT*, appears on screen and should look like the screen shown in Figure 8.10.

The cursor is sitting in the Student Number field. For this example, sort by Grade-% in descending order so that the student with the highest percentage is first on the list.

STEP 4:

> Press: Down arrow, four times
> Type: 1D
> Press: **F2** DO-IT

Both tables can now be seen on screen. The top table is the *ADVCHEM* table, and the bottom table is the *SORT* table. Figure 8.11 shows the two tables. The top table is sorted by the primary key field number. The *SORT* table is sorted by the Grade-% field in descending order, showing Alfie Comet with the highest grade in the class.

```
Sorting Advchem table into new SORT table                              Sort


  Number fields to set up sort order (1, 2, etc.).  If you want a field sorted
    in descending sequence, follow the number with a 'D' (e.g., '2D').
             Ascending is the normal sequence and need not be indicated.


        Student Number
        No.
        Last Name
        First Name
        Grade-%
```

Figure 8.10. The sorting screen for SORT

```
Viewing Advchem table: Record 1 of 6                                    Main

  =No.=======Last Name======First Name======Grade-%=
        1     Astro         Billy           92.26
        4     Pluto         Pete            90.09
        5     Comet         Alfie           98.92
        2     Galaxy        Andre           94.88
        7     Mars          Mike            82.66
        3     Moon          Monica          72.34


  =No.=======Last Name======First Name======Grade-%=
        5     Comet         Alfie           98.92
        2     Galaxy        Andre           94.88
        1     Astro         Billy           92.26
        4     Pluto         Pete            90.09
        7     Mars          Mike            82.66
        3     Moon          Monica          72.34
```

Figure 8.11. The *ADVCHEM* table and *SORT* table on screen

1. Sort a table with a primary key. What happens?
2. After you name the new table and press **Enter**, what happens?

1. *Paradox asks you to name the new table in which the results of the sort should be placed.*
2. *The Sort screen is displayed.*

Sorting a Table by Multiple Fields

Look at another table to test a sort by two fields. The table is *SALARY3*, shown in Figure 8.12. Sort by ascending order in the Name field and by descending order in the Salary field. Start with the cursor in the *SALARY3* table.

```
Viewing Salary3 table: Record 1 of 15                          Main

SALARY3        Name              Salary            Year
  1 ║ Eleanor Poitier          35,000.00           1992
  2 ║ Carlo Borja              19,500.00           1992
  3 ║ Louis Capet              28,000.00           1992
  4 ║ Alexander Poe            38,500.00           1992
  5 ║ Chris Columbus           34,780.00           1992
  6 ║ Eleanor Poitier          38,000.00           1993
  7 ║ Carlo Borja              21,000.00           1993
  8 ║ Louis Capet              31,000.00           1993
  9 ║ Alexander Poe            42,000.00           1993
 10 ║ Chris Columbus           39,000.00           1993
 11 ║ Eleanor Poitier          44,000.00           1994
 12 ║ Carlo Borja              36,000.00           1994
 13 ║ Louis Capet              35,000.00           1994
 14 ║ Alexander Poe            50,000.00           1994
 15 ║ Chris Columbus           40,000.00           1994
```

Figure 8.12. *SALARY3* before sorting

Tip If you tried to sort *SALARY2* by descending order of the Salary field and ascending alphabetical order, you would simply get an alphabetical list of names. The descending order would not appear because each name in the Name field is unique.

In the *SALARY3* table, names are repeated, so three salaries are listed for Alexander Poe. These three salaries can then be sorted in descending order.

STEP 1:

Press: **F10** Menu key
Select: **Modify**
Select: **Sort**
Type: SALARY3
Press: **Enter**

Paradox asks if you want to put the sorted data in a new table or use the same one. In this example, use the same table.

STEP 2:

Select: **Same**

The Sort screen appears with the three fields for the *SALARY3* table on screen.

STEP 3:

Type: 1
Press: **Enter**
Type: 2D
Press: **F2** DO-IT

The table is now sorted first by alphabetical name field and then in descending salary order. Figure 8.13 shows the new table.

Starting with Alexander Poe, who earns $50,000.00 in 1994, the list of names continues with descending salaries until Louis Capet is listed with his lowest salary of $28,000.00.

```
Viewing Salary3 table: Record 1 of 15                              Main
SALARY3            Name              Salary            Year
      1    Alexander Poe            50,000.00          1994
      2    Alexander Poe            42,000.00          1993
      3    Alexander Poe            38,500.00          1992
      4    Carlo Borja             36,000.00          1994
      5    Carlo Borja             21,000.00          1993
      6    Carlo Borja             19,500.00          1992
      7    Chris Columbus          40,000.00          1994
      8    Chris Columbus          39,000.00          1993
      9    Chris Columbus          34,780.00          1992
     10    Eleanor Poitier         44,000.00          1994
     11    Eleanor Poitier         38,000.00          1993
     12    Eleanor Poitier         35,000.00          1992
     13    Louis Capet             35,000.00          1994
     14    Louis Capet             31,000.00          1993
     15    Louis Capet             28,000.00          1992
```

Figure 8.13. *SALARY3A* with double sort in ascending and descending order

Summary

Finding and sorting data is easy with the Paradox **Zoom,** lookup, and **Sort** features. You have performed a lookup that involves several steps but improves the accuracy of the tables you create. Tables can be sorted by single or multiple fields. You have also sorted a table with a primary key defined. The major topics covered in this chapter have been:

- Performing a lookup
  - Using the **Zoom** command
  - Using lookups in related tables
  - Using **HelpAndFill** to check values
- Sorting a table by a single field
  - Sorting a table in ascending order
  - Sorting a table in descending order
  - Sorting a keyed table
- Sorting a table by multiple fields

Exercises

What You Should Do	How the Computer Responds
1. With the cursor in the last name field in a large database: Press: F10 Menu key Select: **Image** Select: **Zoom** Select: **Value** Press: Enter Type: The last name for the record you want to find. Press: Enter	1. The cursor is moved to the record with the last name that matches the one you typed.
2. With the cursor in a field in a database table that is related to another database table: Press: F10 Menu key Select: **ValCheck** Select: **Define** Press: Enter	2. The **ValCheck** menu is displayed.
3. Select: **TableLookup** Type: The name of the table with the descriptions you want to check. Press: Enter Select: **JustCurrentField** Select: **HelpAndFill**	3. Paradox displays a note to inform you that the table lookup has been recorded.
4. Move the cursor to a blank record in the related field. Type data into the field and check if it is valid by: Press: F10 Menu key Select: **ValCheck** Select: **Define** Press: Enter Select: **TableLookup** Press: Enter, or type the name of the correct related table. Select: **AllCorrespondingFields** Select: **HelpAndFill**	4. A message line is displayed that tells you to press F1 for help with the fill-in.

5. Press: **F1**
6. Move the cursor to the data in the related field that you want to insert in the previous table.
Press: **F2**
7. In the table you want to sort, move the cursor to the field by which you want to sort.
Press: **F10** Menu key
Select: **Modify**
Select: **Sort**
Type: The name of the table holding the field by which you want to sort.
Press: **Enter**
8. Select: **New**
Type: A name for the new table.
Press: **Enter**
9. Move the cursor across from the field by which you want to sort.
Type: 1D
Press: **F2** DO-IT

5. The named table appears on screen.
6. The data in the related field is inserted into the field of the previous table.

7. Paradox asks you to decide if you want the sort in the same table or a new table.

8. The sort screen is displayed.

9. The records in the named table are sorted by the field you specify in descending order, that is, with the highest value first and the lowest value last.

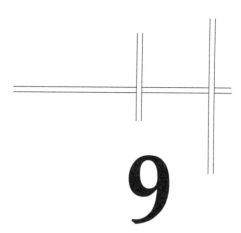

9

Working with the Form Screen

In this chapter you will explore the Form view of Paradox tables. A Form view displays one record at a time. To use forms, you convert the information from the Table view to the Form view of the data. You will also learn some things about the free-form report generator. The main topics found in this chapter are:

- The Paradox form
- Desinging custom forms
- Free-form reports

The Paradox Form

Instead of just displaying columns of data across the screen, a form can display data in the place you choose. Also, comments, highlighting, and some graphics can be added to enhance the look of the form. Examples of forms are invoices, customer profiles, or a single student's assignments and grades.

One advantage of using a Form view is being able to see all the data for one record at the same time. In Table view, some of the data might be in fields that are not visible on the screen. In a long text field, the text can be word wrapped to fit on one screen.

The table view provides an overall look at the entire table while the Form view allows you to zero in on a specific record or series of records. In addition, you can add comments and short descriptions to items on the Form view.

With the Form view, you have the option of increased security. You decide which fields a database user can view and which fields another user can modify. When a table holds confidential or sensitive information, you can protect that information.

Viewing the Paradox Form

In a Paradox form, you specify how you want your table data to be displayed. View a standard form for a Paradox table by using the F7 toggle. Try this out on a table called *INVOICE*. This table is shown in Figure 9.1.

Editing Invoice table: Record 1 of 4					Edit

INVOICE	Invoice No.	Customer No.	Product No.	Date	Quantity
1	8345	123	COM1	1/01/92	2
2	8346	132	COM2	1/10/92	1
3	8347	128	PHM1	1/12/92	2
4	8348	129	COM2	1/14/92	1

Figure 9.1. The Table view of *INVOICE*

With the cursor in the first record of *INVOICE*:

STEP:

Press: **F7**

The first record is displayed in the Form view, shown in Figure 9.2.

Describing the Form View

At the top of the screen for the Form view, Paradox informs you that you are in the Form view, which is displaying record 1 of 4 records. The record you are in and the total number of records is always displayed.

Paradox also tells you that you are viewing form F. Paradox is telling you that you can have more than one form for each table. This is form F, but you can also have form 3 and 10. You can have up to 15 different forms created for each table.

The field columns appear down the left side of the screen, with their corresponding values displayed to the right. In the upper right corner is the In-

```
Editing Invoice table with form F: Record 1 of 4            Edit  ═▼

                                                   Invoice   #     1

   Invoice No.:            8345    ◄
   Customer No.:           123
   Product No.:  COM1
   Date:         1/01/92
   Quantity:               2
   Unit Price:             3.50
   Total Sale:             7.00
```

Figure 9.2.   The Form view of *INVOICE*

voice No., which at this time is number 1.

Notice that the field value 8345 is about ten spaces from the words "Invoice No.:." The next field, "Product No.:," has the product number directly to the right. The "Quantity:" and "Price:" values are farther to the right.

Paradox arranges these numbers this way because it has to make some predictions when it creates a Form view. The Invoice No. was formatted as a number when the table structure was created. Therefore, Paradox leaves enough room for a very large number when the Form view is created.

The next number, "Product No.," has the alphanumeric symbol for that field directly to the right of the field name. When this field was entered, it was formatted as an Alphanumeric field with five spaces. Paradox knows how big this field should be and no prediction has to be made. Therefore, this field is formatted to fit the space specified in the table structure. With the "Quantity" and "Price" fields, Paradox again has to predict how long the numbers will be and leaves a large space for any possibilities.

When Paradox moves you into the Form view, the cursor will be in the same field that it was in while in the Table view. If you go back to the Table view, the cursor stays in the same field.

1. Press **F7**. What happens?
2. Select F from the list of forms. Which form will you see?
3. Insert an Alphanumeric field in the Form view. What mask indicator will you see?

1. *The screen switches from the Form view to the table view.*
2. *The standard form.*
3. *You will see A's.*

Moving in the Form Screen

The keys listed below explain how you can move around in a form screen. Most movement is with the arrow keys and is quite simple.

Right Arrow, **Down Arrow,** Tab, Enter	Each of these keys moves you to the next field. If you are in the last field of a record and you hit one of these keys, the cursor moves to the first field of the next record. If you are in the last field

of the last record and you try to move down one field, Paradox sounds a beep, which indicates that you are at the end of the table.

Left Arrow, Each of these keys moves the cursor to the
Up Arrow, previous field. If you are in the first field of a
Shift-Tab record and you press one of these keys, the cursor moves to the last field of the previous record. When you are in the first field of the first record and you hit one of these keys, Paradox sounds a beep, indicating the beginning of the table.

Home This key moves the cursor to the first record of the table.

End This key moves the cursor to the last record in the table.

Page Down This key moves the cursor to the next record.

Page Up This key moves the cursor to the previous record.

1. Press the right arrow, or the down arrow. What happens?
2. Press **Page Down**. What happens?

1. *The cursor moves to the next field.*
2. *The cursor moves to the next record.*

Exiting the Form View

Press **F7** to go back to the Table view. When you go back to the Table view, the cursor will be in the same field and record as it was while you were in Form view.

Designing Custom Forms

Getting to and moving around the Form view is quite simple. From the *IN-VOICE* table above, design a usable invoice form.

STEP 1:

Press: **Alt-F8** Clear All

This clears all images from the workspace.

STEP 2:

Press: **F10** Menu key
Select: **Forms**

Two options for the **Forms** submenu appear.

STEP 3:

Select: **Design**

Paradox prompts you to name the table for which you wish to design a form.

STEP 4:

Type: `INVOICE`
Press: **Enter**

You see the letter F for the standard form, followed by numbers up to 14. Paradox allows you to design 15 forms per table.

STEP 5:

Select: 1

Paradox prompts you for a description of the new form.

STEP 6:

Type: `Dealer Invoice`
Press: **Enter**

Paradox informs you via the message line that you are designing a new F1 form for the *INVOICE* table. This screen appears in Figure 9.3.

1. Press **Alt-F8**. What happens?
2. Press **F10**, select **Forms** and **Design**. What happens?

```
Designing new F1 form for Invoice                          Form      1/1
< 1, 1>
```

Figure 9.3. Designing form for *INVOICE* screen

1. *All the images on screen are cleared.*
2. *The report design screen is displayed.*

Viewing the Form Design Screen

Paradox tells you what you are doing on the message line, but it doesn't tell you what to do next. Paradox is giving you free reign over the design of the form. At the top right side of the screen, you see the highlighted word "Form." Press F10 Menu key and the **Form** submenu will be displayed.

The "1/1" to the right of the word "Form" means that you are in the first page of a one page form. The "⟨1, 1⟩" that appears on the next line down indicates the cursor location in the form. The cursor is in the first line of the form and in the first space of that line, respectively.

Moving in the Form Design Screen

The special keys used for moving around the form design screen are shown here:

Up Arrow	Cursor moves up one line.
Down Arrow	Cursor moves down one line.
Right Arrow	Cursor moves one character to the right.
Left Arrow	Cursor moves one character to the left.
Home	Cursor moves to the first line of the form design screen.
End	Cursor moves to the last line of the form design screen.
Ctrl-Home	Cursor moves to the beginning of the line.
Ctrl-End	Cursor moves to the end of the line.

1. ⟨1, 1⟩ appears in the upper left side of the screen. What does this indicate?
2. With the cursor in the form design screen, press **Home**. What happens?
3. Press **Ctrl-End**. What happens?

1. *It tells you the cursor location by line and then space.*
2. *The cursor moves to the first line of the form design screen.*
3. *The cursor moves to the end of the line.*

Designing the New Form

In order to make *INVOICE* more usable, it was changed to look like the table in Figure 9.4. The fields are: Invoice No., Customer No., Product No., Date, Quantity, Unit Price, and Total Sale.

```
Viewing Invoice table: Record 1 of 4                              Main

INVOICE┬═Invoice No.═╦═Customer No.═╦═Product No.┬══════Date══════╦══Quantity═
     1 ║    8345     ║     123      ║   COM1     ║    1/01/92     ║      2
     2 ║    8346     ║     132      ║   COM2     ║    1/10/92     ║      1
     3 ║    8347     ║     128      ║   PHM1     ║    1/12/92     ║      2
     4 ║    8348     ║     129      ║   COM2     ║    1/14/92     ║      1
```

Figure 9.4. Restructured *INVOICE* table

Note The *INVOICE* table is set up so that the fields Invoice No., Customer No., and Product No. are primary fields. The Customer No. is set up for a lookup value check with the *CUSTID* table. The Product No. field is set up for a lookup value check with the *PRODSCRP* table. These two tables are shown in Figure 9.5.

Start by putting a title on the form.

Tip In the steps that follow, the location of the cursor will be identified prior to carrying out the steps. This will help you develop a form that looks like the one in the figures for this chapter.

STEP 1:

⟨1, 1⟩	Press: Down arrow, 1 time
⟨2, 1⟩	Press: Space bar, 24 times
⟨2, 25⟩	Type: DEALER INVOICE
⟨2, 39⟩	Press: **Enter**, three times

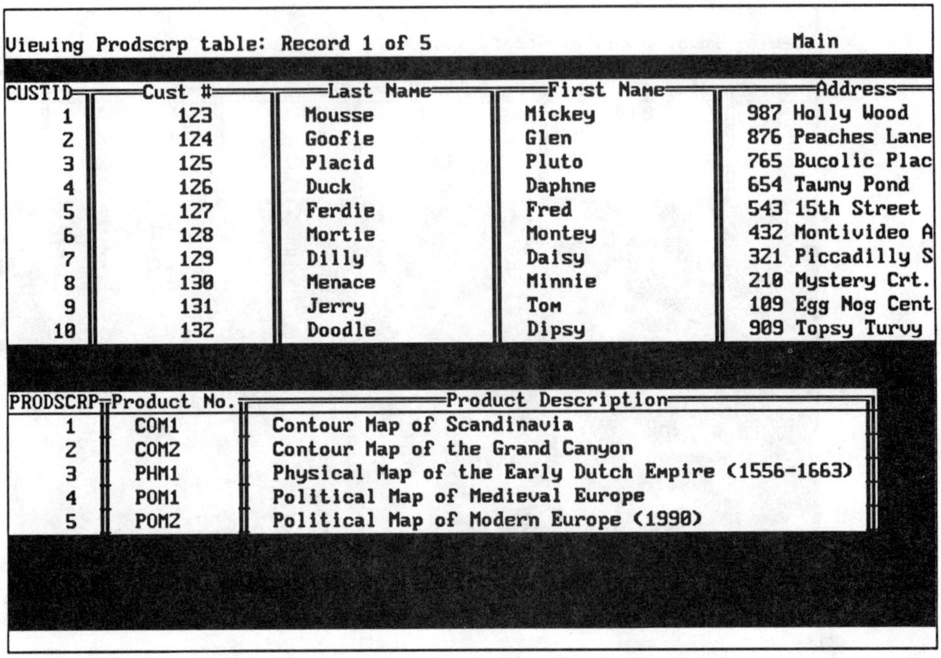

```
Viewing Prodscrp table: Record 1 of 5                          Main

CUSTID      Cust #         Last Name        First Name          Address
    1        123          Mousse           Mickey          987 Holly Wood
    2        124          Goofie           Glen            876 Peaches Lane
    3        125          Placid           Pluto           765 Bucolic Plac
    4        126          Duck             Daphne          654 Tawny Pond
    5        127          Ferdie           Fred            543 15th Street
    6        128          Mortie           Montey          432 Montivideo A
    7        129          Dilly            Daisy           321 Piccadilly S
    8        130          Menace           Minnie          210 Mystery Crt.
    9        131          Jerry            Tom             109 Egg Nog Cent
   10        132          Doodle           Dipsy           909 Topsy Turvy


PRODSCRP  Product No.                 Product Description
    1        COM1        Contour Map of Scandinavia
    2        COM2        Contour Map of the Grand Canyon
    3        PHM1        Physical Map of the Early Dutch Empire (1556-1663)
    4        POM1        Political Map of Medieval Europe
    5        POM2        Political Map of Modern Europe (1990)
```

Figure 9.5. The *CUSTID* and *PRODSCRP* tables on screen

Next, add the invoice number field to the form.

STEP 2:

⟨5, 1⟩	Press: Space bar, 2 times
⟨5, 3⟩	Type: Invoice Number:
⟨5, 16⟩	Press: Space bar, 2 times

The field is named. Now tell Paradox to insert the invoice number in the location designated here.

STEP 3:

⟨5, 18⟩   Press: **F10** Menu key
            Select: **Field**
            Select: **Place**
            Select: **Regular**

Paradox lists the fields from the *INVOICE* table. Select the one you want to be inserted next to "Invoice Number:."

STEP 4:

Select: Invoice No.

Paradox asks you to move the cursor up, down, left, or right to place the field. Since you have already determined the location, take the next step.

STEP 5:

Press: **Enter**
Move the arrow keys to adjust the width of the field. In this example leave at least eight spaces. (There is one dash for each space.)
Press: **Enter**

The first field is labeled and placed in the custom form. Figure 9.6 shows how the DEALER INVOICE form looks at this point.

1. Press **F10** and select **Menu** key, **Field**, **Place**, and **Regular**. What happens?
2. Press **Enter** while in the report design screen. What happens?

```
Designing new F1 form for Invoice                    Form      1/1
< 5,28>

                         DEALER INVOICE


     Invoice Number:      _____
```

Figure 9.6. DEALER INVOICE Form with one field entered

1. *You place a field in the report design screen.*
2. *The cursor moves to the beginning of the next line.*

Adding the Remaining Fields

With your own form, repeat the steps above to finish the form. Follow along below to complete the form design for this example.

⟨5, 28⟩	Press: **Enter**, 2 times
⟨7, 1⟩	Press: Space bar, 2 times
⟨7, 3⟩	Type: Customer Number:
⟨7, 17⟩	Press: Space bar, 2 times
⟨7, 19⟩	Press: **F10** Menu key
	Select: **Field**
	Select: **Place**
	Select: **Regular**
	Select: Customer No.
	Resize field
	Press: **Enter**
⟨7, 28⟩	Press: Space bar, 15 times
⟨7, 43⟩	Type: Date:
⟨7, 48⟩	Press: Space bar, two times
⟨7, 50⟩	Press: **F10** Menu key
	Select: **Field/Place/Regular**
	Select: Date
	Press: **Enter**
⟨7, 61⟩	Press: **Enter**, 5 times
⟨12, 1⟩	Press: Space bar, 2 times
⟨12, 3⟩	Type: Product Number:
⟨12, 16⟩	Press: Space bar, 8 times
⟨12, 24⟩	Type: Quantity:
⟨12, 33⟩	Press: Space bar, 5 times
⟨12, 38⟩	Type: Unit Price:
⟨12, 49⟩	Press: Space bar, 5 times
⟨12, 54⟩	Type: Total Sale:
⟨12, 65⟩	Press: **Enter**, 2 times

⟨14, 1⟩   Press: Space bar, 2 times
⟨14, 3⟩   Press: F10 Menu key
               Select: **Field/Place/Regular**
               Select: Product No.
               Press: Enter
               Press: Enter

⟨14, 9⟩   Press: Space bar, 17 times
⟨14, 26⟩   Press: F10 Menu key
               Select: **Field/Place/Regular**
               Select: Quantity
               Press: Left arrow, 17 times
               Press: Enter

⟨14, 32⟩   Press: Space bar, 8 times
⟨14, 40⟩   Press: F10 Menu key
               Select: **Field/Place/Regular**
               Select: Unit Price
               Press: Enter
               Press: Left arrow, 13 times
               Press: Enter

Tip ‖ Do not add the Total Sale field now. Instead, leave that field off the screen and add it later in the chapter under the section on calculated fields.

Erasing a Placed Field

Erase the field by following these steps after you place the cursor in the field you want to erase.

Press: F10 Menu key
Select: **Field**
Select: **Erase**
Move the cursor to the field you want to erase.
Press: Enter

All of the fields except Total Sale have been entered, and the screen looks like the one in Figure 9.7.

```
Designing new F1 form for Invoice                    Form      1/1
<14,50>
                          DEALER INVOICE


     Invoice Number:    _____

     Customer Number:    ____          Date:    _____



     Product Number:       Quantity:    Unit Price:    Total Sale:

     _____              _____        _____
```

Figure 9.7. DEALER INVOICE form screen

Ending the Form Design

End the form design and save the design.

STEP:

Press: **F2** DO-IT

Paradox returns you to the Main menu.

1. Press **F10**, select **Field** and **Erase,** and press **Enter**. What happens?
2. Select **Field/Place/Regular** from the menu. What are you doing?
3. Press **F2**. What happens?

1. *A field is erased.*
2. *Placing field data into the report design form screen.*
3. *Paradox saves the report design to disk and ends the form design process.*

Using the Custom Form

You have created an invoice form. Now, you want to tell Paradox to use this form instead of the standard Form view (F).

STEP 1:

Select: **View**
Type: Invoice
Press: **Enter**

The *INVOICE* table appears on screen.
Use the **Image** option from the Main menu to tell Paradox to display the *INVOICE* table in the form you have created.

STEP 2:

Press: **F10** Menu key
Select: **Image**
Select: **PickForm**

A list that holds all the custom forms you have developed appears across the top of the screen. At this time, it holds only F and 1. Form number 1 is the only custom form designed at this time. The F form is the standard form.

STEP 3:

Select: 1

The *INVOICE* table is displayed in the custom Form view, just like the one in Figure 9.8.

Selecting the Custom Form

The next time you start Paradox, you want to see this new custom form. If you press **F7** Form Toggle, while viewing the INVOICE table, you will see the standard form (F), not the custom form (1). With the workspace clear, and the Main menu on screen, take these steps to make the custom form the form you toggle to when you press **F7** Form Toggle.

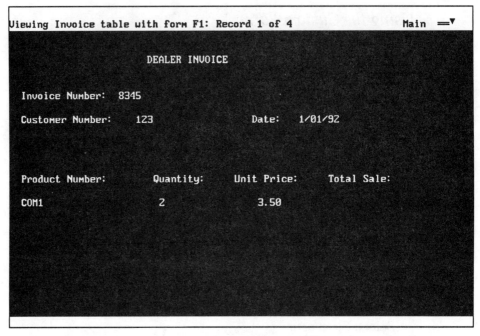

Figure 9.8. DEALER INVOICE form view with table data

Tip

The steps below will get you to the custom form when you press **F7** Form Toggle. To make the custom form the permanent default form, use the **F10/Image/KeepSet** menu options.

STEP 1:

Select: **View**
Type: INVOICE

The *INVOICE* table is displayed on the screen.

STEP 2:

Press: **F10** Menu key
Select: **Image**
Select: **PickForm**

The screen will list the two forms available so far for this table. The first is the standard form (F), and the second is the custom form (1).

STEP 3:

Select: 1

The DEALER INVOICE custom form appears on screen.

STEP 4:

Press: **F7**

The DEALER INVOICE custom form is removed, and the *INVOICE* table is displayed. Now Paradox will toggle between these two forms instead of the standard form (F).

1. Press **F10**, select **Image** and **PickForm**. What action are you taking?
2. Now, with the cursor in the table view, press **F7**. What happens?

1. *Choose a custom form in place of the standard (F) form.*
2. *The screen toggles to the custom form.*

Modifying the Custom Form

In the custom form DEALER INVOICE, the fields have been arranged differently from the standard form (F). There are many things you can do to enhance this custom form even further. Some of the things you can do are move fields in the form, add borders, add color, and add calculated fields. Since this is an invoice form, start with adding a calculated field.

With the cursor in the *INVOICE* table, follow these steps:

STEP 1:

Press: **F10** Menu key
Select: **Forms**
Select: **Change**
Type: Invoice
Select: 1
Press: **Enter**

The cursor is in the DEALER INVOICE custom form. You can make changes to the form now.

STEP 2:

Move the cursor to the line below the Total Sale field.

The cursor location number should be: ⟨14,56⟩.

STEP 3:

Press: F10 Menu key
Select: **Field**
Select: **Place**
Select: **Calculated**

Paradox prompts you to define the expression you want to calculate. In fact, as you see in Figure 9.9, Paradox gives you an example calculation, which is what you should use.

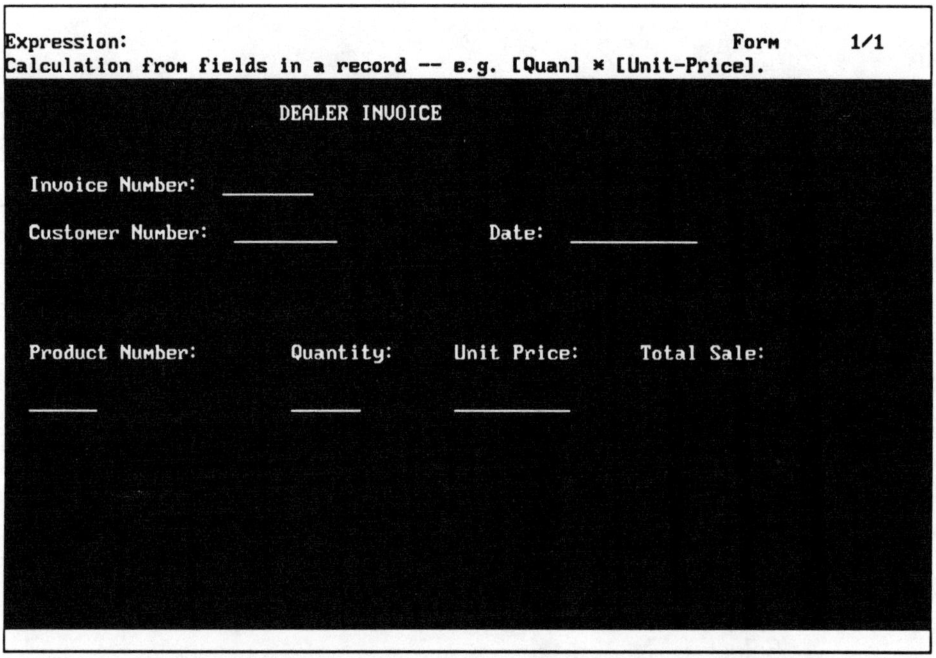

```
Expression:                                             Form      1/1
Calculation from fields in a record -- e.g. [Quan] * [Unit-Price].
                          DEALER INVOICE


   Invoice Number:   _____

   Customer Number:   _____        Date:   _____




   Product Number:      Quantity:    Unit Price:    Total Sale:

   _____               _____       _____
```

Figure 9.9. Expression: prompt with calculations

STEP 4:

> Type: [Quantity]*[Unit Price]
> Press: **Enter**
> Press: **Enter**

Tip

When entering a calculation, use the exact field name as you have used in the form design. Surround each field name with brackets ([]), and use the following operators: + for addition, - for subtraction, / for division, and * for multiplication.

Paradox asks you to determine the size of the field.

STEP 5:

> Press: Left arrow, 12 times
> Press: **Enter**

The calculated field is inserted under total sale. If you move the cursor to the left one more time so that the cursor is in the field, you will see the field indicator describe the field in the upper right corner of the screen. The field description is: Formula,[Quantity]*[Unit Price].

1. Press **F10**, select **Forms** and **Change,** and select a table. What happens next?
2. Press **F10**, select **Field, Place,** and **Calculated**. What action are you taking?

1. *You can modify a custom form from the custom form design screen.*
2. *You are placing a calculated field in the custom form design screen.*

Moving a Field in a Form Screen

While you are still in the act of changing a custom form, move a field. In this example, the "Invoice Number" field will be moved to the upper right corner of the form instead of its location on the left margin.

STEP 1:

> Press: **F10** Menu key
> Select: **Area**
> Select: **Move**

Paradox asks you to move the cursor to a corner of the area to be moved. Move the cursor so that it is at one end or the other of "Invoice Number: _____."

STEP 2:

> Press: **Enter**
> Press: Right arrow, 26 times

Figure 9.10 shows how Paradox highlights the area to be moved.

STEP 3:

> Press: **Enter**
> Press: Left arrow, until the left side of highlighting is even with the "D" in "Date."
> Press: Up arrow, 1 time

The highlighting moves to the right and up one line. You are ready to complete the move.

STEP 4:

> Press: **Enter**

"Invoice Number" and the line that holds the field value move to the new location. If you don't like it here, you can move it anywhere else on the screen. You can use this same method to move larger blocks of text. Whatever you decide to highlight will be moved.

1. Highlight an area and press **Enter**. Move the cursor to a new location and press **Enter**. What have you done?
2. Press **F10** and select **Area** and **Move**. What action are you taking?

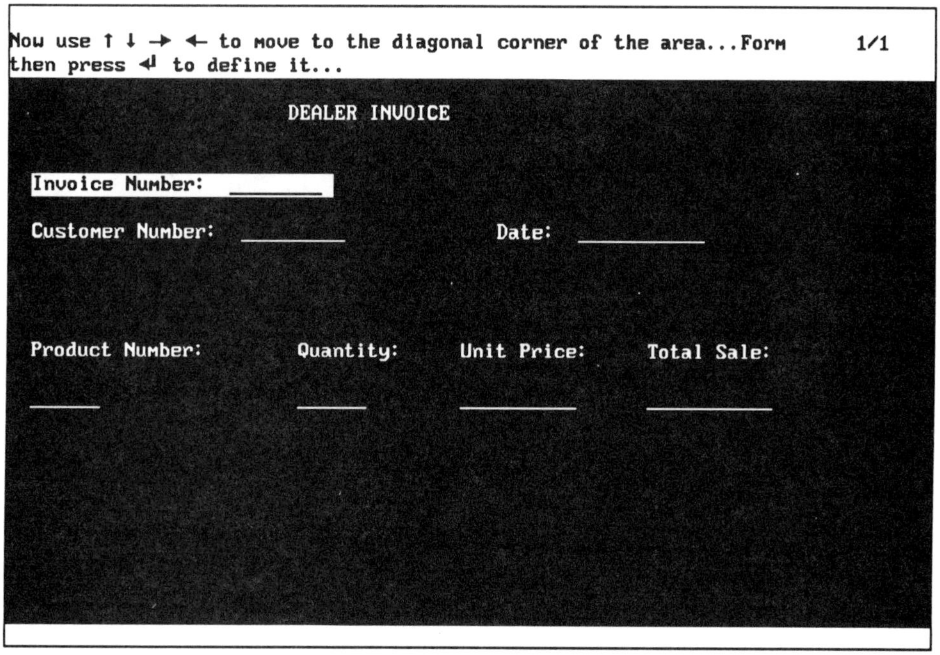

```
Now use ↑ ↓ → ← to move to the diagonal corner of the area...Form    1/1
then press ↵ to define it...

                          DEALER INVOICE


  Invoice Number:        _____

  Customer Number:     _____        Date:    _____




  Product Number:      Quantity:     Unit Price:    Total Sale:

  _____              _____       _____        _____
```

Figure 9.10. Custom form area to be moved

1. *You have moved a field in the form screen.*
2. *You are moving an area.*

Adding a Form Border

Adding a border is as simple as any of the other form design changes.

STEP 1:

Press: **F10** Menu key
Select: **Border**
Select: **Place**

At this point you can see that the option other than **Place** is to erase a border. After you place it and you don't like it, go back to this menu and select **Erase**. You can select a single-line or double-line border, or you can choose another character of your choice.

STEP 2:

Select: **Double-line**
Move the cursor to the lower right corner of the form.
Press: Enter

STEP 3:

Move the cursor to the upper left corner of the form.

The highlighted area that will hold the border appears on screen as you see in Figure 9.11.

STEP 4:

Press: Enter

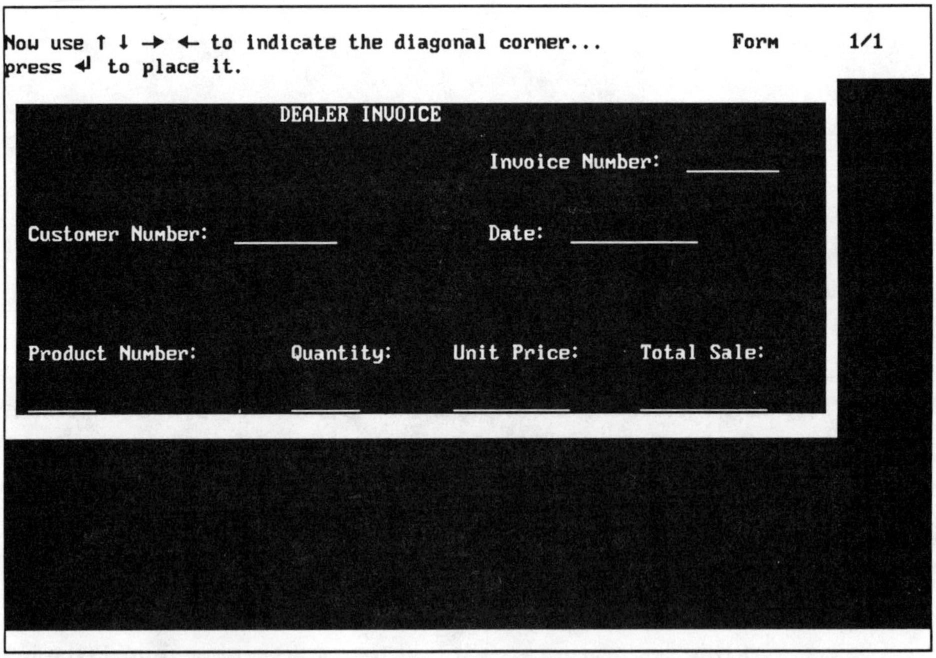

```
Now use ↑ ↓ → ← to indicate the diagonal corner...        Form      1/1
press ↵ to place it.
                              DEALER INVOICE

                                           Invoice Number:   _____


     Customer Number:   _____          Date:    _____



     Product Number:       Quantity:     Unit Price:     Total Sale:
     _____               _____                      _____
```

Figure 9.11. The border highlighted

The double-line border is inserted where the highlighting indicated it should be.

This gives you an example of just a few of the enhancements and changes you can make to a custom form.

Saving the Modified Form

Since you have moved fields, changed fields, and added a border, you have to save the custom design.

STEP:

Press: **F2** DO-IT

Paradox saves the custom form. Now press **F7** to toggle between the *INVOICE* table on screen and the custom form. The custom form with *INVOICE* data inserted in the fields is shown in Figure 9.12.

1. Press **F10**, select **Border, Place,** and **Double-line.** What action are you taking?
2. Press **F2**. What happens?

1. *You are preparing to place a double-line border in the form design screen.*
2. *You end the form design session and save the custom form.*

Free-Form Reports

A free-form report is similar to the form design. Compared to a standard report where the fields are lined up in the table, a free-form report is designed to be much more flexible. You can design the printed page any way you like with a free-form report. Free-form reports are most often used as mailing labels, form letters, and purchase orders.

In this section you will go through the steps to create mailing labels in order to learn about the free-form report. You will have to transfer this

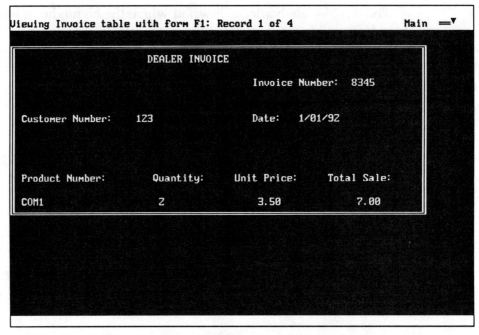

Figure 9.12. Custom form with data inserted

knowledge to create other types of free-form reports. The mailing label is used as an example since it is the most often used type of free-form report.

The mailing labels will print the customer name and address placed in a free-form report. View the table created with the names and addresses of customers. This table is called the *CUSTID* table. It has ten customers listed. You can see this table in Figure 9.13. Create mailing labels for this table or any table you select.

Getting to the Free-Form Report Design Screen

Start by selecting the Report/Design option from the menus.

STEP 1:

Press: **F10** Menu key
Select: **Report**
Select: **Design**

```
Viewing Custid table: Record 1 of 10                          Main

CUSTID┬────Cust #═════╦════Last Name════╦════First Name═══╦════════Address═══
     1 ║      123     ║   Mousse        ║   Mickey        ║   987 Holly Wood
     2 ║      124     ║   Goofie        ║   Glen          ║   876 Peaches Lane
     3 ║      125     ║   Placid        ║   Pluto         ║   765 Bucolic Plac
     4 ║      126     ║   Duck          ║   Daphne        ║   654 Tawny Pond
     5 ║      127     ║   Ferdie        ║   Fred          ║   543 15th Street
     6 ║      128     ║   Mortie        ║   Montey        ║   432 Montivideo A
     7 ║      129     ║   Dilly         ║   Daisy         ║   321 Piccadilly S
     8 ║      130     ║   Menace        ║   Minnie        ║   210 Mystery Crt.
     9 ║      131     ║   Jerry         ║   Tom           ║   109 Egg Nog Cent
    10 ║      132     ║   Doodle        ║   Dipsy         ║   909 Topsy Turvy
```

══════════════ Figure 9.13. *CUSTID* table on screen

Type: CUSTID
Press: **Enter**

Paradox lists the R for standard report and the numbers 1 through 14.

STEP 2:

Select: 1
Type: Mailing Labels
Press: **Enter**

Paradox prompts you to select the type of report to create.

STEP 3:

Select: Free-form

The *design free-form report screen* is now on screen. Take a look at Figure 9.14 to see what is on this screen.

In Chapter 6, you created reports and saw the tabular report design screen. The free-form report design screen is very similar. You will notice

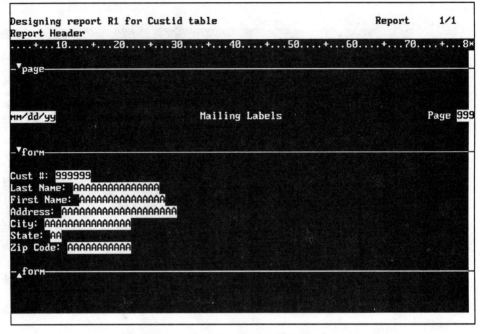

Figure 9.14. The design free-form report screen

one major difference. The fields are listed down the left side of the page in the free-form report design screen. In the tabular report design screen, the fields are listed across the page, just as you would see them printed in the tabular report.

1. Select a free-form instead of a tabular report. What appears on the screen?
2. Look at the screen for a free-form report. Where are the fields?

1. *The design free-form report screen appears.*
2. *In the free-form report screen, the fields are listed down the left side of the screen.*

Designing the Mailing Label Format

Tip

The mailing labels designed here are for standard labels that are 3 1/2 inches wide and 1 inch high (six lines per vertical inch). You will have to adjust the settings accordingly for labels of a different size.

Prepare for mailing labels by removing all the blank lines from the page header and page footer areas. Begin with the cursor in the blank line in the report header.

STEP 1:

Press: **Ctrl-Y**

Continue pressing **Ctrl-Y** until blank lines in the page header and footer are deleted. The report design screen should look like the one in Figure 9.15, where blank lines above and below the form band are removed.

Remove all the lines in the form band, using the same method.

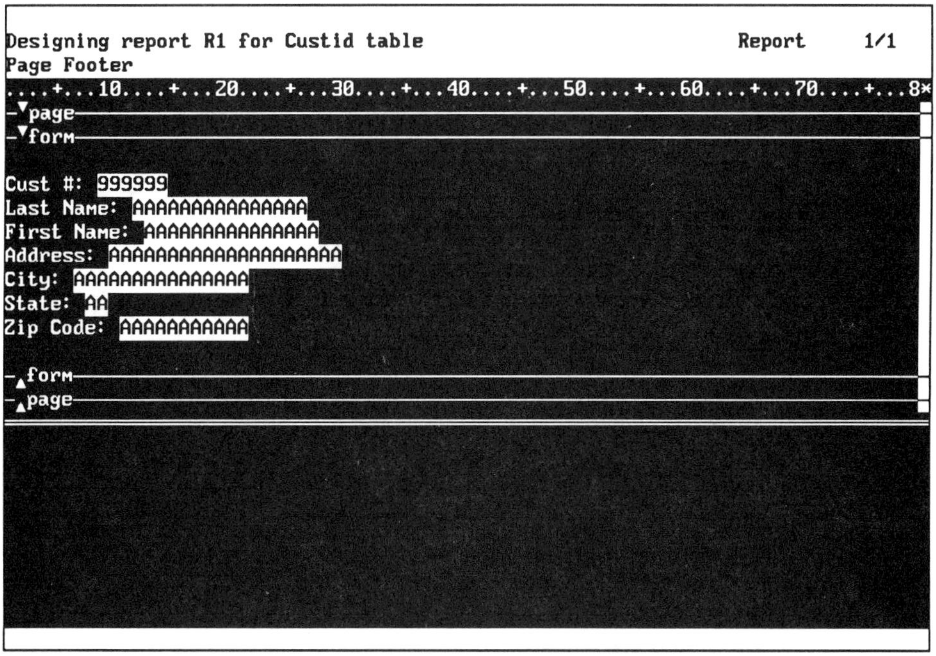

```
Designing report R1 for Custid table                          Report    1/1
Page Footer
....+...10....+...20....+...30....+...40....+...50....+...60....+...70....+...8*
-▼page─────────────────────────────────────────────────────────────────
-▼form─────────────────────────────────────────────────────────────────

Cust #: 999999
Last Name: AAAAAAAAAAAAAAAA
First Name: AAAAAAAAAAAAAAA
Address: AAAAAAAAAAAAAAAAAAAAAA
City: AAAAAAAAAAAAAAA
State: AA
Zip Code: AAAAAAAAAA

-▲form─────────────────────────────────────────────────────────────────
-▲page─────────────────────────────────────────────────────────────────
```

Figure 9.15. Form design screen with blank lines removed

STEP 2:

Move the cursor to the beginning of each line in the form band.
Press: Ctrl-Y

The form band is empty. Now you are going to insert six blank lines in the form band. The cursor should be located at the left of the symbol (up arrow) form, which indicates the lower edge of the form band.

STEP 3:

Press: Ins
Press: Enter, 6 times

Pressing Ins toggles the insert mode in the form design screen. Press Enter six times and six blank lines are added between the (up arrow) form symbols. The next step is to place the fields in the position they should appear on the mailing label.

STEP 4:

Move the cursor to the first line in the form band.
Press: F10 Menu key
Select: **Field**
Select: **Place**
Select: **Regular**

Paradox displays a list of fields for the *CUSTID* table.

STEP 5:

Select: First Name
Press: Enter
Press: Enter
Press: Right arrow, 3 times

The first field is placed in the form band.

STEP 6:

Press: F10 Menu key
Select: **Field/Place/Regular**
Select: Last Name

Press: Enter
Press: Enter

Figure 9.16 shows how the first and last name have been placed in the form band. Notice that the field mask appears on screen (the series of A's); however, no field label appears. When you move the cursor into a field mask, the indicator in the upper right corner tells you what field you are in.

Continue this sequence of commands until the entire address is placed on screen.

STEP 7:

Move the cursor to the left margin of the next blank line.
Press: F10 Menu key
Select: **Field/Place/Regular**
Select: Address
Press: Enter
Press: Enter

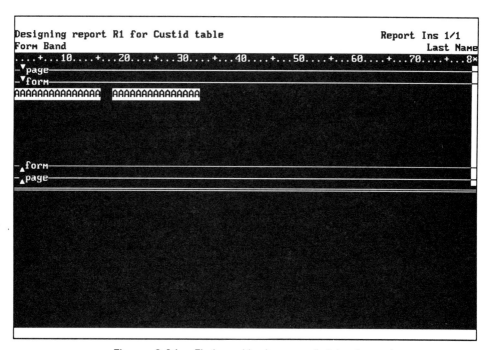

Figure 9.16. First and last name fields placed on screen

STEP 8:

Move the cursor to the left margin of the next blank line.
Press: **F10** Menu key
Select: **Field/Place/Regular**
Select: City
Press: **Enter**
Press: **Enter**
Press: Right arrow, 3 times

STEP 9:

Press: **F10** Menu key
Select: **Field/Place/Regular**
Select: State
Press: **Enter**
Press: **Enter**
Press: Right arrow, 3 times

STEP 10:

Press: **F10** Menu key
Select: **Field/Place/Regular**
Select: Zip Code
Press: **Enter**
Press: **Enter**

The report design screen now looks like the one in Figure 9.17. All the field masks are in place.

1. While in the report design screen, press **Ctrl-Y**. What happens?
2. Press the **Ins** key. What happens?
3. Press **F10** and select **Field, Place,** and **Regular**. What happens?

1. *The line is deleted from the screen.*
2. *You are now able to insert blank lines.*
3. *You have completed the menu sequence for placing fields in the report design screen.*

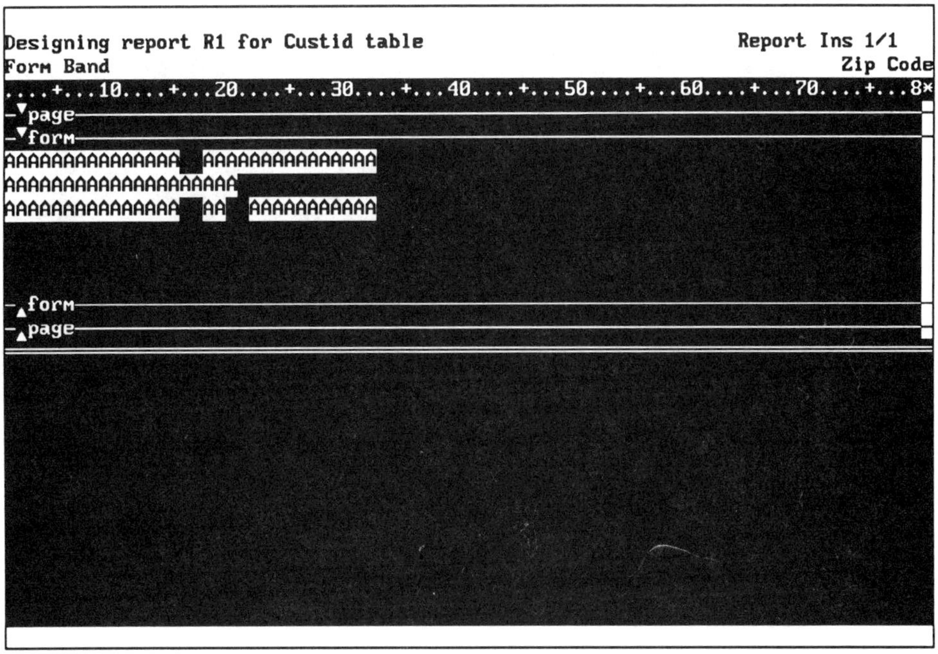

```
Designing report R1 for Custid table                 Report Ins 1/1
Form Band                                                  Zip Code
....+...10....+...20....+...30....+...40....+...50....+...60....+...70....+...8×
─▼page──────────────────────────────────────────────────────────────────
─▼form──────────────────────────────────────────────────────────────────
AAAAAAAAAAAAAAAA  AAAAAAAAAAAAAAAA
AAAAAAAAAAAAAAAAAAAAAA
AAAAAAAAAAAAAAAA  AA  AAAAAAAAAA


─▲form──────────────────────────────────────────────────────────────────
─▲page──────────────────────────────────────────────────────────────────
```

Figure 9.17. Report design screen with fields placed

Previewing the Labels

Take a look at the labels on screen before printing them to see if they look the
way you want them.

STEP:

Press: **F10** Menu key
Select: **Output**
Select: **Screen**

The labels appear on screen as you see in Figure 9.18. While they look
like they will print correctly, notice the excess of blank spaces. Paradox can
easily remedy this problem.

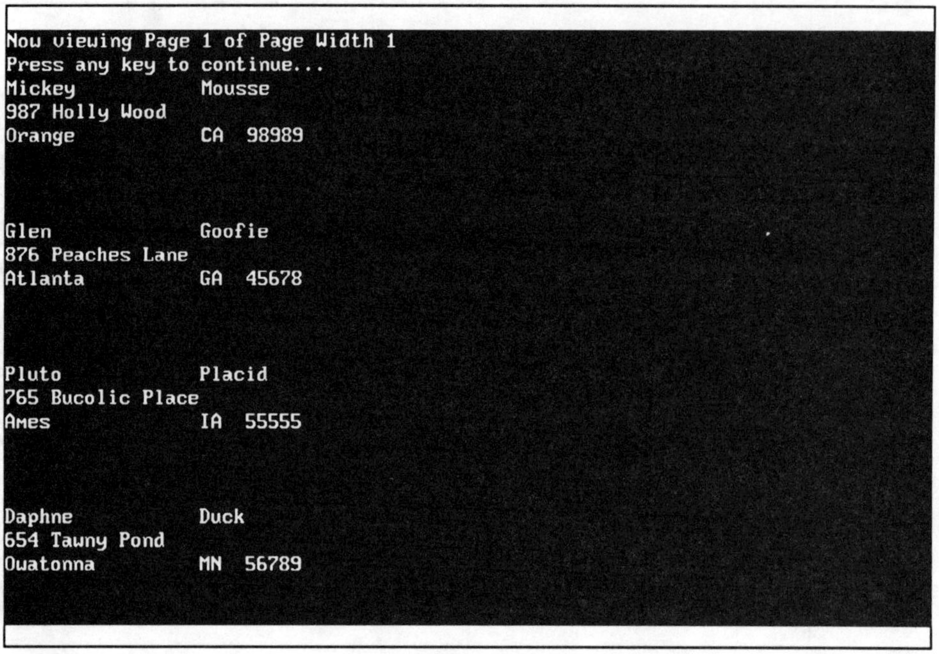

```
Now viewing Page 1 of Page Width 1
Press any key to continue...
Mickey          Mousse
987 Holly Wood
Orange          CA  98989



Glen            Goofie
876 Peaches Lane
Atlanta         GA  45678



Pluto           Placid
765 Bucolic Place
Ames            IA  55555



Daphne          Duck
654 Tawny Pond
Owatonna        MN  56789
```

Figure 9.18.   The mailing labels on screen

Removing Extra Blank Spaces

Paradox will remove the extra blank spaces with the use of the **FieldSqueeze** command.

STEP 1:

Press: **F10** Menu key
Select: **Setting**
Select: **RemoveBlanks**

Paradox offers two choices: the **LineSqueeze** and the **FieldSqueeze.**

STEP 2:

Select: **FieldSqueeze**
Select: Yes

Paradox informs you that the settings for the form design screen have been changed and that the fields are squeezed together.

Figure 9.19 shows how the labels appear on screen now that the fields have been squeezed. Get to this screen by pressing F10 Menu key and selecting **Output/Screen.** The mailing labels look much better without all the unnecessary blanks.

1. Press **F10**, select **Output** and **Screen.** What do you see?
2. Select **FieldSqueeze.** What happens?

1. *The screen view of the mailing labels.*
2. *You are able to remove extra blank spaces in a field.*

Choosing Mailing Label Settings

Now that the mailing labels look great on screen, prepare the printer and paper settings so that labels run continuously and set the page width for labels. Make sure the cursor is in the report design screen before you begin.

```
Now viewing Page 1 of Page Width 1
Press any key to continue...
Mickey  Mousse
987 Holly Wood
Orange  CA  98989



Glen  Goofie
876 Peaches Lane
Atlanta  GA  45678



Pluto  Placid
765 Bucolic Place
Ames  IA  55555



Daphne  Duck
654 Tawny Pond
Owatonna  MN  56789
```

Figure 9.19. Squeezed mailing labels

STEP 1:

> Press: **F10** Menu key
> Select: **Settings**
> Select: **PageLayout**
> Select: **Length**

Paradox displays the prompt: "New page length: 66."

STEP 2:

> Press: **Backspace** key, 2 times
> Type: C
> Press: **Enter**

You told Paradox to print a continuous (C) page instead of a 66-line page. The cursor is back in the report design screen.

STEP 3:

> Press: **F10** Menu key
> Select: **Setting**
> Select: **PageLayout**
> Select: **Width**

Paradox displays the prompt: "New page width: 80."

STEP 4:

> Press: **Backspace** key, 2 times
> Type: 35
> Press: **Enter**

The report design screen now has two vertical lines on screen. Each line is at 35 spaces, showing you how many page widths are available. Remove the extra page widths with the following step.

STEP 5:

> Press: **F10** Menu key
> Select: **Setting**
> Select: **PageLayout**
> Select: **Delete**
> Select: OK

Repeat STEP 5 to delete the page width lines. The upper right corner should display: Report 1/1. The screen should now look like Figure 9.20. The free-form mailing label report is designed.

STEP 6:

Press: **F2** DO-IT

The free-form report design is saved to disk and can be recalled whenever you need to print mailing labels.

Tip

If you wish to print labels with three or four up across the page, adjust the page widths. In the example above, you deleted two vertical page width indicators for a one up label. If you are printing three labels across a page, design the screen as you did above, but set the page width to three instead of one.

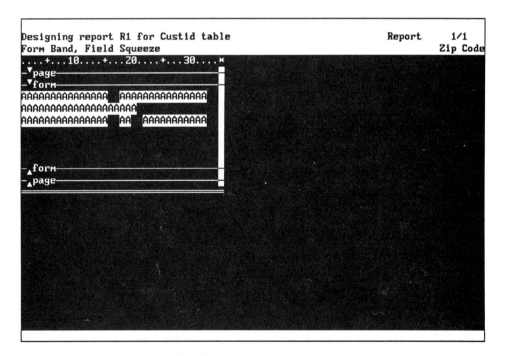

Figure 9.20. The free-form mailing label report design screen

1. Press **F10**, select **Setting, PageLayout,** and **Length**. What action can you take now?
2. At the "Page Length:" prompt, enter C. What happens?
3. Press **F10** and select **Setting, PageLayout, Delete,** and OK. What happens?

1. *You can adjust page length.*
2. *Paradox will print continuously.*
3. *Page width indicators are deleted on screen.*

Printing Mailing Labels

To print the labels, follow the same steps as you do to see the labels on screen, but select **Printer** instead of **Screen.**

STEP:

Press: **F10** Menu key
Select: **Output**
Select: **Printer**

The labels should print to the printer as you have specified. If they do not seem to fit, or are not printing properly, you may have to go back and adjust the page length and width settings.

1. Press **F10**, select **Output** and **Printer**. What happens?

1. *The mailing labels are printed.*

Summary

You have investigated the flexibility of the Paradox form screen, from the standard form to the custom form. In addition to the form screen, you have designed a free-form report with which you can create mailing labels. The steps involved in adjusting the form screen and the printer settings for creating mailing labels are included.

- The Paradox form
  - Moving the form screen
- Designing custom forms
  - Designing the new form
  - Using the custom form
  - Modifying the custom form
- Free-form reports
  - Designing the mailing label format
  - Printing mailing labels

Exercises

What You Should Do	How the Computer Responds
1. With the cursor in any table, press F7.	1. The Form view, with one record per screen, is displayed.
2. With the cursor in any table: Press: F10 Menu key Select: **Forms** Select: **Design** Type: The name of the table for which you want to design a form. Press: Enter	2. Paradox prompts you for a description of the new form.
3. Type: A brief description Press: Enter	3. The form design screen appears.
4. Move the cursor to the location on the screen that approximates where you want the first field to appear in the form. Type: The name for the field. Press: F10 Menu key Select: **Field/Place/Regular**	4. A list of fields from the table for which you are creating the form is displayed.

5. Select the field you want to be inserted after the name of the field.
Press: **Enter.**
Move the cursor to size the field.
Press: **Enter.**

5. The field is inserted in the form design screen. You have typed the label and inserted the field mask.

6. Repeat the process is steps 4 and 5 to place the remaining fields in the form design screen.

6. The fields you choose are placed in the screen.

7. When you have completed the form design to your satisfaction,
Press: **F2 DO-IT**

7. The custom form is saved to disk and be recalled later. You are returned to the **View** mode.

8. With the original table on screen, follow these steps:
Press: **F10** Menu key
Select: **Image**
Select: **PickForm**
Select: **1** (or the number of the custom form you created)

8. The table is displayed in the custom **Form** view. Now you can toggle between the custom form and the table by pressing **F7** Form Toggle.

9. Select **View** and name a table with a list of names and addresses. With the cursor in that table:
Press: **F10** Menu key
Select: **Report/Design**
Type: The name of the table that holds the names and addresses.
Press: **Enter**

9. Paradox lists the R for standard report and the numbers 1 through 14.

10. Select: **1** (or another number that has no report created)
Type: a description of the report
Press: **Enter**
Select: **Free-form**

10. The Design Free-form Report Screen is displayed. The Design Free-form Report Screen lists the fields down the left side of the screen.

11. Delete all the lines on the screen, even those that now hold a field name and field mask. Move to each line and press **Ctrl-Y.**

11. The lines are deleted and the table band lines are the only lines that remain on screen.

12. Move the cursor to the bottom line of the form band.
Press: **Ins**
Press: **Enter,** 6 times

12. Six blank lines are inserted between the form band lines.

13. Move the cursor to the first line in the form band.
Press: **F10** Menu key
Select: **Field/Place/Regular**
Select: First Name
Press: **Enter**
Press: **Enter**
Press: Right arrow, 3 times

13. The first field (First Name) is placed in the form band. This is where the first name will be printed on the mailing label.

14. Repeat number 13, moving the cursor to a new location for each field, until all the fields are entered for the mailing label. This includes city, state, and zip code.

14. Field masks are inserted in the locations you specify so that the mailing label is prepared for printing.

15. Preview the labels on screen.
Press: **F10** Menu key
Select: **Output**
Select: **Screen**

15. The labels appear on screen. Press the space bar to see all of the labels. Press **Esc** to go back to the form design screen.

16. When you are done viewing the labels on screen, the cursor is back in the form design screen. Remove any excess blank spaces by:
Press: **F10** Menu key
Select: **Setting**
Select: **RemoveBlanks**
Select: **FieldSqueeze**
Select: Yes

16. Choose to view the labels on screen again **(F10/Output/Screen)**, and you will see that Paradox has squeezed the data together, eliminating excess blank spaces.

17. Prepare the mailing label settings for the size mailing labels you will print.
Press: **F10** Menu key
Select: **Settings**
Select: **PageLayout**
Select: **Length**
Press: **Backspace** key, 2 times
Type: C
Press: **Enter**

17. When you print the labels, they will be printed continuously instead of at specific page lengths.

18. Change the page width setting to accommodate mailing labels.
    Press: **F10** Menu key
    Select: **Setting**
    Select: **PageLayout**
    Select: **Width**
    Press: **Backspace** key, 2 times
    Type: 35
    Press: **Enter**

18. Paradox inserts vertical lines, showing the page width on the report design screen.

19. Delete the extra page widths.
    Press: **F10** Menu key
    Select: **Setting**
    Select: **PageLayout**
    Select: **Delete**
    Select: OK

19. The vertical page width lines are deleted. Repeat this step until all but one of the page width lines are deleted.

20. Save the custom free-form report design to disk.
    Press: **F2** DO-IT

20. The free-form report is saved to disk.

21. From the report design screen, print the mailing labels.
    Press: **F10** Menu key
    Select: **Output**
    Select: **Printer**

21. Paradox sends the mailing labels to the printer, where they are printed according to your specifications.

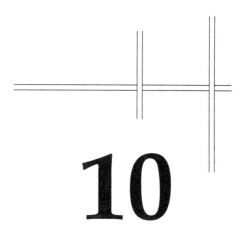

10

Paradox Scripts

W ith a Paradox script, you can automate repeated tasks that have to be accomplished within a database. A script increases accuracy and efficiency while repeating tasks in a database. In this chapter, the question below will be answered, followed by step-by-step instructions for creating scripts.

- What is a script?
- Instant scripts
- Named scripts

What Is a Script?

A script is a series of commands that you give Paradox. These commands are stored in a file and can be called up any time you need a specific task completed. A script is especially useful when you are repeating a task over and over again.

One example of when to use a script is if you have a series of telephone numbers with the 874 prefix. Due to a shift in calling areas, the numbers are changed to a 748 prefix. Paradox can search through the database table, find the 874 prefixes, and change them to 748 prefixes, automatically.

Another example is if in your office you have to provide a weekly sales report. You can design a script that prints this weekly report with just a few keystrokes.

Scripts can be used to insert skeleton records. Skeleton records are those that have the same "skeleton" information, with a few variations from record to record. The script can be designed to insert the skeleton information and then later have someone enter the variant information.

Script files can hold a variety of commands, including recorded keystrokes. A Paradox script can memorize a series of keystrokes, such as menu selections and key commands like **Home** and **Enter**. Scripts can be a stepping stone to harness PAL commands, which in turn can make scripts into programs. You can use IF-THEN-ELSE commands and other control instructions in a PAL.

Note ‖ The use of PAL commands is beyond the scope of this book. Consult the *PAL User's Guide* to learn more about using PAL commands with Paradox.

Tips for Using Scripts

The series of commands you place in a script will be repeated exactly as you record them. For this reason, you need to be aware of where the cursor is when you play a script. If you record a script with the beginning in the Main menu, then you should begin that script from the Main menu every time you play it.

Begin scripts by clearing the screen using the **Alt-F8** Clear All key. This leads to consistency in scripts and makes sure that any images on screen will not affect the script. If you want your script to be played while you are in **Edit, Form Edit,** or **Report Edit** mode, you do not want to clear the screen first.

Before you start recording a script, you might want to practice the series of keystrokes. Paradox will start recording all the keystrokes you make, even mistakes.

If you do make an error while recording a script, press **F10** Menu key and select **Cancel** from the menu. This will stop the recording, and you can start over. Or you can fix the error while recording and then later run the script with the error fixed. Another option is to continue the script with the error in it and then edit the script via the **Script Edit** command.

Instead of making one script that does all your computer work in one keystroke, create several small scripts that can be run separately. Any errors in the scripts can be perceived without ruining your entire database.

Keep your scripts as simple as possible. Even the most complicated tasks can be reduced to several key steps.

If a script isn't working the way you expected, try recording the script again, look at the script to see what might be wrong with it, or use the **Script Edit** command to make alterations in the script. Start by using small scripts and then, as your confidence grows and you are successful, build larger scripts.

Instant Scripts

The simplest form and most often used script is the *instant script*. You begin an instant script by pressing Alt-F3 Instant Script. The next step is to press the keys that carry out the action you want to take. Finish the script by pressing Alt-F3 Instant Script. The series of keystrokes you make between the start and end of the script are saved in a file to be recalled at any time.

Creating an Instant Script

Imagine a situation where you are creating a report. You have designed it according to input from several sources. However, you find that you are constantly adjusting the report. Instead of taking the steps to access the report design screen every time you need to change the report, create an instant script.

Tip | When creating a script, it is a good idea to begin the script with an Alt-F8 Clear All command. Beginning with this command will assure that no other images conflict with the script that you want to record and play later.

STEP 1:

Press: **Alt-F3** Instant Script Record

A message is displayed in the lower right corner of the screen. This message tells you that Paradox is beginning to record the script. At this point, Paradox is recording the series of keystrokes you make.

STEP 2:

> Press: Alt-F8Clear All
> Select: **Report**
> Select: **Change**

At this point, Paradox prompts you to name the table for which the report design screen is created. In the figures that follow, the ADVCHEM screen will be used.

STEP 3:

> Type: ADVCHEM
> Press: **Enter**
> Select: 1 (Student Names and Grades)
> Press: **Enter**

The report design screen you need to access on a repeated basis appears on screen. End the script now.

STEP 4:

> Press: **Alt-F3** Instant Script Record

A message is displayed at the lower right-hand corner that informs you that you are ending the instant script record. Paradox will no longer record the keystrokes you make after this.

You have recorded the keystrokes to get to the report design screen. Now, remove the report design screen by pressing the **F10** Menu key and select **Cancel**. Select Yes and you are returned to the Main menu with a clear workspace.

1. Press Alt-F3 at the beginning of a script. What happens?
2. Press Alt-F3 to begin a script. What do you press to end the script?

1. *Paradox informs you that the script record is beginning.*
2. *Alt-F3.*

Playing an Instant Script

With one keystroke you can repeat the six keystrokes it took to get to the report design screen. Whether you have cleared the screen and the Main menu is at the top of the screen, or you are viewing another table, you can access the instant script. Figure 10.1 shows the screen before you play the instant script.

STEP:

Press: **Alt-F4** Instant Script Play

The series of keystrokes saved in the file is read and reproduced. Just by pressing **Alt-F4** Instant Script Play, the report design screen for the *ADVCHEM* table appeared on screen. Figure 10.2 shows the screen after you pressed **Alt-F4** Instant Script Play.

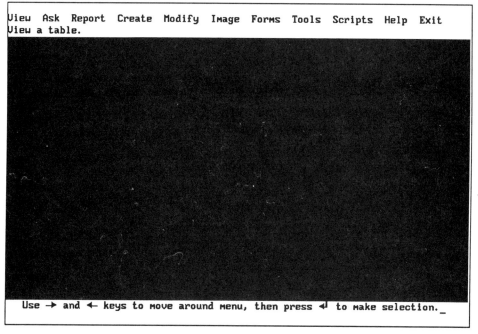

Figure 10.1. Screen before playing the instant script

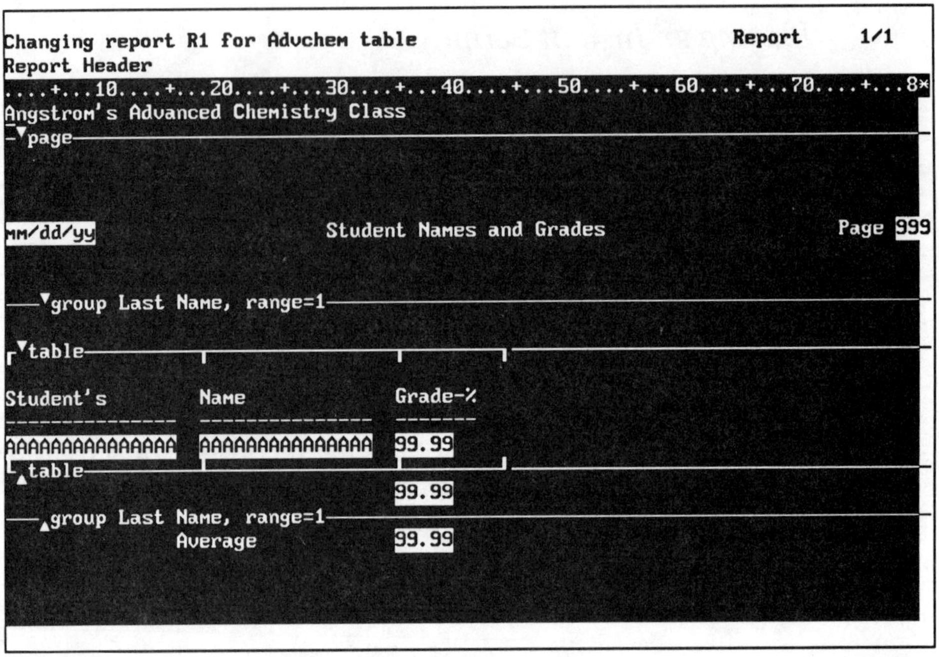

```
Changing report R1 for Advchem table                          Report      1/1
Report Header
....+...10....+...20....+...30....+...40....+...50....+...60....+...70....+...8×
Angstrom's Advanced Chemistry Class
─▼page──────────────────────────────────────────────────────────────────────



MM/dd/yy                        Student Names and Grades              Page 999


    ─▼group Last Name, range=1───────────────────────────────────────────────
  ┌─▼table──────────────┬──────────────┬──────────────────────────────────────

Student's            Name             Grade-%
───────────────      ──────────────   ───────
AAAAAAAAAAAAAAAA     AAAAAAAAAAAAAAAA  99.99
  └─▲table──────────────┴──────────────┴──────
                                        99.99
    ─▲group Last Name, range=1──────────────────────────────────────────────
                     Average            99.99
```

Figure 10.2. Report design screen

Showing an Instant Script

If you created an instant script at one session with Paradox and you came
back later and couldn't remember what the script did, you can show the series of steps recorded in the script.

   With the cursor in the Main menu, use the **Scripts** submenu to display
the series of steps that make up a script.

STEP 1:

   Select: **Scripts**
   Select: **ShowPlay**

Paradox prompts you to name the script you want to play. You can press
Enter for a list of scripts created.

STEP 2:

   Press: **Enter**

Select: **Instant**
Select: **Slow**

The six steps recorded in the script are played back for you at a readable pace, much like an instant replay. Take a better look at the script by displaying the instant script contents.

1. Press Alt-F4. What happens?
2. Select **ShowPlay** from the **Scripts** submenu. What happens?

1. *The series of keystrokes stored in the instant script file is read and replayed.*
2. *You get an instant replay of a script.*

Displaying the Instant Script

Paradox will display the instant script steps when you use the **Scripts/Editor** submenu. Start with the cursor in the Main menu.

STEP 1:

Select: **Scripts**
Select: **Editor**
Select: **Edit**

Paradox prompts you for the name of the script you want to edit.

STEP 2:

Press: Enter
Select: **Instant**

Figure 10.3 illustrates the script step-by-step. At the top of the screen, you see the name of the script you are viewing. You can see that first you selected **Report** from the menu, then **Change**, the table ADVCHEM, the first report created for that table, and finally the description of the report.

While in this screen, you could edit the script by entering different menu selections in the brackets. If you make changes in the script, end the edit session and save the changes by pressing the F2 DO-IT key. If you wish to keep the script as it is, press **F10** Menu key for the **Script** submenu. Select **Cancel** and Yes. You are returned to the Main menu.

1. Press **F10**, select **Scripts, Editor,** and **Edit**. Where are you now?
2. Edit the script. Press **F2**. What happens?

1. *You are at the script editor.*
2. *Edits made to the script are saved.*

Editing a Script

The script editor is similar to the editor used in report generation. In the script editor, there is a line limit of 132 characters, whereas the report generator has no line limit. The keys used in editing a script are shown here.

```
Changing script C:\pdox35\instant                              Script
....+..:10....+...20....+...30....+...40....+...50....+...60....+...70....+...80
Esc ClearAll {Report} {Change} {advchem} {1} {Student Names and Grades}
```

Figure 10.3. Instant script displayed

Right Arrow	Moves one character to the right.
Left Arrow	Moves one character to the left.
Up Arrow	Moves up one line.
Down Arrow	Moves down one line.
Home	Moves to the first line in the script.
End	Moves to the last line in the script.
Ctrl-Right Arrow	Scrolls the screen to the right.
Ctrl-Left Arrow	Scrolls the screen to the left.
Ctrl-Home	Moves to the first character of the line.
Ctrl-End	Moves to the last character of the line.
Ins	Toggle the insert mode between over write and type over.
Del	Deletes the character at the cursor.
Alt-F7	Prints the current script in an instant report.
Ctrl-Y	Deletes all of the characters remaining in the line.
Ctrl-V	Toggles the ruler line on or off.
Back Arrow	Deletes the character to the left of the cursor.
Enter	Inserts a new line when the insert mode is toggled on.

1. Press **Ctrl-End** while in the script editor. What happens?
2. Press **Ctrl-Y** while in the script editor. What happens?

1. *The cursor moves to the last character of the line.*
2. *The characters remaining in the line are deleted.*

Named Scripts

While you need to continually access the report design screen, the instant script you have created works very nicely. But now you want to create another script. If you press **Alt-F4** Instant Script Record and type in another series of keystrokes, this series will be recorded as the "Instant Script." The script that got you to the report design screen will be lost. Try this out by creating another instant script from the Main menu.

STEP:

> Press: **Alt-F3** Instant Script Record
> Select: **Ask**
> Press: **Enter**
> Select: *SALARY*
> Press: **Alt-F3** Instant Script Record

The query form for the *SALARY* table is on screen. Now if you clear the screen and press **Alt-F4**, the query form for the *SALARY* table appears again.

The first instant script has been replaced by another. Clear the screen again (**Alt-F8** Clear All), and this time create a named script that you want to keep for a long time.

Creating a Named Script

Create a named script by going through the **Script** menu. This way you can create and save a named script with a specific name. In this example, you will add skeleton information to a table. You are going to add new names to your database table. In this table, you have a field for telephone numbers. Every record has the same telephone prefix of 555. You are going to design a script that automatically places 555 as the prefix in the telephone field.

STEP 1:

> Select: **View**
> Press: **Enter**
> Select: *Friends*

The *Friends* table appears with three names listed, their addresses, and phone numbers. Move the cursor to the last record in the Phone field. The cursor is shown in the correct position in Figure 10.4.

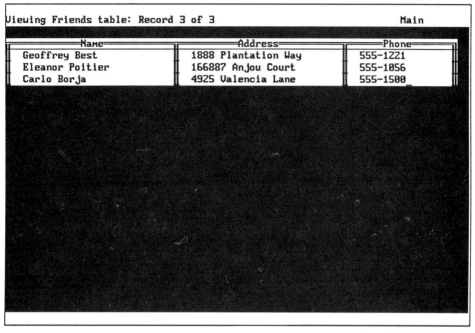

```
Viewing Friends table: Record 3 of 3                              Main
┌──────────Name──────────┬──────────Address──────────┬──────Phone──────┐
│  Geoffrey Best          │  1888 Plantation Way       │  555-1221        │
│  Eleanor Poitier        │  166887 Anjou Court        │  555-1056        │
│  Carlo Borja            │  4925 Valencia Lane        │  555-1500_       │
└─────────────────────────┴────────────────────────────┴──────────────────┘
```

Figure 10.4. Cursor in *Friends* table

STEP 2:

> Press: **F10** Menu key
> Select: **Scripts**
> Select: **BeginRecord**

Paradox leaves a space in which you can enter the name of the script you are creating.

STEP 3:

> Type: 555PREFX
> Press: **Enter**

Paradox puts you back in the **View** mode of the *Friends* table.

STEP 4:

> Press: **F9** Edit
> Press: Down arrow, one time (one blank record is created)
> Press: Right arrow, two times (the cursor is in the Phone field)

Type: 555-
Press: **F2** DO-IT

You have completed entering the data. Now end the script.

STEP 5:

Press: **F10** Menu Key
Select: **Scripts**
Select: **End-Record**

A script with the name *555PREFX* has been created. You can test the script to see how it works for you.

1. Create another instant script. What happens to the old one?
2. Press **F10**, select **Scripts** and **BeginRecord**. What action are you taking?
3. Select **End-Record** from the **Scripts** submenu. What happens?

1. *The first instant script is replaced by the new one.*
2. *You are creating a named script.*
3. *The script is ended.*

Playing the Named Script

The script *555PREFX* was created to add one telephone prefix at a time. This is just an example. In a larger database, you may want to add five or ten at a time. Remember that scripts can be very flexible and are designed to save you time.

Start with the cursor in the *Friends* table. Figure 10.5 shows how the screen should look with the view of the *Friends* table and the cursor just after the prefix you added to create the script.

Tip Because of the way the script was designed, the cursor should be in the Phone field of the last record at the beginning of the script.

STEP 1:

Press: **F10** Menu key
Select: **Scripts**
Select: **Play**

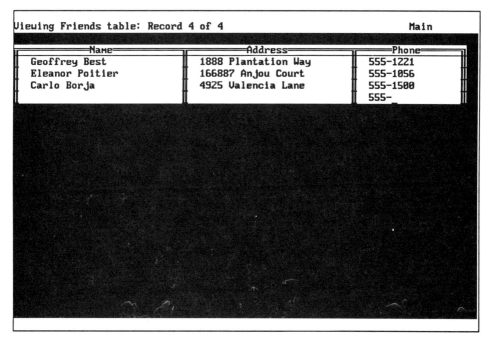

```
Viewing Friends table: Record 4 of 4                           Main

┌══════════Name═══════════┬═══════════Address══════════┬═════════Phone═══┐
║ Geoffrey Best           │ 1888 Plantation Way         │ 555-1221        ║
║ Eleanor Poitier         │ 166887 Anjou Court          │ 555-1056        ║
║ Carlo Borja             │ 4925 Valencia Lane          │ 555-1500        ║
║                         │                             │ 555-_           ║
```

Figure 10.5.   Viewing *Friends* table

Paradox prompts you for the name of the script you want to play.

STEP 2:

Press: **Enter**
Select: *555PREFX*

Now the screen looks like the one in Figure 10.6. You have seen the before and after screen. Play the *555PREFX* script and you will get one record
with the skeleton information of the 555 prefix added to the record. The
table has already been saved, since you built that into the script. Paradox
puts you back in the **View** mode when completed with the script.

1. Press **F10** and select **Scripts, Play, Enter,** and the name. What happens?

1. *The named script is played.*

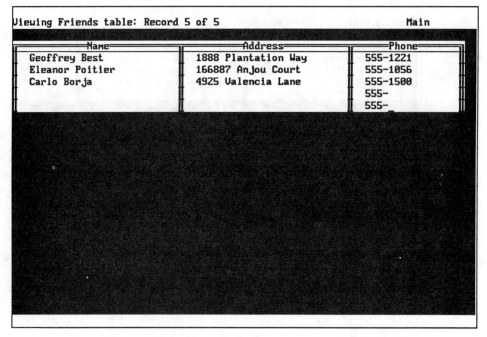

Figure 10.6. The prefix added to the *Friends* table

Summary

Several examples of scripts have been presented in this chapter. You have some ideas of how to use scripts, and with this experience you can see how beneficial and timesaving this Paradox tool can be. You created an instant script and a script that you named. You have used a script to get through the Paradox menus faster, as well as add skeleton information to a table. You can continue working with scripts and get them to work for you. The topics covered in this chapter are listed here:

- What is a script?
- Instant scripts
  - Creating an instant script
  - Playing an instant script
- Named scripts
  - Creating a named script
  - Playing the named script

Exercises

What You Should Do	**How the Computer Responds**
1. Begin the script process by clearing the screen. Press: Alt-F8 Clear All	1. All images are cleared from the screen.
2. Begin the script. Press: Alt-F3 Instant Script Record	2. Paradox briefly displays a note that the keystrokes are being recorded as part of the script.
3. With the cursor in the Main menu: Select: **Image** Select: **Graph** Select: **Modify**	3. The Customize Graph Type screen appears. From this screen you can modify a graph.
4. End the script: Press: Alt-F3	4. A message appears briefly on screen that tells you that Paradox is ending the script.
5. Cancel the modification of the graph because you are not going to change it now. Instead, you are designing a script that will take you to this screen in a hurry. Press: F10 Menu key Select: **Cancel** Select: Yes	5. The Customize Graph Type screen is removed from the screen and you are returned to the **View** mode.
6. Play the instant script you have created. Press: Alt-F4 Instant Script Play	6. The computer responds by playing the script and displaying the Customize Graph Type screen.
7. Remove the Customize Graph Type screen. Press: F10 Menu key Select: **Cancel** Select: Yes	7. The Customize Graph Type screen is removed from the screen and you are returned to the **View** mode.

8. With the cursor back in the Main menu:
   Select: **Scripts**
   Select: **ShowPlay**
   Type: Instant
   Press: **Enter**
   Select: **Slow**

8. Paradox repeats the script you have just played, step-by-step so that you can see what your script is designed to do. You end with the cursor in the Customize Graph Type screen.

9. Remove the Customize Graph Type screen.
   Press: **F10 Menu key**
   Select: **Cancel**
   Select: Yes

9. The Customize Graph Type screen is removed from the screen.

10. View the script on screen. Select: **Scripts**
    Select: **Editor**
    Select: **Edit**
    Type: Instant
    Press: **Enter**

10. The series of keystrokes (in this case, menu selections) recorded in the script are displayed on screen in brackets. In this screen you can add or remove (edit) components of the script.

11. Go back to the Main menu.
    Press: **F10 Menu key**
    Select: **Cancel**
    Select: Yes

11. Paradox removes the script edit screen and returns you to the Main menu and a clear workspace.

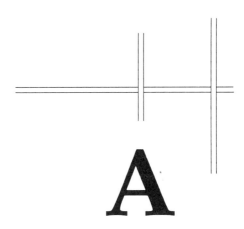

Installation

Preparing to Install Paradox

Before using Paradox, you have to install the software to your hard disk. Paradox takes a large space on the disk, so you will start by finding out if you have enough space on the hard disk to hold Paradox.

Start by getting to the "DOS C:" prompt. If you are not at the "C:" prompt, take these steps:

Type: `C:`
Type: `cd\chkdsk`
Press: **Enter**

On the screen you will see a list of byte amounts and a brief description. The first number tells you the total amount of disk space available. The number you need be most concerned with is the amount of bytes available on disk. To run Paradox you will need at least 3 million bytes or 3 megabytes. After Paradox is installed, it takes less than 3 megabytes.

If the disk check shows that you do not have at least 2 megabytes available, you will have to remove some data from the disk before you can install Paradox.

The programs on the installation disk will create a new directory that will hold Paradox. In addition, they will automatically copy all the files necessary for use with Paradox.

Before you use the new disks to install Paradox, make a copy of the disks. This copy should be stored in a safe place away from extreme heat or cold.

The "C:" prompt should be on screen. Make your hard disk the current drive. Usually, the hard disk is drive C, so the "C:" prompt is where you will install Paradox.

Beginning the Installation

When you open the Paradox package, you will find nine 5.25-inch floppy disks. Find the Installation/Sample Tables Disk. Insert this disk into the A drive (or B drive).

Type: a:install (or b:install if you inserted the disk in drive B)
Press: Enter

The Paradox Installation screen is displayed as you see in Figure A.1.

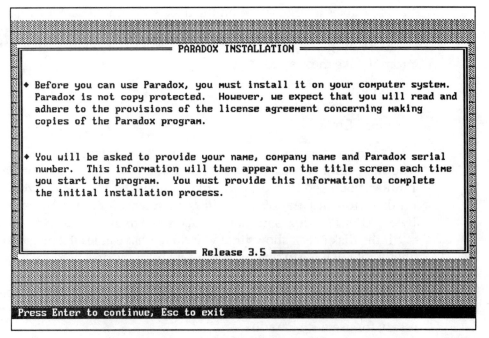

```
╔══════════════════ PARADOX INSTALLATION ══════════════════╗

  ◆ Before you can use Paradox, you must install it on your computer system.
    Paradox is not copy protected.  However, we expect that you will read and
    adhere to the provisions of the license agreement concerning making
    copies of the Paradox program.


  ◆ You will be asked to provide your name, company name and Paradox serial
    number.  This information will then appear on the title screen each time
    you start the program.  You must provide this information to complete
    the initial installation process.




╚═══════════════════════ Release 3.5 ═══════════════════════╝

 Press Enter to continue, Esc to exit
```

Figure A.1. Paradox installation screen

Follow the instructions on this screen. At the bottom you see the message: "Press Enter to continue, Esc to exit."

Press: **Enter**

Paradox asks you to select which type of installation you will be doing. The options are displayed as in Figure A.2. You are doing a "Hard Disk Installation."

Press: **1**
Press: **Enter**

The prompt asks for the source drive. This will be A or B, depending on which drive you inserted the first disk. In this example, the disk is inserted in the A drive.

Type: A
Press: **Enter**

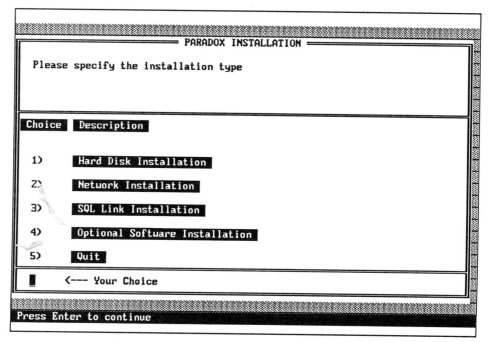

Figure A.2. Installation options

Now name the destination drive as the drive where you find the hard disk. This is usually the C drive.

Type: C
Press: Enter

Name the directory in which you are going to install Paradox. The default directory of PDOX35 is displayed. Type a different name if you want Paradox in another directory. For this example, keep PDOX35 as the directory.

Press: Enter

The next screen lists five country screens. Choose a country and it affects the way data is displayed and sorted. If you are in a country other than the United States, read the *Paradox Introduction* book to find out which country you should choose. If you are in the United States, choose option 1.

Press: 1
Press: Enter

The installation program begins to unpack files and then prompts you to insert System Disk 1 into drive A.

Insert: System Disk 1 into Drive ACT!
Press: Enter

The next screen seen in Figure A.3 has space for your name, your company name, and the Paradox serial number. You will find the serial number on the Installation/Sample Tables Disk.

Type: Your name
Press: Enter
Type: Your company name
Press: Enter
Type: The serial number
Press: Enter
Type: Y if working on a network, N if single use.
Press: F2

The message appears on screen: "Copying files." After the copying is complete, you are asked to insert System Disk 2 into drive A.

Remove: System Disk 1 from drive A

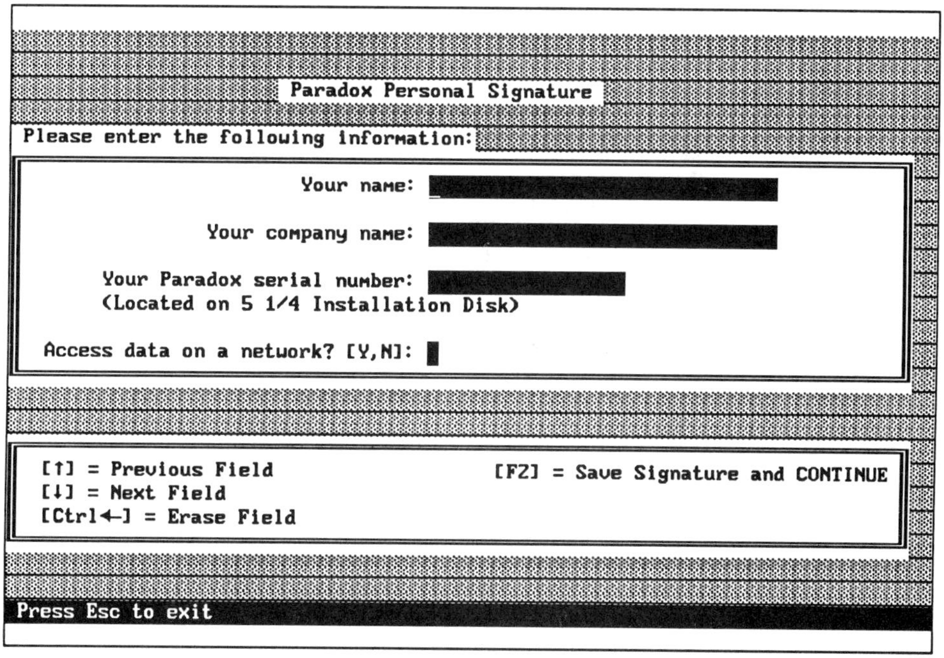

```
┌──────────────────────────────────────────────────────────────┐
│                                                                │
│                 ┌─────────────────────────────┐                │
│                 │  Paradox Personal Signature │                │
│  Please enter the following information:                       │
│  ┌──────────────────────────────────────────────────────────┐ │
│  │                                                          │ │
│  │            Your name: █████████████████████████          │ │
│  │                                                          │ │
│  │    Your company name: █████████████████████████          │ │
│  │                                                          │ │
│  │  Your Paradox serial number: ███████████████             │ │
│  │  (Located on 5 1/4 Installation Disk)                    │ │
│  │                                                          │ │
│  │  Access data on a network? [Y,N]: █                      │ │
│  └──────────────────────────────────────────────────────────┘ │
│                                                                │
│  ┌──────────────────────────────────────────────────────────┐ │
│  │  [↑] = Previous Field        [F2] = Save Signature and     │ │
│  │  [↓] = Next Field                              CONTINUE    │ │
│  │  [Ctrl←] = Erase Field                                     │ │
│  └──────────────────────────────────────────────────────────┘ │
│                                                                │
│  Press Esc to exit                                             │
│                                                                │
└──────────────────────────────────────────────────────────────┘
```

Figure A.3. Paradox personal signature screen

Insert: System Disk 2 into drive A
Press: Enter

Again, Paradox copies files.

Remove: System Disk 2 from drive A
Insert: System Disk 3 into drive A
Press: Enter

Paradox copies the necessary files from System Disk 3.

Remove: System Disk 3 from drive A
Insert: Custom Configuration Disk into drive A
Press: Enter

Paradox unpacks files from the Custom Configuration Disk. The Optional Software Installation Screen appears as shown in Figure A.4.

You can install none, one, or all of these additional software programs. If you intend to work through the samples given in the Paradox documentation, then you want to install numbers 1 and 2. If you are not sure which you

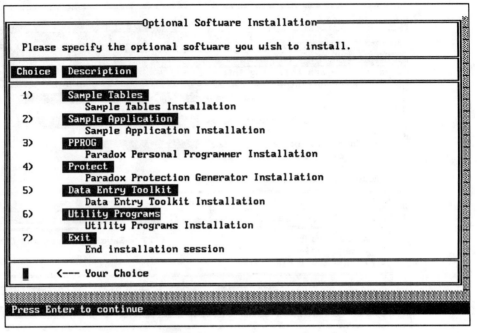

Figure A.4. Optional software installation screen

will use, you may want to install all of the options on this screen in case you ever need them.

Type: The number of the option you wish to install (select 7) to end the optional software installation.
Press: Enter

If you select an option other than 7, you will be asked to specify a directory. If the one entered is wrong, correct it and press Enter. If the directory is correct, press Enter.

Remove: Custom Configuration Disk from Drive A
Insert: Data Entry Toolkit Disk into Drive A
Press: Enter
Installation is completed.

When you select 7 from the Optional Software Installation screen and press **Enter**, the screen appears as you see in Figure A.5.

Follow the instructions given on this screen to read the README file. Get ready to use Paradox by pressing **Ctrl-Alt-Del** at the same time to reboot the computer.

At the "C:" prompt:
Type: cd\pdox35
Press: **Enter**
Type: **Paradox**
Press: **Enter**

The Paradox opening screen appears as you see in Figure A.6.

The installation is complete. If for some reason the installation does not work, review this procedure and then check the procedure listed in the Introduction documentation.

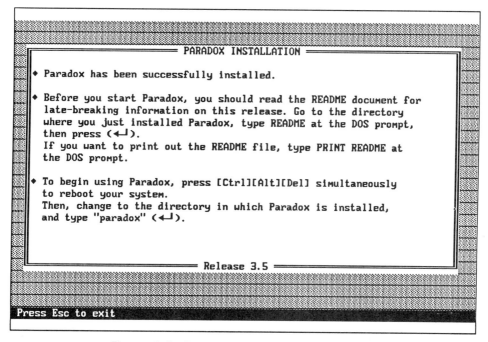

Figure A.5. Paradox installation completescreen

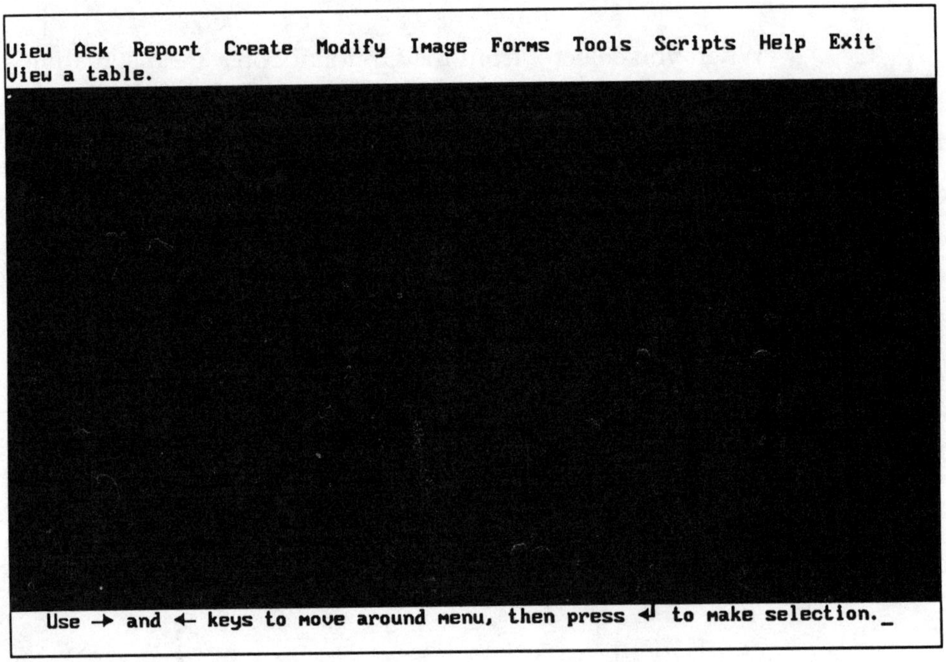

Figure A.6. Paradox opening screen

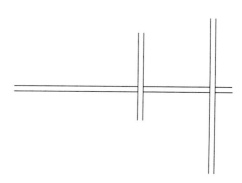

Glossary

Alphanumeric Field A field type that holds letters and/or numbers.

Ascending Order Data sorted from low to high. The alphabet would start with A going to Z. Numbers start with the lowest number. Dates start with the earliest date.

Axis Either the horizontal (x axis) or vertical (y axis) line used to define the range of values plotted on a graph.

Band Found on the report generator, this is a horizontal section that controls the placement of text entered in the band. For example, text entered in the page band will be printed on every page of a report.

Calculated Field Field values that are calculated from the values found in one or more separate fields.

Cancel Found on several submenus, this menu selection stops the action you are doing and returns you to the main workspace.

Character Number, letter, and/or symbol that appears in the workspace.

Checkmark The symbol used in a query table that indicates the fields to be included in the answer table.

Column The vertical segment of a table that holds the fields of data. A column usually has a name that describes the contents of the field in that column.

Crosstab A spreadsheet-like version of three related fields from the same table. The crosstab is used to create graphs comparing two fields to another field.

Cursor The blinking underline that marks the location of on screen activity.

Cursor Control Keys The keys found at the right of the keyboard, either alone or with numbers, that control the right, left, up, and down movement of the cursor.

Data Information or facts held in fields and records.

Database An organized collection of information.

Date Field A field that holds dates.

Default Settings used by the computer and printer that will be used, unless you specifically select an alternative.

Descending Order Data sorted from high to low. The alphabet would start with Z, going to A. Numbers start with the highest number. Dates start with the latest date and go to the earliest.

Directory A DOS term used to describe the location of your files.

Edit Changing information contained in tables by altering, correcting, adding, or deleting information.

Example Element Used in a query to specify how data from one table should be linked to data from another table.

Expression A group of characters combined with operators that result in a value. An example expression is [Quantity] * [Sales Price], which gives the value for the total sales price.

Family A Paradox table and related objects. Forms, reports, and indexes can be part of the family.

Field A single piece of data in a record found in a vertical column. See also **Column**.

Field Type The specified kind of information a column (field) can contain. Field types are alphanumeric, currency, date, numeric, and short integer.

File Related information stored under one name on a disk. Many Paradox objects are held in files, such as tables and scripts.

Form View The view of data seen one record at a time. You specify where the fields are located in form view.

Function Keys The keys labeled F1 through F10 or F12, depending on your keyboard. These keys are designed to carry out complex actions in one keystroke.

Group Records that have certain values in common, placing them in the same set. Groups can be sorted based on similar field values, certain numbers of records, or any criteria you wish.

Group Band One of the horizontal areas in the report design screen that controls how records are grouped in a report.

Help Screen A display of information intended to provide assistance with the task you are trying to complete. Press F1 Help to access the Help screen at any time.

Highlight A reverse video area meant to make some words stand out on the workspace. In reverse video, the characters are dark on a light background, where as normal video has light characters on a dark background.

Image A table viewed in the Paradox workspace. Either the table view or form view can be considered an image. You can have more than one image on the screen at one time.

Index A notation inserted in a table that Paradox uses to search for and locate records. An index makes the search process much faster. See also **Primary Index**.

Insert Mode When in a field edit, you can switch between insert mode and over write mode. In insert mode, characters typed into text push characters that were already there to the right. See also **Over Write**.

Installation The process of placing the Paradox program on a hard disk, preparing it for operation.

Instant Report The result of pressing Alt-F7 while the cursor is in a table. A Paradox standard report without groupings, order, or totals is the result.

Instant Script Begin and end an instant script by pressing Alt-F3. Paradox records and keeps a file of all the keystrokes made between the beginning and end of the instant script so that they can be replayed at a later date.

Key Field Fields established in Paradox that are used to search and locate records. Key fields help prevent duplicate records and help sort and search records more quickly.

Label Found on the axes of graphs to represent the values indicated by the graduated marks on the graph.

Legend Found next to a graph to indicate which line, pattern, or color represent which value on the graph.

Link The association between tables based on the relational data in the tables.

Lookup Table A table that holds information that is referenced by another table. A lookup table is used to make sure values entered in one table are valid, in that they actually exist on the lookup table.

Main menu The options displayed across the top of the screen when you open Paradox.

Mask Symbols that represent field types as displayed on the report design screen. A series of 9's represents a Numerical field and a series of A's represents an Alphanumeric field.

Menu Options listed across the top of the screen. Choose a menu option by pressing the first letter or the option or highlight the option then press Enter.

Message Window The highlighted line at the bottom right of the screen where warnings and prompts appear.

Number Field A field that holds only numbers and a decimal sign, or a positive or negative sign.

Object Any one of the following files in Paradox: table, form, report, index, settings, or validity check file. A family is made up of a Paradox table and the related objects. See also **Family**.

Operators The indicator that tells which kind of action will take place with numbers or field values. Examples of operators are: + (addition), - (subtraction), * (multiplication), / (division), <= (less than or equal to), and = (equal). Operators can be used to create field values, report values, or indicate query selections.

PAGEBREAK Used in the report generator to indicate where a new page should begin.

PAL The acronym for Paradox Application Language.

Primary Index A key field index used to help sort and locate records in a Paradox table.

Prompt A message from Paradox, placed at or below the menu line. The prompt usually is set up to accept some typed information from you or to inform you what you are doing at the moment.

Query A question asked about, or a task specified, of the data held in Paradox tables.

Query By Example Providing an example of what you are looking for when you ask a question of the information contained in Paradox tables.

Query Form The image that appears on the workspace where you place the examples representing the questions you want to ask about your data.

Record One row in a database table that holds a group of related fields. See also **Row**.

Relational Database A database based on the relational model of information, as opposed to a flat database.

Report Organized information, taken from database tables, that is printed on paper.

Restructure To move fields, change fields, or adjust the field type in a table.

Row The horizontal segment of a table that holds a group of related fields.

Scale The range of values indicated on a graph by tick marks on either the vertical (y) or horizontal (x) axis.

Script A record of commands held in a file that can be played back. These commands instruct Paradox to complete certain tasks.

Scroll Moving the image on screen up, down, left, or right in order to see additional records.

Sort Arranging records based on the values in a field (column).

Structure The organization of a table specifying the order of fields, field types, key fields, and the number of fields in a table.

Submenu A menu that appears after selection of a Main menu item or while acting in the workspace. A submenu provides more detailed options for which to carry out your activity.

Table Categories of information held in rows (records) and columns (fields).

Table View The database information displayed in vertical columns and horizontal rows.

Undo A command that reverses any edits or changes made in reverse order.

Validity Check A check you place on values to determine whether the data can be entered or not (whether it is valid according to another table). In addition, conditions such as minimum, maximum, picture specifications, and required entry can also be validated.

Word Wrap In a larger volume of text in a report or form, the word wrap option allows words to be held within a certain margin. Text will be continued on the next line if it cannot fit on the current line.

Working Directory The directory in which Paradox objects are located.

Workspace An area on the screen where images and characters can be placed to be worked on.

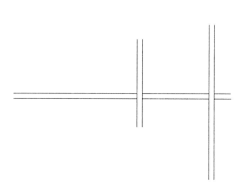

Index